PRAISE FOR
BRYSON CITY SEASONS

As I read Walt Larimore's *Bryson City Seasons*, I was transported to that Smoky Mountain community. The folks he loved and served, the colleagues he worked with, the situations he dealt with—some funny, some sad—were all so real. The whole book is delightful and very readable. My only criticism: there wasn't enough of it!

Margaret Brand, M.D., co-laborer with
Dr. Paul Brand in leprosy work in India

I love to hear Walt's stories. He's kept me entertained for years with tales from his life in the Smokies. Some of them are even true. I learn something from all of them.

Bill Peel, bestselling author of
What God Does When Men Pray

Another charming winner. At times medically messy (do you really want to follow the coroner into the woods?), at times soaring and suspenseful, this second-year sequel exposes the triumphs and tragedies of medical practice in the Smoky Mountains. Hide yourself in the medical bag of this Carolina physician for a bumpy roller-coaster ride to see why small-town medicine is so full of unexpected risks and rewards.

Richard A. Swenson, M.D., bestselling author of *Margin*

The Doc knows exactly what we need—an easy and enjoyable yet empowering memoir. Walt takes us to that Smoky Mountain hideaway town in our hearts—to teach us, bless us, and entertain us. Get yourself a good cup of dark roast, ease back into your favorite rocker or Lazy Boy, and start reading!

Dr. Dennis "The Swan" Swanberg, speaker,
author, TV host, humorist

I feel strongly that life is too short for me to read books that fail to move me deeply or take me to places I've never been. *Bryson City Seasons* succeeds wonderfully on both counts.

Joe L. Wheeler, Ph.D., editor of the bestselling
Christmas in My Heart series

Resources by Walt Larimore, M.D.

Bryson City Secrets

Bryson City Seasons

Bryson City Tales

Alternative Medicine: The Christian Handbook
(coauthored with Dónal O'Mathúna)

God's Design for the Highly Healthy Person
(with Traci Mullins)

God's Design for the Highly Healthy Child
(with Stephen and Amanda Sorenson)

God's Design for the Highly Healthy Teen
(with Mike Yorkey)

Why ADHD Doesn't Mean Disaster
(coauthored with Dennis Swanberg and Diane Passno)

Lintball Leo's Not-So-Stupid Questions About Your Body
(with John Riddle, illustrated by Mike Phillips)

*Going Public with Your Faith: Becoming a Spiritual
Influence at Work*
(coauthored with William Carr Peel)

*Going Public with Your Faith: Becoming a Spiritual
Influence at Work* audio
(coauthored with William Carr Peel)

*Going Public with Your Faith: Becoming a Spiritual
Influence at Work* ZondervanGroupware™ curriculum
(coauthored with William Carr Peel,
with Stephen and Amanda Sorenson)

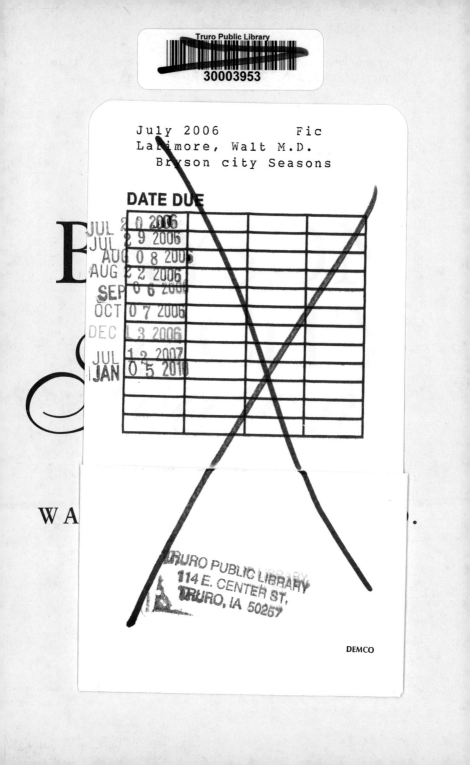

We want to hear from you. Please send your comments about this book to us in care of zreview@zondervan.com. Thank you.

ZONDERVAN™

Bryson City Seasons
Copyright © 2004 by Walt Larimore

This title is also available as a Zondervan audio product.
Visit www.zondervan.com/audiopages for more information.

Requests for information should be addressed to:

Zondervan, *Grand Rapids, Michigan 49530*

Library of Congress Cataloging-in-Publication Data

Larimore, Walter L.
    Bryson City seasons : more tales of a doctor's practice in the Smoky Mountains
/ Walt Larimore.
      p. cm.
    ISBN-10: 0-310-25672-0
    ISBN-13: 978-0-310-25672-4
    1. Larimore, Walter L.   2. Physicians—North Carolina—Bryson City—
Biography.   3. Medicine, Rural—North Carolina—Bryson City.   I. Title.
    R154.L267A3 2004
    610'.92—dc22

                                         2004012811

Published in association with the literary agency of Alive Communications, Inc., 7680 Goddard Street, Suite 200, Colorado Springs, CO 80920.

Interior design by Michelle Espinoza

Map by Terry Workman

Printed in the United States of America

---

05 06 07 08 09 10 /❖ DCI/ 10 9 8 7 6 5 4 3 2 1

To Maxine Larimore and Inez Shaw—

both of you have been incredible examples to me
of what it means to be a woman, a wife, a mother, and a friend.
I'm in awe of how you've each encouraged,
equipped, and empowered me.
I love you both very much.

CONTENTS

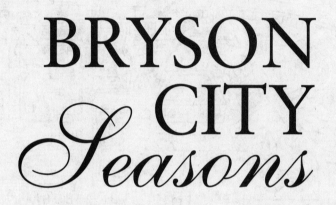

BRYSON
CITY
Seasons

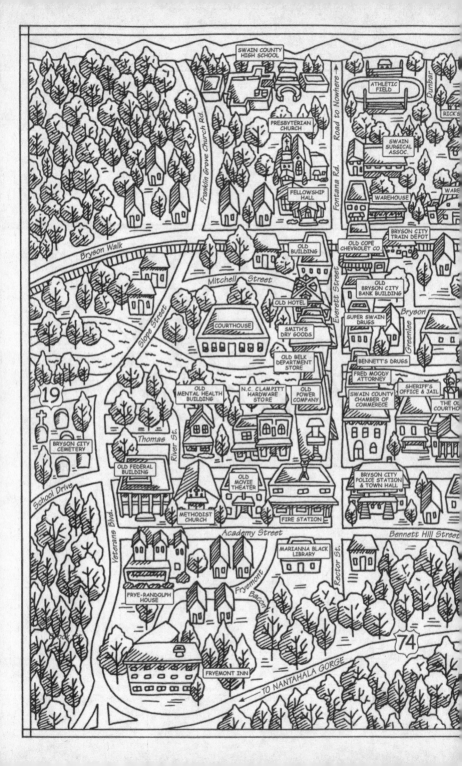

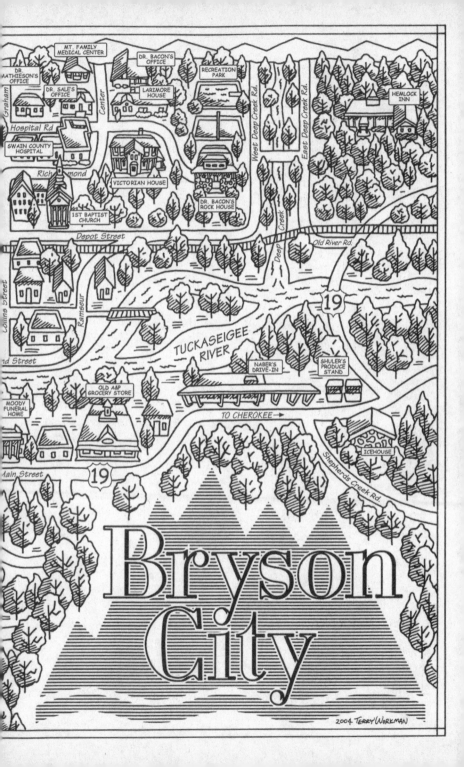

part one

SUMMER

chapter one

DEAD MAN STANDING

℘t was one of those sweltering summer afternoons in the Smoky Mountains that are unknown to outsiders and a distinct surprise to first-time visitors—humid, sticky, and unyielding. The heavy air lay over us as though it didn't want us to even move.

"You didn't tell me, Walt," my bride of nine years complained. We were heading toward our tenth wedding anniversary that fall, and I had already begun scheming, behind her back, with the help of our friend Sally Jenkins, to give Barb a bedroom makeover and a special trip out of town.

"About what?" I asked, trying to feign innocence but suspecting she had somehow found out about my shenanigans. One thing that was almost impossible in Bryson City, North Carolina, was having a secret remain a secret. Somehow news wafted through our town as easily as mountain breezes.

"About this heat!" Barb exclaimed. "If I had known it was going to be this hot in the mountains, I might have just stayed in Durham and let you come up here by yourself!"

Barb turned to smile at me—one of those "you know I'm kidding" smiles I loved. She turned back to face the mountains. "At least I would have asked the hospital to put an air conditioner in the house!"

We were sitting on the park bench we had placed in our backyard when we moved to Bryson City, North Carolina, over a year ago. It looked out over an exquisite view across Swain County Recreational Park, then up and into Deep Creek Valley, and finally over nearly endless ridges all the way to the most distant mountain ridges—deep in Great Smoky Mountains National Park—that separated North Carolina from Tennessee.

"Maybe I could call down to the Bryson City icehouse and have them send over a block or two for us to sit on."

"You mean that old building down by Shuler's Produce next to the river? It doesn't look like it's been open for years. How about you go get us a glass of ice water?"

I nodded and ran into the house to get a glass for each of us—being quiet so as not to wake up our napping children—and then tiptoed to the back screen door and out to Barb.

The view was mesmerizing, and we had now seen it through each of the four seasons—my first year as a practicing family physician—since finishing my family medicine residency at Duke University Medical Center.

"I didn't know it would be this hot," I commented. "But then there were so many things we didn't know about this place until after we settled here, eh?"

Barb threw back her head and laughed. My, how I loved her laughter!

"True enough!"

We both fell silent, reflecting on the beginning of our medical practice here. I had left residency so full of myself. Indeed, I had been very well trained—at least for the technical aspects of practicing medicine. But when it came to small-town politics and jealousies, the art of medicine, the heartbreak of making mistakes and misdiagnoses—all piled on the difficulty of raising a young daughter with cerebral palsy, dealing with one very strong-willed, colicky little boy, and transitioning a big-city girl into a rural doctor's wife—well, the task was not only full of unexpected events, it was downright daunting.

Barb turned her ear toward our house for a moment. I could tell she was listening for the children. Kate and Scott were napping, so we had the windows open—both to capture any passing breeze that might happen along and to hear the children if they were to awaken.

My thoughts turned to our small hospital—a sixty-mile drive west from the nearest medical center, which was in Asheville. In the early 1980s, Swain County was still a slow, small, sheltered mountain hamlet. Most of the folks were natives, as were their parents and their parents' parents. Most all of the physicians, and the nurses for that matter, were in at least their third to fourth decade of practice. They had their way of doing things and didn't "hanker to outsiders"—whom they called "flatlanders" if they liked you, or "lowlanders" if they did not. They especially resisted any "newfangled" ways. "Be careful if you say anything negative about anyone, son," Dr. Bill Mitchell, or Mitch as everyone called him, warned me. "It'll get back to them—and me—lickety-split."

Rick Pyeritz, M.D., my medical partner and also a classmate in our family medicine residency at Duke University Medical Center, was on call this day for our practice and for the emergency room. In Bryson City, the on-call doctor was on call for hospital inpatients, the emergency room, the jail inmates of the Swain County Sheriff's Department and Bryson City Police Department, the National Park Service, the coroner's office, the local tourist resorts and attractions, and the area rest home and nursing home. The fact that one of us would cover all the venues in which medical emergencies might occur made it very nice for the other six physicians not on call that particular day.

"When the kids get up, how about we all take a stroll up Deep Creek?" Barb asked.

"Sounds like a great idea!" Deep Creek was the southern wilderness entrance to the Great Smoky Mountains National Park. The creek was wide, tumbling, and ice-cold—a great place to go tubing or to just hike in the solitude of the park.

We looked across the valley. I looked at Barb as a small breeze caught her hair and blew it across her forehead. She swung her head to flip it out of the way. "But until the kids get up," I inquired, "maybe their parents need a nap?"

"Just what do you mean by *nap*?" Barb wondered out loud, tossing a suspicious look my way.

It was my turn to smile and silently look up at the ancient creek and across the ageless mountains.

Suddenly we were startled by a loud sound. We turned to see a car screeching around the hospital and heading down Hospital Hill toward town at a rapid rate of speed.

"Wasn't that Rick?" asked Barb.

"It was! Wonder where he's going?"

In a small town it doesn't take long to find out almost anything.

⟆

Even though on call that Saturday afternoon, Rick had found some time to lie down on his couch for a nap. Living in houses owned and provided by the hospital, we were just across the street from the hospital. We had been friends since our internship year at Duke. Our varied backgrounds, interests, and character traits— he a New Englander and I a Southerner; he a single man and I a married one; he a backpacker, naturalist, ornithologist, jogger and I a sedentary family man; he an introvert and I an extrovert—drew us together like opposite ends of the magnet. However, we shared a love of family medicine and a desire to serve the families that honored us by choosing us to be their family physicians—and we were both equally attracted to this rugged wilderness area.

During our days in training at Duke, Rick and I became best friends—while Barb became Rick's surrogate sister, confidante, and friend. The three of us did many things together, and during the third year of residency, we decided to go into practice together. I arrived in Bryson City a few months before Rick, and during those months, I'd been learning the ropes of private practice, settling into this mountain community and gaining, ever so slowly, a sense of confidence in my own style of practice. And with Rick's arrival I now had a colleague with whom I shared roots and history, mutual respect, comparable training, and medical perspective—as well as a similar outlook concerning the value of spirituality and faith.

Sometime in midslumber, the shrill ring of the phone snatched Rick from his sleep.

"Dr. Pyeritz," barked the official-sounding voice, "this here's Deputy Rogers of the Swain County Sheriff's Department. We're at the site of a terrible accident and need the coroner up here. Louise Thomas in the emergency room notified me that you're the coroner on call. Is that correct, sir?"

"That's right," Rick replied, in his most official, trying-not-to-sound-just-awakened, coroner-type voice.

"Then, sir, we need you at the scene as soon as possible."

"Where's that?"

"Where's what?"

"The scene—you know—where's where you're at?"

"Not sure I can tell you, sir."

Rick paused for a second as he tried not to laugh. Smiling, he continued. "Well, Deputy, if you can't tell me where you're at, how am I supposed to get there?"

"Well, sir, that's what I'm tryin' to tell you. I mean, I'm not sure I can explain it. We're up in the national forest—up on Frye Mountain. It's not far from town, but it's not easy to get here. Well, at least it's not easy to tell someone how to get here. Especially if they're not from here—uh—sir."

Rick was beginning to get irritated. "Well, Deputy, you tell me. Just what *am* I supposed to do?"

There was silence for a moment. "I reckon I have an idea, Doctor. How 'bout you drive to the station and catch a ride up here with the sheriff. He's a comin' up here. And he's from here. So he'll know how to get here."

"Okay, Deputy. I can do that. When do I need to be there?"

"Where? Here?"

Rick laughed. "No, not there! When do I need to be at the sheriff's office?"

"Oh! Well, Doc, you best git on down to the station purty quickly. The sheriff's gittin' ready to leave 'bout now."

"Sounds good. Let me phone Louise and let her know, and then I'll be right there. Okay?"

"Here?"

"No, Deputy! The sheriff's office. I'll call Louise, and you radio to the sheriff that I'm coming to his office. Okay?"

There was silence on the other end for a moment. Then this warning: "Doc, it's purty gruesome up here. Best be prepared." Then the deputy hung up.

———

Rick was glad he had ridden with the sheriff.

Indeed, the site of the death was not far from town as the crow might fly. But the accident scene was far up the rugged side of Frye Mountain and required the sheriff to navigate a number of small, winding, steep lumber roads and execute several frighteningly tight hairpin turns.

During the trip up the mountain, the sheriff was, as usual, quiet and nontalkative. He was concentrating on driving and on smoking a cigarette. Rick didn't bother him.

Finally they pulled up behind another patrol car—which was parked behind an old logging truck. Beyond the truck, Rick could see the crime scene tape, about four feet off the ground and strung from tree to tree, surrounding the logging truck and then going up a small ridge.

Rick and the sheriff got out of the car and walked past the other vehicles. As he crushed out his cigarette, the sheriff lifted up the tape to let Rick walk underneath.

The deputy came walking down the hill toward them.

"You won't believe this one, Sheriff. Never seen nothin' like this, I'll tell ya!"

"What happened?" asked the sheriff.

"You just come look. You gotta see this." Deputy Rogers turned and began hiking up the hill. The sheriff and Rick followed.

They crossed a small ridge. When Rick saw the scene below him, it stopped him in his tracks. *What is this?* he thought. His eye squinted as he stared—almost gawking—at one of the strangest sights he had ever seen.

His first impression was that he was seeing a scarecrow. What appeared to be a human body, standing straight up, was dressed in old overalls and a denim shirt—the standard dress of the lumberman in the western North Carolina mountains. *But,* Rick wondered to himself, *where are his lower legs?* The man looked to be standing on his knees—with both arms hanging down at his sides, his gloved hands nearly touching the ground.

"What in tarnation?" muttered the sheriff, who had stopped beside Rick.

"I told you!" the deputy exclaimed. "I done told you! I ain't never seen nothin' like this here. Never!"

Rick and the sheriff began to walk forward toward the body. It was standing straight up—leaning against a large poplar tree, but with no other support whatsoever. In front of the body was the trunk of a recently felled tree. Rick stepped across the log, continuing to stare. *This can't be a body!* Rick thought. *It's got to be a fake!*

As he slowly walked around it, Rick noticed that the man's hard hat was nearly crushed flat—almost like a beret—and was resting on his shoulders. But there was no head! Rick bent down to look more closely. He could not see a head, and the shirt was terribly bloodstained front and back.

"Who is this?" asked the sheriff.

"Clyde Frizzell. Has his home over in Graham County—not far from Robbinsville. Been lumberin' in the national forests out here his whole life."

"What happened?" asked Rick.

"His partner is Bobby Burrell. Bobby done said he was usin' his chain saw to cut down this big ole poplar tree." Rogers pointed to the tree that lay about three or four feet in front of the body—not far from its freshly cut stump.

The deputy continued. "When that cut tree began to fall, Bobby done yelled, 'Timber!' just like he always did. Clyde was standin' right here leanin' against this tree. He shoulda been safe here, but he just couldn't see that the tree Bobby was fellin' was connected to this one just behind him by one big ole vine."

The deputy pointed out the vine and continued. "When that vine pulled tight, it snapped off the top of the tree Clyde were leanin' against, and that trunk crashed down and fell right smack-dab down on top of Clyde's head. It just bonked him on the head and drove him straight into the ground, just like you see him. He done never seen it comin'!"

"Where's Bobby?" Rick asked.

"I sent him on to the hospital. He was purty tore up. Figure he needs a serious sedative. The men had been lumbering together the best part of four decades."

Rick set his black bag on the ground and opened it. He reached in and removed a set of latex gloves. Then he stood and began to walk slowly around the body as he pulled on the gloves. When he came back to the front of the body, he first reached for the man's arm. It was still supple and moved easily. *He hasn't been dead that long,* Rick thought. He felt for the radial pulse he didn't expect to feel. There was none.

Then he slowly reached out toward the hard hat. It was driven into the tissues of the shoulder, and it took a bit of wiggling and pulling to remove it. When it slipped up, Rick gasped and fell back. He couldn't believe his eyes, and an overwhelming sense of nausea overcame him.

chapter two

Eyes Wide Open

The phone rang, waking me—but not Barb—out of our afternoon nap. I rolled over to answer the phone. I picked it up during the first ring—to keep it from waking the children.

"Hello," I muttered. Unlike Rick, I tried to sound as tired as possible. I wanted whomever was disturbing my nap to know they were doing so. Admittedly, it was a rather selfish tactic.

"Don't you play like you're a sleepin'! I know you've been sittin' outside on your bench with Mrs. Larimore."

It was Millie on the other end of the line. Every doctor knew Millie. She was one of the dispatch officers for the Swain County Sheriff's Department. Millie knew just about everything about every doctor in the county—all seven of us. She always knew where we would be and what we would be doing at almost any time of any day. Equally important to me was that Millie knew every road and every nook and cranny of the county.

"I *was* sleeping!" I complained.

"No you ain't. Louise in ER told me she seen you and Mrs. Larimore out on your bench behind your house."

"Millie," I tried to sound irritated, "Mrs. Larimore and I *were* on that bench, but that was over an hour ago. More recently, we were trying to lie down for a nap."

I heard her snicker. "Hmm. Just what do you mean by 'nap'?"

"Millie, you've been reading too many of those romance novels." I tried to snarl at her, but not very effectively.

She replied with her typical, very condescending "Yes, I know." Then there was a long pause before she continued. "Well, anyway, the sheriff and Dr. Pyeritz just called me. They wants ya to come help 'em at the scene of an accident."

I sat up. "I saw Dr. Pyeritz light out of here a little while ago. What happened?"

"Logging accident. One dead. No others injured."

"What does he need me for?"

"How am I supposed to know?"

"Millie, it seems to me you know almost everything around here."

"Well, I ain't no smarty-pants, know-it-all doctor, I'll tell you that!"

I realized I was treading on thin ice. "Where's Dr. Pyeritz located?"

"Dr. Larimore, I'm not even sure *I* could get up there. It's up near the top of Frye Mountain. But if you get down to the ambulance squad, you can ride up there with them. So you stop your romancin' that beautiful wife of yours and git movin'. Ya hear?"

I felt like I was being lectured by my mother. I hung up and got out of bed. Barb was sound asleep—as were our children. I softly closed the kitchen screen door behind me as I left the house.

———

I met Don Grissom and Billy Smith, two of Swain County's finest paramedics, at the sheriff's office. They had the ambulance engine warmed up and the cab cooled down, and they were ready to go. The air-conditioned unit felt wonderful. I hopped into the back and pulled down a small seat so I could sit just behind and between them. On the way up the mountain, I told them what little I knew about the case.

Billy commented, "Sheriff and Rogers both say hit's the strangest thang they done ever seen."

Don chimed in, "That Rogers just got a soft belly. Don't take much to get him green-faced."

"Yeah," added Billy, chuckling. "Kinda like you were in your first coroner's case, Doc."

The memory of that accident scene was seared into my memory. Two men were drunk and got into a fight. One of them pulled out a loaded shotgun. The two wrestled over the gun, it went off, and one of them had his head blown off and his brains splattered all over the walls and ceiling of a small bedroom.

"Gotta admit it. I looked as green as I felt on that one," I said, chagrined.

"'Member when we first met you?" Don asked.

I thought for a second and then smiled. "Yep. It was my first home delivery. Millie called me out on my first night on call here in Bryson City. I asked her to call you guys to come back me up."

Billy laughed. "I'd a liked to have seen yer face when you walked in that barn with that farmer and saw his white-faced heifer locked in breech. I'd pay anything fer a picture of that moment."

"Yep, my first home delivery in private practice was that little calf." We all chuckled.

"Doc, you know if Clem still got that calf?"

"He does. In fact, I just saw her last week."

"Did you shore 'nuff?"

"Yep. I go see her from time to time—after all, Clem did name that little calf after me."

"No way."

"He did. Named her Walter."

The two paramedics cackled.

"Seems like so very long ago, doesn't it?" I commented, more to myself than to them.

"Well, time does fly when you're having fun!" commented Don. "But, Doc, I'll tell ya this—you'll be needin' to git a lot more miles on ya. A year or two of practice out here is just a beginnin'—at least compared to your older colleagues."

I smiled. "I know." As Don drove up a steep valley, I thought about the other physicians in town. Harold Bacon, M.D., was nearly eighty and the dean of the medical community. Bill Mitchell, M.D., was in his seventies and a general surgeon who had served as a captain in the Army in World War II. We all called him Mitch. Along with Ray Cunningham, M.D., who was a Bryson City native, they formed Swain Surgical Associates.

Ray also was a surgeon, but much younger than Mitch, and was the only residency-trained and board-certified physician in town besides Rick and me. Mitch and Ray had helped recruit Rick and me to the area, and they were allowing us to practice medicine with them until our new office was completed.

The ambulance bumped and swayed as it left the paved road and began climbing up a narrow, graveled mountain road. I continued to think about the other local doctors. Paul Sale, M.D., was about fifty years old and a general practitioner. Like Harold and Mitch, he had practiced in Bryson City his entire career. However, Ken Mathieson, D.O., had retired from practice elsewhere and then settled in our small town to set up what would be his last practice. Like Rick and me, he was still seen as an outsider.

The ambulance strained as it climbed the steep lumber roads.

"Good thang this here has four-wheel drive," Billy commented—to no one in particular.

Finally we arrived at the scene and got out.

Rick had heard the ambulance struggling up the mountain road and met us at the tape.

"What's up, partner?" I asked him.

"I've never seen anything like it, Walt! Just wanted you to see. You know, create a memory together." He tried to smile—but couldn't. He turned, and we followed.

The four of us walked over the ridge to where the deputy met us—the sheriff having left to return to town. There was no banter as we all turned to fix our eyes on the shocking scene in front of us. As we walked around it, Rick explained what he had learned. "Obviously, the cause of death is blunt trauma to the head."

"How's he still standin'?" asked Don.

"I wondered the same thing," Rick answered. "Obviously, the blow drove his lower legs deep into the mud. And it must have crushed his spine in such a way that he's stuck upright. Of course, having the tree right behind him helps."

Don commented, almost to himself, "Seems like he'd bend over frontward at the hips, don't it?"

"I agree," I said. We three continued to walk around the body—not believing what we were seeing.

Then I noticed the crushed hard hat sitting on the shoulders. I looked at Rick. "Have you taken the hat off?"

"I did. But you may not want to, Walt. It's pretty ugly."

The deputy chuckled. "I thought Dr. Pyeritz here was gonna toss his lunch. He got even greener than you did at the shootin' over at the Grissom place, Dr. Larimore."

"Well, Rick," I muttered, "at least our reputations are established among the law enforcement community, eh?"

"I'm just kiddin' you boys," the deputy said. "Don't take no offense. Happens to every new doctor comes out this way. You just don't see these types of things in the city, do ya?"

"True enough!" I responded. "Well, let's take a look."

I took a deep breath and then lifted the flattened hard hat off the shoulders of the dead man. I'm sure my instant shock was apparent to anyone not transfixed on what I was seeing. It wasn't the skull, squished like an eggshell, that stunned me. It wasn't the brain, open and exposed like a bowl of pasta, that surprised me. It wasn't even the dead man's face, crushed but facing up, that dazed me. It was his eyes—wide open, protruding, bugged out, and staring straight up toward heaven. I slowly placed the hard hat back on the dead man's shoulders, feeling a bit green.

"Reckon he never knew what hit 'im," Don whispered.

Then there was a moment of quiet. No one spoke until the deputy broke the uncomfortable silence. "Dr. Pyeritz, anything else you need?"

"I don't think so, sir."

"Well, let's see if we can get him out of the mud and over to Sylva for the autopsy. Then I'll go over and talk to his wife. It's not the best part of my job."

"It's not the best part of ours either," Rick whispered to me.

We turned to head back to our vehicles. Don and Billy put the body in the back of their rig. Rick and I rode with the deputy.

On the drive back into town, I thought back on the start of my professional life in Bryson City—on the sudden turns and unexpected tragedies like the one I had just witnessed, on the fragility of life and the part I played in that drama. As I looked across the forest, it dawned on me, unexpectedly, that no life is insignificant—that each one of us is playing a critical part in a great production being overseen by an incredible director. Even though I wasn't sure of all the whys and all the reasons for the many events in my life and my patients' lives that sometimes seemed haphazard or random, I knew there was One who did.

I looked out the window and turned my eyes toward the heavens. I wondered how prepared I was for whatever was coming next.

chapter three

AUSPICIOUS ACCIDENTS

In a rural community, building a practice can be a slow process—especially when there are established professionals already well entrenched.

Without a doubt, Mitch and Ray accepting us and letting us begin practice with them was an invaluable boost—an implied seal of approval, both implicit and explicit. Nevertheless, there is only so much such a sanction or blessing can do. One still has to build his or her reputation with individual competence, character, and compassion. However, there are those tiny blessings that can make so much of a difference.

I received two on the same day.

Helen Gibson, Mitch's longtime nurse and my assistant when I was in the office, came walking up to me—more quickly than usual. Because the door to a patient's room was open just behind me, she bent over to whisper, "Dr. Larimore, there's a cut butt coming in."

I turned to look at her. "What?"

She put her finger to her lips and then indicated we should take a walk. I followed her to the end of the hall.

"What's up, Helen?"

"Good news. There's a cut butt coming over here to get sewed up."

31

"Why's that good news?"

"It's Michelle Robertson's butt!"

"Who is that?"

"Don't you know?"

I smiled. "Helen, as you are painfully aware, there is much I don't know when it comes to this small town. Good thing I didn't start practice in a big city. Imagine what I wouldn't know then."

"Well, her husband, Charles—everyone calls him Charlie—is a big-time CPA here in town. Both his reputation and his physique are enormous. He's one big man! But he's always taken himself and his family to Asheville for their medical care. I don't think he thinks much of our medical community. Worst of all, he's a big supporter of the Democratic Party!"

This is an important piece of medical history in this particular office! I thought, smiling to myself. Mitch was one of the leaders of the local Republican Party—and party affiliations seem to be more poignantly important in this small town.

"Anyway," Helen continued, "his wife, Michelle, is a well-known artist. She makes her own paper. It's beautiful!" Helen paused—I guess for effect.

"And . . ."

"Well," Helen went on, "apparently she and her boys were out walking down a hill below their home. Michelle slipped and slid for a bit. She apparently hit a sharp piece of rock and cut her derriere. She's on her way over here now."

"Thanks for the heads-up, Helen."

Now it was her turn to smile. "Just thought you oughta know."

So my first view of this prominent artist was her south end—as she was lying on her side facing north. Helen had cleaned the wound, and it was ready for me to stitch. But I thought a brief introduction—getting to know the patient a bit—would be appropriate.

"Mrs. Robertson, I'm Dr. Larimore. Sorry to have to meet you like this."

She smiled. "I agree." Michelle was a beautiful woman, with long brown hair, brown eyes, and a gorgeous smile.

"Mind if I take a look back there?"

"Not my best side. But help yourself."

The laceration wasn't too long or deep, but it was still actively oozing blood. "Shouldn't take too many stitches, but I suspect it will leave a nasty bruise."

"Drats!" she commented. "I'll have to watch the afternoon soaps on my stomach!" She laughed, and I smiled.

As I numbed and stitched her derriere, Michelle explained that she had met Charlie in Washington, D.C., had two young boys, and moved to Bryson City, where Charlie began his CPA practice. I suspected Michelle may have had some French blood in her. She asked questions about my training, background, and family. I felt as though I was being interviewed. In fact, I probably was.

"You know," she said, "I believe I met your wife."

"You did?"

"Yes. I was taking the children trick-or-treating last Halloween up on Hospital Hill. Don't you live in Eudora Gunn's house by the hospital—that long green house next to the white Victorian?"

In many towns, this would be considered an inappropriately personal question. However, in Bryson City almost everybody knew everybody's business—personal or otherwise.

"Yes we do. At least until we can find something more permanent."

"Well, your wife's a lovely woman. If I remember, she looked like she was pregnant, and she had a pretty young lady at her side."

"Yes, she *was* pregnant. Scott was born that Christmas, and that was Kate at her side."

"Well, I was dressed as a witch. One of my boys was dressed as a mouse and the other a cat. Your wife seemed surprised at how ugly I was. Of course, it was just the makeup." She laughed again.

When we were done, I had Helen update Michelle's diphtheria-tetanus immunization, since it had been over ten years since her last one.

"It was a pleasure to meet you, Michelle."

"You too, Doctor. I expect we'll be seeing you again."

Later, Reva Blanton, one of the two receptionists at Swain Surgical Associates—the practice owned by Mitch and Ray in which Rick and I worked while our office was being built up on Hospital Hill—told me Michelle had asked that charts for the entire family be set up at the office. She also signed for copies of their medical records to be forwarded to us.

———

As I was rounding at the hospital that evening, Vernel, one of the nurses, came up to me. "Dr. Larimore, Louise called from ER. She says she needs you to come by when you have a moment."

When I finished my last note and set of orders, I walked to the ER. Louise was sitting at the counter reading a magazine.

"Hi, Louise. How may I be of service?"

Louise scowled. "You ain't no waiter, and I ain't no customer. But I got one for you. Chain saw done tore up a hand." She began walking toward a cubicle where the curtain was pulled shut, expecting me to follow. I did.

Louise Thomas had run the Swain County emergency room for as long as anyone could remember—and she ran it the same way Patton ran his army. You could do it her way or hit the doorway—as she was fond of saying.

During my first year of practice, Louise and I had some runins. But we now had a truce. In fact, I liked and admired Louise—a lot! Louise would usually see the patients when they arrived in ER. She would take a history and make an assessment. If tests or X-rays were needed, Louise would order them.

If the case was simple or only needed some first aid, Louise would take care of it and not even bother the doctor on call—who would simply sign the ER sheet the next morning. In this case, however, this was apparently more than just a minor complaint. As we entered the ER bay, I saw a beautiful and familiar-looking woman lying on the gurney with her hand soaking in dark-brown

Betadine water. Betadine is an iodine-based antiseptic used to cleanse wounds. Next to the patient was a ruggedly handsome man. Both were thin and well tanned. Louise did the introductions. "George and Elizabeth, this here's Dr. Larimore. He's one of our newer doctors."

"Oh, for heaven's sake, Louise. I've been here over a year. When am I no longer new?"

Louise turned to sternly face me. "When I say so."

George smiled and reached out to shake my hand. "Good to meet you, Dr. Larimore."

I turned to Elizabeth. "Sorry to have to meet like this."

She looked up. "We've met."

I thought for a moment but couldn't make a connection. Doctors get used to this. We see so many people that it's hard to remember every person—although most expect us to. "You'll have to forgive me. I simply don't remember where."

Elizabeth was gracious. "I know you meet a lot of folks. But I work part-time as a maître d' at the Fryemont Inn. We met when you and your wife celebrated your anniversary with us."

"I do remember you. We're up there quite often. Please forgive me for not remembering"—and I should have, as Elizabeth was a tall and strikingly beautiful woman.

"Well, I suspect people look different lying down than they do standing up." Elizabeth laughed.

"True enough. Actually, you and Katherine both served us that night. Katherine cooked us a special dinner." I was referring to Katherine Collins, not only the owner and proprietor of the Fryemont Inn but its celebrated chef.

"She loves doing that for special people." She furrowed her eyebrows. "Let's see. If I remember, Katherine served you her special prime rib."

"That's right. It's still our favorite entrée there. We also had the smoked Smoky Mountain rainbow trout appetizer, Katherine's silver queen corn chowder, and a salad with fresh mozzarella cheese on top of the best tomatoes I've ever tasted."

"Dr. Larimore, sounds like you've got a better memory than you let on to."

"Not really. It was just a memorable evening."

"Do you remember what you had for dessert?" George asked.

I didn't even have to think about it. "It was the fresh-baked peach and blackberry cobbler smothered in vanilla bean ice cream."

Our laughter was interrupted by a throat being cleared. "If you all are through with your reunion, we've got work to do here." Louise had her protocols, and we were obviously breaking one of them. So it was time to go to work.

"Well, what happened?" I asked.

Elizabeth seemed to blush. "I was cutting some firewood at our home. The chain saw bucked on me. My hand flew off the saw, turning off the saw, but somehow before the chain stopped, it ripped through my glove and into my hand."

"I thought the blade stopped immediately when you let go of the trigger or whatever."

"Yeah, it's supposed to. Guess we have an older model."

I had Elizabeth pull her hand out of the water. There were a series of parallel lacerations—we call them staccato lacerations—on her palm and fingers. I had her move her fingers through a variety of movements to check each tendon. Then I checked the sensation and blood flow to each finger. "Elizabeth, no major damage here. All the tendons, nerves, and arteries seem to be intact. I think if we clean this up really well and stitch it up, your hand should be fine."

She and George seemed visibly relieved. "We were worried," George confided. "Elizabeth is quite the artist. I can't imagine what she'd do without full use of her hand."

"I'd love to see your work sometime."

"Oh," Elizabeth responded, "your partner already has a couple of pieces."

"Mitch?" I asked.

Elizabeth laughed. "No! That man has no taste or interest in art. I'm talking about Rick."

I nodded. I should have known. I suspected the connection was Katherine.

———

Elizabeth and Michelle both recovered with minimal scarring—physically or psychologically. And for Rick and me, their misfortune was a blessing.

There is a truism all physicians in a rural practice must accept and understand when they begin their practice: Until patients come to see them, they are unable to care for them. And in most small towns like Bryson City, people tend to be cautious and conservative. They simply won't visit a new physician until either they have to or someone they know well and respect recommends they do so.

This may seem self-evident, yet I've seen new physicians expect that just by hanging up a shingle, folks will come—that somehow new physicians, due to their years of study and hard work, deserve to have people come to them and trust them. But it just does not happen this way in a small town. Trust can only be earned—and such opportune times infrequently cross the physician's path.

Michelle and Elizabeth, both of whom were highly respected in our town, seemed to provide the tipping point for our practice. Indeed, up until their injuries, the kind words of the Clampitts, the Shells, the Mattoxes, the Jenkinses, the Douthits, and Katherine Collins—not to mention some of the nurses at the hospital who would speak well of Rick and me—had provided the recommendations we needed to be tried and then trusted by some Bryson Cityites. But once Michelle and Elizabeth bestowed on Rick and me their "seal of approval," our practice seemed to grow exponentially.

chapter four

ANSWERED PRAYERS

I had just finished seeing the last patient of the morning. Helen passed by my workstation and commented, "Barb's in Mitch's office when you're done."

Barb would usually drop by the office with the children several times a week. I loved seeing them and wanted them to know they were a priority. Besides, just seeing them and watching the staff and patients enjoy them would often make my day. In addition, Mitch's staff and the patients enjoyed seeing the children. I quickly finished my chart work and walked down the hall.

Barb was reading a magazine and quickly put it down as I entered. "Got time for lunch?"

I smiled. "You bet." Then she must have seen the furrow in my brow.

"Walt, is this a bad day?"

I laughed. "No, just wondered where the kids are."

"It's Nancy Cunningham's day off, and she wanted to take them on a walk around Hospital Hill while we go out for lunch!"

"That's a nice surprise." I called out, "Helen."

"Yes, Dr. Larimore?" she called back from the nurses' station. It was the closest thing we had to an intercom.

"Believe we'll walk down to Doc John's for lunch." I was referring to Super Swain Drugs, owned and operated by pharmacist

John Mattox and his wife, Becky. In the drugstore, they had an old-fashioned grill, one of the many places where locals could enjoy breakfast and lunch.

As we walked out the office door, Pastor Ken Hicks was stepping out of his office at the Bryson City Presbyterian Church, just across the street from the offices of Swain Surgical Associates.

"Doc and Barb!" he hollered. "Are you heading to lunch?"

We nodded and waited as he closed the door, crossed the street, and joined us as we headed to the café.

"How's the new office coming along?" Ken asked as we walked toward town. He was referring to the new office the North Carolina Office of Rural Health was building for Rick and me up on Hospital Hill.

Barb answered, "The trusses are going up. They're predicting that Rick and Walt will be opening their practice up there the early part of next year—maybe March or April."

"How do Mitch and Ray feel about it, Walt?"

"Well, I think they're happy about it. The office is awfully crowded when the four of us are there. But I'll tell you this, Rick and I have appreciated them letting us use their office and their staff this last year. It's been a great way to get introduced to the community—and we've learned so much that we couldn't have known had we gone straight into our own practice. We're probably going to start interviewing for our staff just after Christmas. If you know anyone who wants to interview, let me know."

"What are you looking for?"

"An office manager—someone to do the accounting and billing—and two nurses, one for me and one for Rick. Mitch has agreed to let them work with Rick and me the last four to six weeks we're in his office. That'll allow our new staff to learn from his. It will be a bit crowded, but I appreciate Mitch's offer."

Ken nodded. "Mitch sure talks fondly about you, Walt."

Barb beamed. I wanted to hear more.

"Really?" I asked.

"It's true. I think he's proud of you and Rick—and how you boys are a positive addition to our community."

*W*e entered the building and heard a shout from the back from none other than Doc John himself. "Have mercy! Two of the town's healing arts professionals and a lovely lady have just entered the Super Swain drugstore together. Goodness gracious!" Several people sitting in booths near the soda fountain counter clapped their approval, with Doc John serving as the maestro.

Doc John was one of the old-timers in the profession of registered pharmacists—able to bottle up the most recent prescription medications but also to take raw ingredients and compound them into pills or potions or ointments or poultices or extracts or teas or powders. You name it; Doc John could mix it—whether for oral, rectal, or topical application. Doc John was a "generalist" in the best sense of the word. He did it all. He was known far and wide for his "home remedies."

Uncommon was the patient I saw in the office who had not first tried one of "Doc John's Tried-and-True Home Remedies." What came to surprise me over the years was just how many seemed to work. He wasn't really a formal doctor-of-anything, but he had always been "Doc" to the locals.

Ken, Barb, and I smiled as we slid into a booth. Whenever I stepped into the grill at Super Swain Drugs, I was immediately swept up in feelings of nostalgia. The store looked almost identical to Maxwell's Rexall Drugstore in Tiger Town—the commercial area on the edge of Louisiana State University that my family patronized when I was growing up in Baton Rouge. I had warm, deeply meaningful memories of my father taking me to the grill/soda fountain there on many occasions before school for biscuits and bacon. It was "just us guys." Bob Price, the registered pharmacist and a close family friend, would always greet me by name whenever I'd walk into his store. I can remember each of us having a cup of coffee, mine mixed as café au lait, and feeling very grown-up.

"The usual?" shouted Becky, the short and effervescent wife of the town's most gregarious pharmacist—serving today as pharmacist aide, short-order cook, and waitress.

We all nodded our assent. Although Barb and I were still considered newcomers by many of the locals—and would be for some time to come—at Super Swain Drugs we were now considered "locals" and valued customers.

We were quietly chatting as Doc John came up and threw himself into the seat next to Ken. As his large frame landed on the upholstered bench seat, we could hear a large whoosh of air escape as Ken bounced into the air and then settled back down into the cushiony softness of the seat.

"Can't tell ya how surprised I was to see you three walk in together," Doc confessed. "Ever had that sudden sense that God's answerin' your prayer right before your eyes?"

"I know what you mean, Doc," Barb answered. "What's up?"

Doc John took a deep breath. "Had a fella talk to me yesterday. He's a pastor, and his daughter just had a baby over in Waynesville, and the baby's got Down Syndrome. The whole family is tore up over it, and I keep wonderin' how God could let something like this happen. Truth is, I've been askin' God 'bout it all morning. It just don't make no sense, given this man's served the Lord so well and for so long. Anyways, I was just thinkin' 'bout that, and who walks in but a pastor, a doctor, and a mother. And not just any doc and mother, but ones with a little girl who's got some kind of birth defect herself."

Pastor Ken seemed startled. "Doc John, do you think a man of the cloth is protected from trials or tribulations?"

"Well, seems like he should be—at least somewhat. Shouldn't he?"

Ken chuckled. "Well, in my observation it doesn't happen that way. In fact, one well-known man of the cloth, Saint Peter, wrote that we shouldn't be surprised at the painful trials we suffer, as though something strange were happening to us. But we should rejoice, he said, that we participate in Christ's sufferings, so that we may be overjoyed when his glory is revealed."

"I see what you're saying," Doc John conceded, "but I'm not sure I understand why God allows terrible things to happen to innocent children. I mean, I know he knows what he's doing. But somehow it just doesn't seem fair."

"John, God doesn't promise us that life will be fair," Ken observed. "But he does promise that he himself is good. And he promises that if we love him and are called according to his purpose, then all things—even things that appear bad or unfair or unjust—will work together for good. So I hang my hat on his promises. To be truthful, though, I've not had to walk down the road your friends have. I can't imagine how difficult it must be."

"Well, I can tell you," Barb added, "that it's an incredibly hard path to walk. In fact, it's the hardest thing I've ever done."

I had a strong sense God was prompting me to tell Kate's story. I hesitated and then glanced at Barb. She nodded, and I knew this was one of those God-ordained moments.

"Doc," I began, "we'd love to tell you our story about Kate. I'm sure it won't answer all your questions, 'cause the truth is, we still have lots of questions ourselves. But the question you're asking is one we've lived with and learned from through our experience with Kate. Do you have the time now to talk a bit?"

"I'll make the time," Doc John answered. "I have a feeling God sent the three of you in here just for me today."

Just then Becky brought the tray with our lunches. After she doled out the food and made sure we didn't need anything else, she asked, "Y'all mind if I pull up a chair? Things have calmed down a bit. And I want to be sure this pharmacist isn't telling any tales out of school!"

John laughed. "No, dear. No tall tales today. I'm just askin' these good folks 'bout a serious topic."

Becky looked askance at her husband. "*You're* being serious?"

John smiled. "For once I am. I guess I'm just tore up 'bout that little girl over in Waynesville, and Walt here was gettin' ready to tell me 'bout Kate."

Becky nodded. "Now *that's* a story I'd like to hear, if it's okay."

I nodded. "After Kate was born, her development seemed delayed—she wasn't doing some of the things babies her age normally do. Kate's physician and I weren't concerned. But Barb strongly sensed something wasn't right. Kate's lack of development finally became obvious to me and her doctor, and so we had her evaluated at the age of six months. They made the dreaded diagnosis: Kate had cerebral palsy."

"What causes cerebral palsy?" Ken asked.

"For some reason, blood to part of the baby's brain is blocked before the baby is born. The loss of oxygen and nutrients causes a part of the brain to die. It's almost never recognized at birth, but usually at four to six months of age it starts to show some effects. Once it's diagnosed, it's pretty much a shock for the parents, who thought their child was normal."

"So what did they tell you?" Becky inquired.

"Kate had a CT scan, and the pediatric neurologist said it showed virtually no right brain and a severely shrunken left brain—leaving her with about a third of a brain. As alarming as that news was, he then told us, 'She'll never walk or talk. She'll grow bigger, but she'll never get better.' He told us we could put her in an institution, or we could just take her home and love her."

"It must have been devastating to both of you," Becky remarked.

"It really was," Barb noted. "And it was a real strain on our marriage. It nearly tore us apart as a couple."

Ken chimed in. "That's no surprise, Barb. I've read that about 70 percent of married couples who have a child with severe disabilities end up getting divorced."

Barb nodded. "I had heard the same thing, Ken. So I determined two things: Walt and I *were* going to make it, and I was going to do everything in my power to give Kate a fighting chance."

"So what did you do, Barb?" asked Doc John.

"Well, I read all I could about the diagnosis and talked to other parents who had raised children with cerebral palsy. And I was attracted by the then-novel theories that children's brains could be shaped by plenty of physical therapy. So my prescription for Kate was lots of therapy and a large dose of reading and singing, combined with a healthy measure of daily prayer and unconditional love."

I picked up the story. "While Barb went to work on Kate's development and therapy, I've got to admit I chose a darker, more dismal road. I wallowed in anger and self-pity. I could imagine having to care for Kate not only as a disabled child but as a profoundly disabled adult. For Barb that thought generated great love and empathy, but for me it generated great anger. All my hopes for her—of becoming an athlete or thespian; of dating and loving; of finding her soul mate for life and of having me, her daddy, walk her down the aisle to him; of enjoying my grandchildren—were pounded and pummeled by her prognosis. So I chose to bury myself in the world of medicine."

"Wow!" exclaimed Doc John.

"Let me tell you, John," added Ken, "Walt's response isn't unusual. In fact, many parents get really mad at God when they have to walk this path. Did you feel that way, Walt?"

Embarrassing as this was to share, I continued. "My anger at Barb—and at God—for 'doing this terrible thing' to me was intensified by a discussion with a pastor one afternoon."

"A pastor?" asked Ken.

"Having heard about Kate and the difficulties in our marriage, he came over to our house one evening. After a few formalities, he launched into the purpose of his visit."

"I remember it like it was yesterday," Barb commented. "He began with, 'Walt and Barb, I've come to help you.' Walt and I looked at each other expectantly. I mean, we felt we would have cheerfully accepted any help—especially since parents who have been told there is no hope will desperately seek any morsel of help."

"That's true," added Ken. "So what'd he tell you?"

"Ken, what he said next stunned us. He said something like, 'I can tell you, based upon the authority of God's Word—the Bible—that God did not design Kate to be like this, that God does not want Kate to be like this. He wants her healed—and isn't that what you want?"

John looked at Ken. "Is that true, Pastor?"

"Some think so," answered Ken.

"Well," I added, "Barb and I sure wanted to believe it. In fact, we both nodded our heads affirmatively to his question. After all, who wouldn't want their child healed?"

"Well, I'll tell ya this," said Doc John. "The fella whose grand-daughter has Down's sure would want her healed."

Becky nodded and looked at Barb. "So then what'd he say?"

"Well, he kinda shocked us. He told us there were people who would say that Kate is just an accident. Then he said, 'But we know that's not true. The Bible says God knit Kate together in your womb, Barb. She's not an accident; she's an accomplishment in God's eyes. Some would say the Devil did this. But the Bible says the Devil can't do anything that God won't let him do. Amen?'"

"We had no idea whether this was true or not," I commented. "But we nodded our heads because we were hoping what he was saying *was* true."

"And?" asked John.

"He said to us, 'I must ask you a very important question.' He paused for a moment and then asked us, point-blank, 'Do you want Kate healed?'"

"What did you say?" asked Becky.

"Of course!" Barb exclaimed.

"Obviously, my answer was the same," I commented. "But for some reason my suspicion meter was rising. It didn't feel quite right to me. Then he completely shocked us. With an absolutely straight face he told us, 'Then you have to understand that her sickness comes from sin.'"

John's and Becky's mouths dropped open. "Are you serious?" John asked.

"That was my exact thought, Doc John!" Barb commented. "In fact, I looked him in the eye and said, 'From sin? How can a little girl have sinned?' He smiled at me and then explained, 'Oh, Barb, it's not *her* sin.'"

"Oh no!" exclaimed Ken. "I know just where he was going."

"Well then, what sin?" Doc John asked.

"The answer shocked us," I added. "He looked at Barb and me and whispered, 'It's *your* sin.'"

"Yours!" John and Becky cried in unison.

Barb picked up the story. "That's exactly what *we* said."

"How'd he answer you?" asked Ken.

"He told us yes!" I answered. "He said, 'You want Kate healed. God wants her to be healed. Then you need only ask him to heal her, and he will. You've got to ask in his holy name. You've got to say the word—to declare it, to profess it. You've got to claim his great promise. But, first and foremost, you've got to confess your sin. The only thing that keeps him from healing her is your failure to admit and confess all of your sins and then claim his healing for her.'"

"You kiddin' me?" exclaimed Doc John.

Ken spoke up. "There are plenty of people who believe that theology, and they're just plain wrong!"

Barb added, "In my heart of hearts, I *knew* he was wrong. *What a horrible injustice!* I thought when he said that. I mean, to blame a little girl's disability on her parents!"

"I'm no pastor," I said, "and certainly no theologian, but when he said that, I thought to myself, *That dog just plain won't hunt!* Yet my soul ached for Kate. And I knew I'd do almost anything to see her healed."

"So what did you say?" Ken asked.

"I simply asked him what we needed to do."

Barb continued. "He led us as we kneeled in our living room and asked God to forgive our sins—even those of which we were not yet aware and had not yet been convicted. Then he placed Kate, in her child seat, between us. He laid our hands on Kate's head and his hands on ours. He claimed God's healing for Kate and thanked God for the healing that only he could bring. The prayer was loud and intense. How it didn't wake little Kate, I'll never know."

John chuckled. "Man oh man! So what happened?"

I continued the story. "Well, the prayer session finally ended. The pastor gave us a few final instructions. We were to expect Kate to begin to develop normally. We were to believe it. We were to continue to claim it in daily prayer. We were to expect the Devil to be defeated—along with *his* disease."

Becky and John were silent. Ken looked at them and then at Barb. "Well, I guess it's obvious Kate wasn't healed, right?"

"That's right," answered Barb. "Over the next few months, she didn't improve. I poured even more time into her therapy. And Walt poured even more time into his medical training."

"How'd you feel, Walt?" asked John.

"It was bad enough that we were growing apart; however, what was even worse was that in the depth of my soul I believed Kate's disease was caused by me and my sin."

"Did you buy that drivel, Walt?" asked Ken.

"I did, Ken. But God was about to demonstrate how he answers prayer—in a way neither the name-it-and-claim-it pastor nor we expected or anticipated."

Barb picked up the story. "As Walt worked thirty- and thirty-six-hour shifts, I looked for a small home to purchase—finally finding one in a quaint neighborhood halfway between Durham County General Hospital and Duke Hospital—the two hospitals at which Walt worked. It was a beautiful little house with hardwood floors in a very quiet neighborhood with nice trees. The backyard would be a perfect place for children to play safely. This house—or rather the neighborhood in which it was located—was the source of many answered prayers for Walt and me. Yet our buying it also answered some of the prayers of others."

"The prayers of *others*?" asked Becky.

Barb smiled. "Absolutely!"

"How so?" asked Ken.

"Well, across the street, Gertrude and Walter Eakes were praying that a young couple would buy the empty house and that the couple would have one or more small children who could become their 'adopted' grandchild or grandchildren."

I added, "Next door, Richard and Margaret Scearce, who loved to coach and come alongside young couples, were praying that a couple, young in their spiritual journey and needing mentoring, would move in."

Doc John chuckled.

I continued. "Next door to the Scearces, and two doors from our house-to-be, lived several single men—all medical or psychiatry residents and all strong in their faith—who were praying that a young doctor who was really messed up would move in."

Now John, Becky, and Ken all began to laugh.

"Better yet," I added, "kitty-corner to the empty house sat a small neighborhood church that had a fresh-out-of-seminary pastor named Mac Bare. One day the pastor was visited by a nurse, one of his parishioners, who worked at the Lennox Baker Cerebral Palsy Hospital. She had a desire to begin a ministry on Sunday mornings to the families of children with profound disabilities. She asked him, 'Why not use one of our Sunday morning nursery rooms to serve as a respite room for these children? Parents could leave their children with us for Sunday morning. If they want to attend church, fine. But if not, if they just need time to themselves—respite time—then that's okay too. We'd just be here to serve them.'"

"What'd he say to that?" asked Ken.

"The young pastor liked the idea; however, neither the nurse nor the pastor knew of any parents in the neighborhood who needed such services. So the nurse said to the pastor, 'Well then, let's pray that some will move in!'"

"Little did Barb and I know that simply by being led to buy this house, we were answering so very many of *their* prayers."

"That's an incredible story," John remarked. "God really did use you to answer a lot of prayers!"

"You bet, John. And in the same way, ours were being answered in ways we could not have imagined."

Barb picked up the story. "For the next two years, these wonderful folks ministered to Kate, me, and most especially her dad."

Barb reached over to give my arm a squeeze. I could feel my eyes filling with tears as Barb explained. "They renewed our faith and our strength. And I watched Walt fall back in love with our daughter, me, and our God."

I took Barb's hand. "Along with Barb's prolific prayers and lavish love, Kate began to respond in remarkable ways. And then one day the little girl who was supposed to never talk said 'Mama.' And her second word was 'Da.' I've gotta tell ya, it was the sweetest sound I'd ever heard."

Becky smiled sweetly. "I bet it was, Walt."

"And that's not all. One afternoon, while I was seeing patients at the family medicine clinic, my nurse came up to me and said, 'Dr. Larimore, you need to go home—now!' I asked what she was talking about. She told me, 'Barb just called. There's no emergency, and she and Kate are fine. But she needs you to come home *now.*' Well, of course, I protested. I still had a couple of patients to see. But another doctor agreed to see my patients. My nurse looked me in the eye and simply said, 'Trust me, Dr. Larimore. Go home. *Now!*' The short drive home seemed an eternity. I parked in the driveway and rushed into the house. When I reached the den, I cried out for Barb. I could hear her in the living room. She sounded so calm. I rushed through the den and dining room and found Kate and Barb laughing as they sat on the floor. 'Why'd you call me?' I asked."

Becky leaned forward as Barb continued. "I remember smiling at him. I told him to sit down so I could show him an answered prayer."

"So what happened?" asked Becky gleefully.

"It was such an incredible moment," I explained. "First Kate grinned from ear to ear. Then Barb reached over and took her hands. Kate struggled to stand, and with Barb's help she gained her balance. Barb let her lean back against the sofa and moved a few feet away. Then Barb said, 'Come on, Kate. Let's show Daddy!'"

"Did she?" asked Ken.

"I wish you could have seen it, Ken. Kate smiled and laughed. Then she slowly leaned forward and took a couple of very wobbly steps before she lunged into Barb's waiting arms. It was the first day she had ever taken a step. I couldn't believe it! I was seeing my little girl walk! Sure, her steps were wobbly and weak, but they were steps!"

"Kate was laughing hysterically," Barb added.

"And Barb was cheering like crazy." Then I paused a moment. "And I bowed my head into my hands and wept like a baby. My prayers *had* been answered. My baby had now talked and walked. She was never supposed to do either."

Becky's eyes filled with tears. "What a wonderful story," she whispered.

"It gets even better. After I finished my residency, Barb and I determined we needed to spend several months of time with thirty-month-old Kate—who was sitting and scooting around the house. Her left side still worked very poorly, and her right side was weakened. By then she could speak a few words. She loved to be read to and sung to, and her smile was effervescent. It became increasingly clear Kate was a special blessing, and I didn't want the burdens and responsibilities of starting a new practice at this critical stage in her life."

"I don't blame you," John commented.

"I wanted—and needed—to be with her and her mom because we were still rebuilding our marriage. So we put our furniture in storage, borrowed my mom and dad's camper, and went on a three-month camping vacation out West. We visited national parks and seashores and devoted time to each other and Kate."

"Three whole months?" asked Becky.

"Yep. During that trip Barb and I devoted a lot of time to the physical, speech, and occupational therapy Kate had begun at the CP hospital. With the help of special braces, she had begun to stand more confidently and to take even more steps. We saw her develop so much in those three months, and I've never regretted investing the time in my family."

"I bet you all have lots of special memories," Ken remarked.

"We sure do. In fact, one of the most special memories occurred in Yellowstone National Park, among its spectacular vistas and wildlife. Kate seemed especially interested in the buffalo and the elk. We enjoyed taking park ranger–led nature walks, and Kate apparently absorbed more than we imagined. At a roadside viewpoint, we had pulled over to observe a large herd of elk near the road, quietly grazing in the knee-high grass of the roadside meadow. We were sitting on a bench, watching the spectacle, when Barb asked Kate, 'Can you call the elk?'"

"I wish you could have seen it," Barb added. "Kate took her good hand, her right hand, and held it next to her mouth, as she had seen a park ranger demonstrate earlier that day. She drew in a big breath, threw back her head, and bellowed, 'Heeeeeeeeeeeere elk!' Several of the nearby elk looked up and stared at us while chewing their lunch."

"Kate began to giggle and then laugh almost hysterically," I recalled. "As we watched the elk, Kate pointed to a small calf that had apparently injured its leg and was limping. She said, 'Look, Daddy. That baby has a bent leg, just like me.' I tell you, I had a lump in my throat as I picked her up and held her tight against my chest."

I lowered my head as I felt tears streaking down my cheeks. I was glad Barb carried on with the story. "When we arrived here in Bryson City, one of our concerns was that there were no services for children with cerebral palsy. But the folks who cared for Kate at Duke had recommended the Cherokee branch of the Child Development Center at Western Carolina University. So I take Kate to the center at least twice a week for physical, speech, and occupational therapy, and I continue the therapy at home every morning and evening. And our love for her deepens in ways we never could have imagined."

I wiped the tears from my eyes and looked up. There was silence at the table. I took a deep breath and let it out. "So, John, I'm not sure I have an answer for your friend except to say that this side of heaven I don't believe a whole lot of our 'Why, God?'

questions will be answered. And I've come to believe the real question is 'What?'"

"'What?'" asked John.

"Yep. Like 'God, *what* are you trying to teach me?' or 'God, *what* are you going to do in and through me with this difficult situation?'"

"Or," Barb added, "maybe what appears to the world to be an adversity is, in fact, one of the greatest blessings you'll ever receive. Maybe that's why one of my favorite Scripture verses is the one that says, 'And the God of all grace, who called you to his eternal glory in Christ, after you have suffered a little while, will himself restore you and make you strong, firm and steadfast.'"

John nodded. "Well, like I told ya, I've been askin' God 'bout this all mornin' long. And I reckon y'all are an answer to my prayer. I suspect God's gonna answer *their* prayers too. Maybe not today, maybe not the way they want, but certainly in ways they'll never suspect."

"Amen!" my spirit welled up in agreement.

chapter five

ROTARY LUNCH

*S*uper Swain Drugs became my lunchtime home for two or three days a week—the other days reserved for lunch at the hospital or at one of the other town cafés. But I reserved one day a week for the Rotary Club meeting at Sneed's Restaurant on Main Street.

I don't remember who first invited me to attend the weekly lunchtime Rotary Club meeting. It could have been Rick or perhaps Ray. Since we worked in the same office, I may have just decided to join them one day and invited myself. Nevertheless, one day I decided to go, and before long I had become a Bryson City Rotarian.

The weekly meetings involved lunch, lots of talk and gossip, a few announcements from the president of that particular year, and an "important" guest speaker. Now, "important" has different meanings in different communities. In big cities, the Rotary speaker may be a congressman or famous journalist, a sports or theater celebrity, or a famous musician or novelist. In midsize towns, the speaker may be a governor or state senator, a college football or basketball coach, or perhaps a local who made it big in the business world.

In Bryson City, it could be the mayor or the county agricultural agent or a park ranger. Or it could be the president of the garden club or a new developer in the area who was trying to attract for-eigners—our name for rich folks from Florida who knew neither how to drive on mountain roads nor the true value of mountain property (as they always paid way over market value). They clogged our roads in the summer and ran up our property prices in the spring and fall. Then they abandoned us for the winter.

In fact, one day my dad called. "Walt, your great-aunt Leota, when she passed away, left me and your mom her beach house in New Smyrna Beach, Florida. If there's any chance you and Barb might live in Florida one day, we'd be glad for you all to have the home and manage it."

"Dad," I told my father, "I wouldn't move to Florida if it was the last place left on the planet where I could practice." If only I had known how my words would one day mock me.

At this Rotary meeting I sat at a table for lunch with Pastor Ken, Doc John, and Fred Moody, a local attorney and a member of the hospital board of directors. Pastor Ken was the only non-member; he was with us as a guest that day.

The fact that I was sitting with these particular men on this specific day, especially in light of the discussion Ken, John, and I had had the day before—added to the distressing phone call I'd received from an attorney the night before—was to me an answer to an unvoiced prayer. The thought of that call had kept me incensed off and on all morning long. I was interested in hearing my tablemates' response to the account—although it wasn't easy to get a word in edgewise with these three guys at the table!

Fred gave me the opening I needed. "What's happening in the wide world of medicine, Walt? You save any lives yet today?"

"Ah, it's still early, Fred."

The men chuckled.

"But I did receive a strange phone call last night. I'd be inter-ested in y'all's advice about it."

It grew silent at the table as six eyes peered at me.

"Well, after supper the phone rang. I picked it up, and the voice on the other end said, 'Is Mr. Larimore there?'"

"Mister?" asked Doc John.

"Yeah, made me think it was someone who didn't know I was a physician."

"Probably a solicitation," predicted Fred.

"In a way you're right, Fred. The man told me he was an attorney from Raleigh. He said he'd recently been told that my daughter was diagnosed as having cerebral palsy, and he wanted to know if that was true."

Fred put down his fork. "Are you kidding me, Walt?"

"I wish I was, Fred."

"Go on."

"Well, feelings of distrust immediately sprang up in my mind. So I said, 'Why do you ask?' He commented that my question was fair, and then he told me that his law firm represented the parents of many children with CP. He told me that in virtually every case cerebral palsy is caused by some sort of medical misadventure."

"Misadventure!" exclaimed Fred. "Nonsense! That's just a euphemism for malpractice. This guy was a malpractice attorney, wasn't he?"

"I'm sure you're right."

"So what'd he say next?"

"He carried on with his speech by saying something like, 'Actually, it's *usually* caused by a mistake. Now, of course, these mistakes are usually unintended, unplanned—an accident, if you will. And certainly the excellent doctors and nurses at Duke usually provide exceptional care, and they certainly mean well, but there is the occasional mishap—misfortune, if you will.'"

Fred's face was flushed. "Walt, what this guy's doing is unethical!"

"I know, Fred. I was outraged too. I tried to sound calmer than I was feeling. So I told him I was sure there were no, as he had said, 'mishaps'!"

"So what'd he say to *that*?" asked Fred.

"Well, he stayed calm—at least he sounded calm. He told me it usually seemed that way. 'But,' he said, 'almost always a mistake has been made and then hidden from the child's family.' He went on to tell me that even if he couldn't find a mistake or prove that one was made, juries could be easily convinced of the need to compensate parents for the expensive care that their child was going to need for life. He told me it could mean hundreds of thousands of dollars toward Kate's medical and long-term care expenses."

"I can't believe my ears!" Ken exclaimed. "Isn't that illegal, Fred?"

"It oughta be, that's for sure!" Fred growled.

"Well," I continued, "I couldn't believe my ears either. I mean, this weasel—excuse me, Fred—but this weasel wanted to sue our doctor to compensate for Kate's care expenses. All I could mutter to him was that there was no way we'd ever sue Dr. Vest. In fact, after she heard of Kate's diagnosis, she thoroughly reviewed the medical records. When she could find nothing wrong, she had a hospital committee review the case. She was devastated by Kate's disability—just devastated. I'd never consider suing such a competent and compassionate physician. No way!"

"How'd he respond?" asked John.

"Well, I almost didn't find out. I started to hang up on him because I was so mad. But before I could, he continued. He said something like, "Mr. Larimore, I understand completely. Who in their right mind would want to sue such a wonderful person? I would *never* suggest such a thing. As you say, *No way!*'"

"Oh, this guy is sly!" commented Fred.

"Hey, Fred, doesn't it take one to know one?" quipped Doc John.

"Well, you know," Fred responded, "there's evil sly and then there's shrewd sly. I just so happen to be the latter."

"I'm lost," Ken confessed. "Where was he going with this?"

"Well, I asked him that. He told me he'd never suggest suing the doctor—only the malpractice insurance company. No harm would be done to the doctor that way, he told me. He'd only be asking an impersonal and uncaring company—one that makes outlandish, even obscene, profits—to compensate what he called 'our poor little daughter' for her handicap. And then he threw in the kicker. He said, 'Perhaps you and your wife can get some well-deserved compensation for some of *your* pain and suffering.'"

"See what I mean, John?" Fred muttered. "This guy is evil. This type of firm is what gives my profession a bad name."

"So, Walt, how did you respond?" asked Ken.

"Ken, my anger was reaching a boil. This clown had *no* idea what malpractice suits do to doctors and their families—especially when the doctor has done nothing wrong. This person was a bottom-feeder, in my opinion. All I could mutter was, 'What's in it for you?'"

Fred smiled. "Ah, the rubber meets the road."

I continued. "He told me his firm would only take a reasonable percentage of the settlement—and only after the settlement was paid. He said we'd have no out-of-pocket expenses. He said they'd take all the risk and do all the work; then he said—and I quote—'Then your poor daughter will reap the benefit from our effort and expertise.'"

"Yeah, yeah, yeah," Fred muttered. "I bet they'd take 30 to 40 percent of the award. What they call reasonable and what I call reasonable aren't in the same ballpark, I'll tell ya that!"

John laughed. "You mean you'd charge more?"

Fred smiled. "Cute, Doc John. Cute."

"So what happened?" asked Ken.

"Well, my anger had intensified to a brisk boil. 'Mister,' I asked him, 'how'd you get this information?'"

"Great question, Walt!" Fred commented.

"Well, maybe so, but he didn't bother to answer. My anger erupted. I told him my wife and I had never signed a consent for the release of our daughter's confidential medical records to him or any other law firm. Then I told him that to my knowledge none of this information was available legally in *any* public forum. I told him that as far as I was concerned, he must have obtained it illegally."

Fred laughed. "Way to go, Walt! I couldn't have done better myself. What'd he say?"

"Nothing. 'Umm' was all I could hear on the other end of the line. So then I said to him, 'And further, sir, as a physician myself, I would *never* sue another physician—especially one I was convinced had done her very best for us.'"

Laughter erupted around the table. I could see other Rotarians shooting glances at us.

"Bravo, Walt!" Fred exclaimed. "What'd he do then?"

"There was silence at the other end of the line, but I could hear the snake still breathing. I asked him, 'Would you give me your name and phone number?' Suddenly the phone line went dead, and I slammed the receiver down in its cradle."

"Wow, what a story!" Doc John exclaimed.

"I bet I could find out the name of the firm if you want me to, Walt," added Fred.

I smiled. "No, probably just best to let it drop. I don't think it's a dog I want to chase."

Ken smiled at me and reached over to pat my arm. "I think you're wise. Sometimes it's best, as the good Lord said, to just 'shake the dust off your feet.'"

That evening, Barb and I sat on the bench behind our home. I was thinking about the last two days. I was ever so slowly coming to the realization that God knew exactly what he was doing when he allowed Kate to have the gift of cerebral palsy. What others, even a misguided but sincere pastor in Durham and an unethical lawyer in Raleigh, had seen as a mistake or a terrible disease, was actually for Barb and me—and all who were to meet and get to know Kate—an incredible miracle and blessing.

Once I had prayed for her healing. But from this time forward, I was able to sincerely and gratefully give daily prayers of thanks for one incredible little girl and the healing that God gave us with and through her—and through a wonderful community of friends and neighbors.

chapter six

DEATH BY EMOTION

Tim Johnson had been one of my patients since I'd started practice in Bryson City. He had been a soldier, and since leaving military service he'd been unable to let go of a massive, seething pot of anger about the Vietnam War that churned deep in his soul.

At several past appointments I had gently confronted Tim about his anger. He recognized that he had trouble losing his temper, but he wasn't willing to invest the time to seek counseling for anger management, or even to do a bit of journaling.

One day he came to the office with an injured hand. I looked at the X-rays with Helen.

"Boxer's fracture?" she asked.

"Yep," I replied as I looked at the strangely angulated fracture of the end of the fifth metacarpal—the bone in the hand just proximal to the little finger.

"Usually caused by punching something, isn't it?"

"Yep."

Helen looked askance at me. "You're Mr. Chatty today, aren't you?"

I looked at Helen and smiled. "Yep."

She smiled back. "Let's go to work, Dr. Chatty Kathy."

We walked into the procedure room. "Well, Tim, it's broken. What did you hit?"

Tim blushed and held his head down. "A wall."

"How's the wall doing?"

Tim looked up and smiled.

I went to work, first numbing the fracture site with an injection of lidocaine and then setting the fracture and placing the hand in a plaster cast. After Helen took the follow-up X-rays and we saw the fracture was adequately reduced, I had a brief talk with Tim. I gave him cast care instructions and then asked if he had any questions.

"I do," he replied. Quiet for a moment, he gathered his thoughts, then continued. "I guess I'm ready to take up your advice and begin dealing with my anger."

"I think that would be a good idea. Loneliness and anger are two emotions that are more likely to ruin your health than almost any other. So I'm pleased you want to do something about it. It'll be good for you—and your walls."

Tim smiled.

"I'll have Helen call Ed Dawson. He's a terrific psychologist. His office is over on Deep Creek, and I think he'll be a real help to you. But I still want you to do some of the journaling we talked about before."

"Doc, I don't know if I'm real comfortable writing about my war experiences."

"Tim, I wouldn't expect it to be comfortable—or easy. But I can almost guarantee you it'll help in your healing."

"I'm willing to try anything if it will help."

I was looking forward to seeing if he would really follow my advice. If he would, healing would be possible. If not, the prospects were frightening for one simple reason: anger kills. And so does loneliness.

❦

While Tim struggled with the emotional disease of anger, Anne Smith was plagued by other more silent killers—lonesomeness, isolation, and seclusion.

One evening Anne came to ER and was seen by Louise, who diagnosed her sore throat as strep throat. What was unusual this particular time was that Anne actually had something physically wrong with her.

Usually, in the case of a sore throat, especially if the patient was a local, Louise would call the on-call doctor, get an order for penicillin, and administer the injection. Maybe it was because I was so new to practice, or maybe it was the way I was trained, but I was not comfortable *not* seeing each patient myself—which Louise took as an affront to her professional competence. Nevertheless, after Louise called, I walked over to ER to see Anne, much to Louise's consternation.

I came to know Anne, a dull and dreary fifty-nine-year-old woman, through her frequent ER visits. She seemed to take a liking to the younger doctors in town, and after a while she would only come to ER when Rick, Ray, or I was on call—since we were the only docs who would actually come into ER to see her. I learned that Anne and her husband moved around a great deal during his long Army career, raised five children, and reveled in their close-knit family life. But the kids grew up and left home to start their own families. Then Anne's husband died unexpectedly at the age of fifty-one. And Anne, instead of finding purpose and enjoyment in her new life, retreated into loneliness. Instead of finding new friends and rewarding vistas, she segregated herself from any of their former friends.

Anne had a strong religious faith but adamantly refused to go to church or to be involved in any other relationships. Instead of making new friends or volunteering her many skills and personal charms in service to church or community, she choose day after sad day to spend most of her time alone—pining for her past losses.

Anne usually came to ER complaining about not feeling well, and she would often complain that she was not long for this world. Her medical checkups almost always indicated a normal degree of physical health for her age. Louise thought it best that the doctors not come visit her in ER, as she felt that only encouraged Anne.

But I both felt sorry for her and enjoyed seeing her. She easily could have had another thirty or forty years of vibrant life ahead of her—if only she would have chosen that option! But instead of choosing to live, she was, although I didn't recognize it at the time, choosing to die—a slow, lonely, and emotionally painful death.

Her children, as was appropriate and healthy, had moved on with their own spouses and loved ones. Anne, unfortunately, was stuck in the past—and stuck there alone. It was slowly killing her—but neither she nor I saw it coming.

One Sunday afternoon I was on call when Millie called the house. "Doc, we got a home death we need you to go see."

At that time in North Carolina, if someone didn't die in a medical facility, the medical examiner had to be called to the scene, just to be sure there was no foul play. So I left our home on Hospital Hill and drove up Deep Creek Valley.

The old ramshackle home was located on a dirt road just up "Toot Holler." A Swain County sheriff's car was parked perilously at the edge of the road—leaning menacingly toward the small creek ten feet below. I parked—in the middle of the road—and walked up to the house. Deputy Sheriff Dan Rogers met me at the door.

"Doc, sure looks natural. This ole lady's been up here all alone for years. Hardly ever left the house or had any visitors."

As I ducked to enter the undersized door, he followed me, continuing his soliloquy. "She had a friend who came up once in a while. It was her friend who found her here this evening and called us."

And there she was. Anne Smith. Her porcelainlike skin was white and smooth. She had surprisingly few wrinkles for someone born well over a half century earlier. I suspected she saw very little sunlight in her days. She was stone-cold and stiff as a board. Rigor mortis had set in.

There was no sign of foul play. No indication of a struggle or a seizure. By all outward signs she had died quietly, peacefully. As I examined her, I ran through possible causes of death in my mind. Heart attack? Heart irregularity? Infection? Stroke? Brain hemorrhage? Poisoning? All were possible, but only an autopsy could tell for sure. As I was contemplating the possibilities, the deputy lobbed a theory I hadn't seriously considered.

"I'll tell ya what she done died of, Doc," he began slowly, almost thoughtfully. "This here woman died of loneliness." He stood there looking down at the body, rubbing his chin whiskers. "You can put whatever you want on that death certificate, but I'll tell you what, son, she done died of loneliness. I see it all the time."

He turned and walked out.

The autopsy results arrived at my office the next week. The conclusion? Anne had arteriosclerosis (hardening of the arteries) and very early and very mild coronary artery disease. She also had stones in her gallbladder, fibroids in her uterus, and benign tumors in both of her breasts. There were signs in her brain of mini-strokes, and her teeth were in poor shape. But there was no obvious cause of death. No evidence of a massive stroke or heart attack or poisoning or infection. The pathologist declared it to be a natural death. I guessed that the medical cause of death was cardiac arrhythmia—her heart had developed an abnormal and irregular beat that proved to be fatal.

But I suspected in my heart of hearts that the deputy sheriff was right.

The next day Pastor Ken Hicks and I had lunch together at Super Swain Drugs. I shared with Ken my experience with the deputy and Anne Smith.

"It just makes sense," Ken commented. He had completed seminary the year before and had come to Bryson City Presbyterian Church, his first church, with his wife, Tina. Ken's dad was an internist and also a well-known lay minister.

"Walt, what we were taught in seminary—and what I'm finding to be true—is that when people feel loved, nurtured, appreciated, valued, and cared for, they are much more likely to be happy."

I nodded. "I think you're right, Ken. In my psychology course in medical school, we were taught that people who are involved in social groups have a much lower risk of getting sick. And if they do become ill, they have a much greater chance of surviving."

"That's interesting. We were taught pretty much the same thing in seminary. In fact, one of my professors taught us that if we wanted to stay healthy in the pastorate, we needed to be involved in healthy relationships. I think he was right."

We each took a bite of our sandwiches, and Ken continued. "I think the Creator understood the problems that can result from being alone. I remember my Hebrew class. We were studying in Genesis where it says God formed man from the dust and breathed life into him. Just after he created man, God said it was not good for the man to be alone. Walt, the Hebrew word translated 'alone' means separated, or lonely or alienated. But even more interesting to me is that it can mean the man was incomplete. It's almost like God is telling us that if we're lonely, we can't be complete."

I chewed slowly—on both the sandwich and his words. Before I could swallow either, he continued. "I learned another interesting fact. Many Hebrew people consider aloneness to be the exact opposite of really living. To them, encouraging social relationships in the family and in the community is critical. For them, true life is not individual; it's social. It's living in harmony with others. That's why Tina and I feel fellowship and small groups are such a vital part of the church's mission in the community."

I thought about his words for a moment and then reflected on some of my medical school training. "Ken, it sounds like this is one area where theology and medicine agree. I was taught that loneliness can cause psychiatric disorders and mental breakdowns, and even physical illness and premature death."

"Makes sense to me, Walt. Basically the Bible teaches that real, authentic living occurs when we share life and love with God, family, and community."

I nodded and continued with my lunch. What Ken said made a lot of sense. It certainly explained why those patients I saw each day who were healthy spiritually and consistently involved in a faith community seemed to be so much healthier physically and emotionally than those who avoided friendship and fellowship.

In fact, I would see another prime example that very night in the emergency room.

Don and Billy had just finished dinner at the ambulance station when the 911 call came in from Millie, the dispatcher.

"You boys 'bout done fillin' your tummies?" she asked.

"Millie," Don laughed, "we'll never be done with *that* chore."

"Well," she grumbled in her usual curmudgeonly fashion, "'bout time for you boys to get some exercise. The Millers just called in from the downtown boarding house. They say Sam Cunningham's in a terrible mess and needs to be picked up right now."

"Is he drunk again?"

"Nope. Apparently his foot's rotting off and stinkin' up the place. And if that ain't bad enough, he's talkin' crazy."

Only thing new there is his foot, Don thought. "Okay, Millie. We'll roll on over there."

Mr. Miller was waiting for Don and Billy as they rolled the stretcher up to the front porch of the boarding house. As they walked up the steps, he stood. "It's a shame, I tell you."

"What's going on?" Billy asked.

"Me and the missus began to notice an unpleasant smell coming from Sam's room, which is right next to ours. We don't normally bother Sam. He ain't very friendly and ain't never returned any kindness we offered. Just last week my wife left a small vase of flowers and one of her homemade pies at his door. He never said thank you—just left the empty vase and dish in front of our door a few days later. Didn't even wash 'em."

"You see him very often?" Don asked.

"Nope. And on the rare occasions we did, he'd just sneer or grunt at us. So we didn't bother him. But when the smell got bad, we knew we had to do something."

"So what'd you do?" asked Billy.

"Well, we went over and knocked on the door. He didn't even come to the door until after the fifth knock. When he opened the door, he looked terrible—and he smelled worse. He was confused and disheveled. And his foot was wrapped in a rag—but soaked with pus that was stinkin' up the whole place. Sam almost seemed to stare past us, and then he began to laugh—real strangelike—and suddenly he slammed the door. That's when we called 911."

"Would you show us the way?" Don asked. They followed Mr. Miller up the stairs. As they reached the second floor, Don could see Billy crinkling up his nose. The smell was disgusting.

When they finally arrived outside the door, Billy knocked several times, but there was no answer. He bent over and turned the doorknob, which was not locked, and slowly pushed the door open. "Paramedics!" shouted Billy.

A revolting odor wafted out of the room. Then Don heard Billy whisper, "Oh my goodness!"

Don quickly walked over to Billy's side. There was Sam lying on the floor, surrounded by piles of garbage. He was unconscious—which was best, given the putrid look of his foot and the horrid smell.

---

*D*on and Billy brought Sam to the emergency room. He was obese and filthy. He was what we doctors call "chronically dirty." Every wrinkle had the rankest grime at its base. His toenails were thickened, long, and curled over around and under his toes, and his toe webs were nasty. But his right big toe was the worst. It was gangrenous.

Sam was delusional, probably from the infection that was spreading from his toe throughout his body. His blood pressure and blood sugar were both highly abnormal. Louise and I worked fast and hard to stabilize him, fearing his diseases were going to beat us to the finish line.

I walked down to the X-ray suite and found Carroll Stevens there. He was the director of our X-ray department and an excellent radiological technician. He not only provided all the basic X-ray services we needed; he had a CT scanner come to our hospital once a week on a trailer truck. This was a really big deal, as CT scanners were fairly new technology back then.

Although Bryson City had no radiologist in town, a consulting radiologist from a nearby city came over three days a week to read X-ray studies and to perform procedures like upper GI series and barium enemas. In an emergency, a radiologist could be called to travel the twenty-five or thirty miles to help us out.

Carroll found the patient's films, and as he was putting them on the view box for us to look over, the overhead paging system began to crackle. "Code blue, emergency room!" Carroll and I turned and sprinted to ER.

Sam's heart had started to fibrillate, beating rapidly and erratically, and then he had a seizure. We did CPR for quite some time—but to no avail.

———

That night, after the kids were asleep, Barb and I sat out on the bench. The moon was nearly full, and Deep Creek Valley was an iridescent, shimmering silver. I shared with Barb about Mrs. Smith and Mr. Cunningham. I told her about my discussion with Pastor Hicks. "I'm not sure which is worse," I commented, "loneliness or anger. But I think they both can kill."

"Walt," Barb asked, "when it comes to loneliness, what do you think about people who are introverts—those who seem to enjoy being alone? Is being alone the same as loneliness? I mean, I'm kinda introverted, you know."

I thought for a moment. "Barb, I'm not talking about people who are natural introverts—who get recharged from being able to spend time thinking and reading alone. By and large, I think healthy introverts understand, enjoy, and appreciate close relationships. You do, don't you?"

She laughed and moved closer. I put my arm around her shoulder and gave her a hug. "I think I do!" she said. We were quiet for a few moments—just enjoying the cool and beautiful summer evening. Barb sighed.

"Penny for your thoughts," I commented.

"Well, I guess to stay healthy we'll just have to stay married, eh?"

It was my turn to laugh. "That's a prescription I'll be happy to take."

I thought of our upcoming tenth anniversary in the fall. I had already begun meeting with Sally Jenkins to discuss the details. Sally was a part-time decorator and travel agent, and the full-time wife of R. P. Jenkins, a member of our hospital board of directors. They lived near us on Hospital Hill.

Barb had shared with me over the years her ideas about the ideal bedroom furniture. She wanted a four-poster rice bed—a replica of the type of bed common in the Charleston, South Carolina, area toward the end of the eighteenth century—along with a Philadelphia highboy armoire, a Philadelphia chest on chest, a couple of lowboy bedside tables, and a beautiful cherry lingerie cabinet. There was just no way we could afford this furniture, unless we bought it one piece at a time over many years. However, Sally knew of furniture factories in western North Carolina that made this type of furniture, and she convinced me that, when ordered wholesale, it would be extremely affordable. Sally also wanted to draw up ideas on how to completely decorate Barb's new bedroom. My job would be to pay for the whole affair.

I couldn't wait!

—

When I filled out Sam's death certificate a couple weeks later, I wrote that the cause of death was a heart arrhythmia exacerbated by obesity, hypertension, arteriosclerosis, tobacco abuse, alcoholism, diabetes, sepsis, and gangrene. But if the truth were told, Sam, like Anne, died of loneliness.

For whatever reasons, Sam had tended to be angry, hostile, and cynical. By choosing a life of isolation, he had cut himself off from others who could have brought balance and perspective to those deadly emotions.

By the age of twenty-nine, he was a pathological loner and an extreme example of the negative health effects of the loneliness that Pastor Hicks and I had talked about. Sam's story drove home to me the point that loneliness, like anger, kills—unless the patient is willing to do something to quell the pain. Most don't—but one did.

—

It was 2:00 a.m. when he called and woke me out of a deep sleep.

"Doc!" he almost shouted. "You won't believe it. It's gone!"

"Who is this? What are you talking about?" I asked, being roused from a deep sleep.

"This here's Tim Johnson. I did it! I really did it! It worked! It really worked!"

"Tim, you did what?"

"Doc, I began seeing Dr. Dawson—you know, that psychologist over on Deep Creek. Anyway, he told me to follow your advice—about keeping a journal. So I began writing about the war. And I began writing letters. I wrote Sarge and Binky. I wrote the Vietcong. I even wrote Johnson and Nixon. I tell you, I was one angry guy. I had no idea how angry! But, Doc, it's gone! It's really gone!"

He then broke into sobs for what seemed like several minutes. As he composed himself, I asked, "Tim, are you okay?"

"Doc, I've never been better. The pain's gone. I feel so much better. I want to bury these memories. Will you come over and help me?"

I paused for a second. I was extremely tired, but I knew what was right to do. "You bet, Tim. I'll be right there."

I rolled out of bed. Barb didn't move. Over the years she had grown used to my leaving during the night to attend a hospital admission or a birth.

The early morning air was still warm. Tim's house was just a few miles away, nestled in a small hollow. When I drove up, he met me on the front porch. He looked very serious—not angry, but grave and solemn.

"Follow me," he whispered.

We walked to the edge of the backyard. He had dug a hole, and I could see the shovel and a pile of dirt in the moonlight. He pulled a roll of papers from his belt, knelt down, and gently placed them in the bottom of the hole.

He struck a match, and we watched his hatred flame and then cool into ash.

"Doc, I know you're a man of prayer. Would you say one for me—and Sarge and Binky?"

So I prayed. Then, together, we filled that hole with dirt.

Tim buried that pain. It was gone! And so was a bunch of Tim's distress.

Researchers have now found that loneliness and anger are two of the leading causes of death—primarily by dramatically increasing the risk for heart disease. Even in the 1980s, an increasing number of well-designed studies involving hundreds of thousands of people around the world concluded that loneliness and anger not only hurt people physically, emotionally, and spiritually but could actually kill.

Love, social support, intimacy, security, safety, satisfaction, and community—these terms all relate to a common theme found not only in romance novels and popular fiction but also in the medical literature.

It was even true way out in Bryson City, North Carolina.

chapter seven

THE INVITATION

*B*arb and I drove across town and up into the hills just south of the main traffic light. After a little dogleg around the library, we pulled past the Frye-Randolph House and into the parking lot of the Fryemont Inn. We had left the children with Dorinda Monteith, their most frequent and most favorite babysitter.

After parking, we strolled up the front driveway toward the main entrance—a large front porch with several occupied rockers—and stopped to gaze at the nearly endless view across town and up Deep Creek Valley. The famous Smoky Mountain haze was setting in as the sun retreated behind the distant peaks. The air was just starting to cool down from the warm summer day.

Barb and I stood arm in arm for a few minutes, slowly and deeply breathing in the clean mountain air. There was no particular fragrance to the Smoky Mountains this time of the year—but the ever clean, crisp air and the view and surroundings were all invigorating to us.

Barb sighed. "This place has really been growing on me."

I thought a moment and then replied, "Me too."

Barb gave me a hug. "And these romantic dates really help!"

I smiled as I hugged her back. I couldn't stop thinking about my secretive planning for our tenth anniversary. That week I had talked to the manager of the Polynesian Resort at Disney World. He had found our registration information from ten years ago and would be sure we were registered for the same room in which we had celebrated our honeymoon. I was excited about being able to surprise Barb.

We turned and walked into the lobby—suddenly feeling right at home in the large, comfortable room full of rockers and over-stuffed couches occupied by the inn's guests. Some were reading, while others were enjoying board games. There was no TV blaring—none even in sight—which we found to be very pleasant. The air contained the heady scent of an open fireplace, delectably mixed with the earthy smell of the leather sofas—aromas that beckoned us to sit for a spell. Nevertheless, we walked through the lobby, turned to our right, and followed the long, narrow, creaking hall to the foyer just outside the dining room—which displayed framed magazine and newspaper articles from scores of food critics and travel correspondents—all lavishing praise on the inn and its chef-owner, Katherine Collins. The pictures showed a beautiful woman with a stunning smile and long sandy-blond hair.

As I opened the entry door into the dining room for Barb, we heard in the background the familiar sound of the ever-playing 1940s music that Katherine so enjoyed. Just as Katherine intended for her guests, we were transported back into another era.

The dining room was nearly seventy feet long and about forty feet wide, with a floor of wide maple planks. Large, dark timbers supported the vaulted ceiling—and the room was packed with diners. Elizabeth Ellison, the maître d', welcomed us and showed us to our table.

As she seated us and placed linen napkins in our laps, I couldn't help but notice her hand. "Elizabeth, it looks like your hand's healing well." I hadn't seen her since her chain-saw accident. Rick had taken out the stitches and told me that the wounds were healing fine.

"Oh, I'd almost forgotten!" exclaimed Elizabeth. "Here, look at your handiwork." She stretched out her hand, palm up, and slowly opened and closed her hand.

"What happened?" asked Barb.

"Oh, just a silly accident with a chain saw. But your husband put me back together pretty well, wouldn't you say?"

"It does look like you've healed very well, Elizabeth," I noted.

"And I have you to thank, Dr. Larimore."

"Not really," I answered. "We doctors can put the pieces back in order, but the healing really comes from the Great Physician."

"Well," she commented, laughing, "I think that with you and Rick, he's chosen some mighty fine assistants! Let me get you some water and lemon wedges."

The Fryemont Inn had become our favorite place to go for a romantic dinner. Here in Katherine's dining room we could escape the pressures of parenting, medical practice, and the many storms of modern life that bombarded us in the daily news. Her dining room's ambience—that of an earlier time and another place—helped us break away from our day-to-day responsibilities and enjoy focusing on one another. Katherine's exceptional ability to transform mere food into culinary creations was exceeded only by her skills as a hostess.

Better yet, she had become a dear friend to us—and an even dearer friend to Rick. Sadly, she was in the process of a divorce, so her and Rick's relationship had been fertile fodder for the local gossip mill.

Although Rick had been single throughout his entire education, I had never known him to be lonely. During our residency and first days of practice together, I was sometimes jealous of how rich and full a life he seemed to live. However, Barb disagreed. She felt he was missing the experience of someone special with whom to share life and love—and I had begun to suspect she was right.

I must admit I enjoyed no longer being the town's newest doctor. Unfortunately, at least for me, since Rick—the *now* newest doctor in town—and I were practicing together, we were together considered the town's newest doctors, and it was a designation we would keep as long as we practiced in Bryson City.

—

$\mathcal{A}$s Barb and I were finishing dessert, Elizabeth came to the table to check on us. Just then, Bryson City's oldest doctor and his wife, Mercedith, stopped to greet us on their way out.

"Walt, do you, Barb, and the children want to join me for a barbecue?" asked Dr. Harold Bacon. "Mercedith will be out of town, but I'll be barbecuing on Saturday afternoon. Would love it if y'all could join me."

The invitation was a total surprise. Even though Barb and I lived next door to him, and even though he had seemed polite and friendly, he had never invited us over for a meal. Dr. Bacon continued. "Four o'clock at my place. I am the best barbecue chef west of Asheville. You'll see."

I am sure my jaw was still locked in the open position as he and Mrs. Bacon turned to leave.

When we first moved to Bryson City, Dr. Bacon had been opposed to adding any new physicians. I was quite sure that he, along with Drs. Mathieson and Nordling, had opposed our recruitment. The latter rented office space from Dr. Bacon, and the former was one of the newest doctors in town himself, having "retired" to Bryson City after a long and productive career as an osteopathic physician. I always wondered if they were threatened by the arrival of newer and more recently trained physicians.

This trio grudgingly accepted Ray Cunningham into the community just a few years before our arrival—probably because Ray had been raised in Bryson City and because he was Mitch's partner. But Rick and I had neither of these attributes. The fact that Mitch had invited us to work in his practice somewhat mitigated their irritation with us—but not much.

When Dr. Mitchell and the hospital board of directors overruled their opposition to our recruitment, the three had decided to watch us carefully, looking for any mistakes. After finding a couple of missteps early in our tenure, one of the three—we never knew which one—brought official charges against us to the medical staff. We were told later that at the hearing to revoke our privilege to practice medicine in the hospital, a vociferous debate ensued, and by a vote of three to two, Rick and I barely kept our medical staff privileges and our professional skins.

Although we never knew exactly who voted for or against us, Dr. Nordling left town shortly after the vote, and Dr. Mathieson avoided speaking to us for quite some time. We suspected that Mitch, Bacon, and Paul Sale had voted for us—while Nordling and Mathieson had not. Ray, as chief of staff, could only vote in case of a tie. So I've always believed that Harold Bacon was the swing vote that saved our careers in Bryson City. But that's just a guess.

Thus, his invitation was not a total shock—but it was a surprise. As he and Mrs. Bacon walked away from our table, Elizabeth chuckled. "You can close your mouth now, Dr. Larimore."

"Did he just invite us to his house for dinner?"

"That's what it sounded like to me," Elizabeth answered. I looked at Barb, who nodded.

But why? I thought.

⟞⟝

The next day began as a deliciously lazy morning. I awoke just before dawn, and since Rick was covering the practice and the emergency room, I would be free for the entire weekend. At the blissful thought of two obligation-free days ahead, I drifted back to sleep. However, the just-after-dawn patter of eighteen-month-old Scott's little feet and Kate's "sawmill whisper"—"Wait for me! Wait for me!"—woke me up. Now four years old, Kate stood boldly at my side of the bed, next to her little brother, and then loudly whispered, "Daddy, do you want to help me and Scoot make *pain perdue* [French for "lost bread," otherwise known as "French toast"], or do you want us to do it by ourselves?"

I smiled. Even Kate had picked up our pet nickname for her little brother, calling him Scoot instead of Scott. Kate's language skills had progressed remarkably. When she began speaking—at about three years of age—she spoke in complete sentences, which stunned both her parents and therapists. And, as was her habit, she would usually be up with the sunrise, and Scott followed not too much later. I wasn't sure if her question was manipulative or just innocent—but either way it had the effect of rousing me. Imagining these two young children trying to cook with an electric skillet was more than I could stomach.

After cooking breakfast and enjoying it with the kids, I cleaned up the kitchen and waited for Barb to get up. While the kids were playing in their room, I had just enough time to step out of the back door and sit on our bench to enjoy the rapidly warming day and a second cup of coffee.

Why would Dr. Bacon invite us over for dinner? I wondered. He had seemed somewhat warmer toward Rick and me—especially since the time I worked an entire evening with him the year before to save the life of one of Dr. Mathieson's young patients, who was dying from bacterial sepsis. He seemed to have been thankful for my work and would occasionally say howdy or nod his head in my direction when we passed in the hall.

I tried to figure out the good motives he might have—but I confess I felt suspicious.

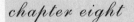

chapter eight

BARBECUE AND BACON

It was my first time in the Bacon home. Like the homes of the rest of the Bryson City doctors, it was plain—not at all pretentious.

There were two reasons for this. First, the physicians in the area made much less money than their contemporaries in virtually every other area of the country. Second, in a small town, everything you do or buy or say is common knowledge—or soon will be! Living simply is simply a necessity. Living other than modestly is simply not acceptable.

Dr. Bacon was known for his apple orchard, his barbecue skills, and his love of flying—although he no longer practiced the latter. Rumor was that his last flight resulted in his landing his single-engine plane on the four-lane instead of at the airport—sending four- and eighteen-wheelers careening off the road to avoid the oncoming Cessna. He was said to have claimed that he ran out of gas. However, the FAA inspector is reputed to have found the tank over half full and the engine working just fine. It was the good doctor's last flight, and a matter he adamantly refused to discuss.

When the appointed hour came, I walked across our yard and up the driveway to Dr. Bacon's home. Barb had sent me ahead, saying she and the children would follow in a bit. I found Harold on the back porch, and the sight of him made me chuckle. He wore a chef's hat and a large, rather messy apron, and he stood at an enormous grill. Smoke was wafting up and out the grill's stone chimney. He was hard at work. It was already a hot day, and the added heat of the fire had him sweating profusely.

He backed away from the grill. "Well, howdy, Walt! Glad you're here. Come on over."

He dove back into the smoke, turning a variety of meats and occasionally backing up to escape an attacking waft of smoke. He slathered a dark brown-black solution over the meat, which only aggravated his battle with the smoke.

"Where are Barb and the kids?"

I settled into an Adirondack chair on the deck that overlooked the town and explained they'd be over soon. He turned back to the grill. "One of the things I love about North Carolina is that this is where barbecue sauce and barbecuing began."

I had no idea if his belief was historically accurate, but he surely delivered his pronouncement with gusto. "What are you grilling?" I asked.

"Well, let's see. These are pork ribs from Clem Johnson. He always pays me in ribs. And these are beefsteaks from Mitch and Gay. They give me a bunch of steaks every Christmas. I think they come from his herd. This is boar tenderloin from one of my Cherokee patients, and over here's a bit of venison and bear."

I didn't ask him where the latter came from. I knew Harold didn't hunt, and I suspected he was paid, as we all were from time to time, in food instead of money. Sometimes the meat was legally harvested—and sometimes not.

He continued his lecture. "Walt, this is my favorite barbecue sauce, my private secret recipe. Mitch and Ray would love to know how I do it. But I'm not telling." He smiled and slathered more sauce on the meat, creating more clouds of smoke as the sauce dripped onto the coals below.

Harold backed up and smiled, never taking his eyes off his work, and he continued his lecture. "Barbecue sauce is a critical part of barbecuing. But there are other facets to remember too. For example, when I barbecue, I slow-cook my meat for a long period, which must always be done over low, indirect heat. I started this batch this morning after rounds. But the coup de grâce is *always* the sauce."

He began turning the meat as he continued his soliloquy. "Some make the mistake of only putting the sauce on the table. But barbecue sauce is meant only for foods that are grilled, *while* they are being grilled." He paused for a second and then looked at me. "What type of barbecue sauces do you like?"

I feared this was a trick question or some sort of quiz to check out what he would come to find was my very, very limited knowledge of a subject that many in North Carolina consider a religion.

"I'm not sure I've tried very many, Harold. Barb and I liked the barbecue sauce they used around Durham when I was in residency. But I'm not sure whether it was a particular type or not."

"Hmm," he crooned as though deep in thought. "Durham is in the middle of the state, but they still tend to use a western North Carolina sauce—as opposed to the eastern North Carolina sauce."

"What's the difference?"

He looked at me and smiled. I suspected he was pleased to find a subject he could teach to his young colleague. "Well, most North Carolina barbecue sauce is vinegar based. Most folks traditionally put it on pulled pork shoulder at the table. Like I say, that's a travesty. Meat's meant to be cooked *with* the sauce, and the vinegar sauce is too thin to stick. Anyway, the sauce tends to be clear in eastern North Carolina and tomato-red in the western half."

He attacked the meat with a new coating of what appeared to be a very dark sauce—clearly not from the eastern end of the state. He continued. "But there are different barbecue sauces all around the country. I've tried them all—or at least most of them."

I was in new territory, and my professor could smell my ignorance. He proceeded. "What I call Kansas City–style sauce is the most common across the country. It has a tomato or ketchup base, and you can taste sweet, sour, and smoky elements in it. The smoky taste usually comes from one brand or another of a bottled liquid smoke—that's the secret. St. Louis barbecue sauce, on the other hand, has a tomato base but none of the liquid smoke—which makes it worthless in my book."

As he flipped the meat once again, his lecture continued. "In most, but not all, of the sauces in Georgia, South Carolina, and Mississippi, mustard is the main ingredient. I like to use a little, but not as much as those folks do. In Alabama, folks love what they call white barbecue sauce. They use it a lot on chicken, and it has a base of mayonnaise, cider vinegar, and black pepper. Absolutely awful if you ask me."

I didn't have time to put a word in edgewise as he continued his culinary tour. "In Texas the sauces tend to be watery and way too spicy for my taste. They'll use beer and chilies in their sauces. As you head into the Southwest, tomato salsa and pico de gallo are called barbecue sauces—but they aren't, at least in my book. You ever have pico de gallo?"

I shook my head.

He smiled, obviously enjoying the fact that he could teach me so much in a single swoop. "I haven't either. Mercedith tells me it's a blend of cumin, lime juice, and garlic. Sounds like it would taste awful." As he slathered on the sauce, the lesson continued unabated. "My first homemade sauce was too tomatoey. I suspect I didn't cook it long enough. If you're determined to make your own sauce, and I recommend it, it's best to start with ketchup."

"Why?"

He smiled to himself, now knowing for sure he had a rookie barbecue aficionado on his hands. "It's simple. Ketchup already has a sweet and sour component to it. Also, it obviously has tomatoes and spices." He turned to look at me, pointing the barbecue fork at me as he continued the lecture, "You can add to the sweetness by adding molasses, brown sugar, maple syrup, or honey—or a mixture of them. You just have to experiment."

I nodded my understanding. He continued. "If you want a sour tang to balance the sweetness, you can add a tad of vinegar."

He looked to the side of the porch, perhaps to see if anyone was listening. "I use a bit of cider vinegar myself. Mitch uses a bit of lemon—but I think that's a waste."

I nodded again.

"Besides adding a tad of mustard, I've learned to add a bit of Worcestershire sauce, garlic, onion, and black pepper. Mitch uses ground cayenne or Tabasco—but that makes it too hot for me. Ray—you know how he likes the fancy wines—will add a bit of red wine or port. But my personal secret is a bit of liquid smoke. In my opinion, you can't have a good barbecue sauce without some liquid smoke. It's impossible."

He turned back to the grill to turn the meat. As he did so, clouds of delicious-smelling smoke encircled Harold and the grill. I savored the moment.

A gentle breeze cleared the smoke and left my professor facing me and pointing his lecturing fork at me. "Walt, you gotta understand that consistency is critical—a sauce that's just a tad thinner than ketchup works best. If it's any thicker, the sauce will hang heavy on the meat like goop. If it's a thinner version, it'll just slosh off before it can do any good."

He paused just long enough for me to insert my first question. "Harold, do you put the sauce on throughout the cooking process?"

He looked at me like I had two heads. "Why, of course not. Remember, a prize barbecue sauce always contains a bit of sweet— some kind of sugar—and if you put it on the meat too early, it'll just burn on the outside before the inside is done. Since I slow-cook my meat, I don't start putting the sauce on until ten to twenty minutes before it's done."

We heard the sounds of giggling children and Barb's happy voice and turned to see them climbing Harold's driveway. "Now here's the last secret I'll tell you," he said conspiratorially. "Never let the sauce do all the work for you—you gotta season the meat well before and during cooking. I use a spice rub that Mitch makes up for me. He doesn't share his recipe with me, and I don't share my barbecue sauce recipe with him. We figure this arrangement will preserve our friendship."

He let out a rumbling laugh and slapped his knee—sending pellets of sauce flying off the end of the fork.

After the meal, Harold called me into the kitchen. He looked back toward the family room to be sure no one was looking and handed me a folded piece of paper as he whispered, "Walt, here's my recipe. You can have it, but just don't ever let Mitch or Ray know. And for sure don't let Paul Sale know you've got this. You know, they'd kill for this recipe. Let's just keep it between us, okay?"

I took the paper and held it like a treasure. "Harold, thanks for your trust. I promise you I won't betray it."

"Well, after I'm gone to the hereafter, you can share it with folks. But not before, hear?"

I nodded, and we turned to walk back to the family room. Dr. Bacon slapped me on the back. "I've always liked you, Walt."

Having never before this day seen any indication of evidence that would corroborate such a statement, I was appropriately, but happily, befuddled.

Later that evening, I opened the treasured piece of paper. Written in a scrawled handwriting, barely readable, was "Basic Barbecue Sauce." Below the heading was a list of the secret ingredients:

2 cups ketchup
1/4 cup cider vinegar
1/4 cup Worcestershire sauce
1/4 cup firmly packed brown sugar
2 tablespoons molasses
2 tablespoons mustard
2 teaspoons liquid smoke

1/2 teaspoon freshly ground black pepper
1/4 teaspoon onion powder
1 crushed garlic clove

Combine all ingredients in a saucepan and bring to a boil over medium-high heat. Reduce heat to medium and simmer 15 to 30 minutes or until sauce is dark, thick, and rich.

I vowed to myself to keep Dr. Bacon's secret—at least as long as we both lived in Bryson City.

$\mathcal{A}$s we turned off the light to go to bed, I hugged Barb.

"Did he give it to you?" Barb asked.

"What are you talking about?"

"Did Dr. Bacon give you the barbecue recipe?"

"Why do you ask?"

"Well, someone at the hospital, who will remain unnamed, gave me Mitch's secret recipe for spices to rub into the meat before barbecuing."

Hmm, I thought to myself. "What's in the spices?"

"I could tell you," Barb whispered, "but then I'd have to kill you." She chuckled and then snuggled against me. "It was nice of him to have us over."

"It was," I agreed. "But why do you think he waited until Mercedith was out of town?"

"I was thinking about that," Barb replied. "You know, I think he's sensitive that she's so much younger than he is. Maybe that's part of it. Or since she's so involved in Democrat politics here in town, and all the doctors are Republican, maybe she just didn't want to mix."

"Well, I'm just thankful to get to know him a bit better."

"Me too," Barb whispered. "Makes me feel a bit more at home here."

I was quiet for a moment. I did feel a bit more at home here. And then I laughed out loud.

Barb rolled back toward me. "What are you laughing about?"

"I was just thinking about the fact that, with you having Mitch's secret spice rub recipe and me having Dr. Bacon's secret barbecue sauce recipe, we'll just have to stay married."

Barb laughed softly and then whispered in my ear, "Indeed 'tis an arrangement that may well keep us together."

chapter nine

A TOUCHY SUBJECT

Eschar is the medical name for a scab.

I mention this fact because, as most small-town doctors know, patients will frequently use an encounter with the doctor at a local business establishment as an opportunity to "catch up" their case histories or "ask a question or two." One of the most amusing encounters I ever had involved an eschar.

An elderly couple was sitting at Super Swain Drugs when I walked in with Ken Hicks for lunch. I had seen the woman for a venous stasis ulcer that had been located just above her ankle. Of several potions tried, one of Doc John's recipes had dramatically reduced the size of the eschar and begun to promote "proud flesh" formation more successfully than any other treatment.

Doc John called it "Betadine-sugar paste." It was very easy to mix, and I used it off and on for my entire practice career. The paste contained eight parts granulated sugar, one part Betadine ointment, and one part Betadine solution. Additional ointment or solution could be added as necessary to obtain a paste, as Doc John would say, "the consistency of granular peanut butter."

Ken and I stopped at their booth to say hi. As we turned to go to our booth, the husband remarked to me, "Doc, the dressing you suggested for Ruth's escargot was wonderful. Her escargot is the best it has ever been!"

Once I realized what he was saying, I chuckled out loud.

As we walked to our booth, Ken seemed rightly confused. "What was *that* all about?"

$\mathcal{D}$uring our lunch together, for some reason we got on the topic of specialists—which was, early in my career, a somewhat sore subject with me.

Ken began innocently enough. "Walt, what do you think about the hospital's desire to bring some specialists into the community?"

"I hadn't heard about it."

Ken cocked his head and explained. "I thought you would have known. Anyway, Earl Douthit, the administrator, mentioned to me that they're thinking of buying the home next to Rick's house. It's for sale."

"What would they do with the home?"

"He says they'll convert it into an office and have specialists from Sylva come over to see patients here in Bryson City."

I paused, certain my neck was changing color. "Why would we need them?"

"Well, a lot of people from this town travel to Sylva to see a dermatologist or urologist or pediatrician."

"I know," I complained.

"Well, maybe it'd be easier for folks if the specialist came here once or twice a month."

"Ken, seems to me we already have too many physicians here. In fact, Dr. Mathieson thinks we have t-w-o too many physicians."

Ken chuckled. "May be true, Walt. But sometimes the specialists in Sylva will tell our people that GPs may not be the best for their care. They say there's just so much any one person can know."

Now I was certain the emotion showed in my face. Before I could think, I shot back, "Ken, many subspecialists are academic, ivory-tower types. They usually care only for one gender or for one age group or for one organ system. And they believe there's so much medical knowledge that no rational person could ever consider becoming a competent generalist physician. Such sentiments are, I believe, hogwash."

Ken sensed my emotion. "Whoa, Walt! I'm on your side. I'm just telling you what I hear folks saying."

I took a deep breath and a sip of my soft drink. "Ken, since Sir William Osler's time at the turn of the century, the discipline of general practice has been an academic discipline with its own curriculum, research base, and peer-reviewed journals, but it's also the cornerstone of most national health care systems—that is, with the notable exception of the United States. What a GP has to know to be a competent physician is different from but no less demanding than that of any specialist in any university center—much less Sylva!"

Ken looked at me and then said gently, "I can see this is a touchy issue."

"Well, it really is, Ken. As residency-trained and board-certified family physicians, Rick and I are trained to handle over 95 percent of the problems that come into the office. And we have additional training in maternity care, orthopedics, nursery and child care, and surgery."

"You know, my friend, I don't think most people around here know that. I think we need to get you some PR."

"Ken, if they'd think about it, it would make sense to them." Then I chuckled.

"What's so funny?"

"I was just remembering a quote from a fictional character who was the oldest man in the world. His name was Lazarus Long."

"Oh, I remember him!" exclaimed Ken. "He was in one of Robert Heinlein's science fiction novels."

"Yep, that's him. And he said something like this: 'A human being should be able to change a diaper, plan an invasion, butcher a hog, conn a ship, design a building, write a sonnet, balance accounts, build a wall, set a bone, comfort the dying. We should be able to take orders, give orders, cooperate, act alone, solve equations, analyze a new problem, pitch manure, program a computer, cook a tasty meal, fight efficiently, die gallantly. Specialization is for insects!'"

Ken laughed. "Okay, okay. I see your point."

"Of course, Ken, I'd never publicly admit to so deeply enjoying a quote such as this."

"I understand, my friend. But I still think we need to get you and Rick some PR."

I let the comment pass. We finished lunch and walked back to our offices. We were both absorbed in our own thoughts. My concern was whether Rick and I would ever be able to fit into this small, closed medical community. In so many ways they wanted us there. Yet in so many ways they did not.

Only time would tell.

chapter ten

FAMILY TIME

$\mathscr{S}$eptember in the mountains marks the end of summer and brings the first of the color season to the high country. As Bryson City began to shed the last of the summer's scorching heat, the ancient Great Smoky Mountains began to breathe the cool and colorful commencement of autumn. To me, the fragrances in the air were sweeter then than at any other time of the year.

Fall creeps slowly into the Smoky Mountains—almost unexpectedly early at first—at least to those of us who were used to the flatlands. It begins around the forested peaks and the craggy balds of the higher mountains and slowly creeps down the slopes to form soft layers of mist and fog that begin to descend each morning into the lush, fertile hollows and coves.

By the end of September, chilly breezes sweep down from the ridgelines early in the morning, and the folks in the Smoky Mountains know autumn is just around the corner.

Even though autumn's peak color generally occurs around the middle of October, trees growing above four thousand feet will not uncommonly begin to proudly show off their coats of many colors between mid-September and early October.

After Labor Day and before mid-October, the summer crowds are gone and the swarm of color gawkers is yet to come. On most weekdays during this time period, locals have the national park to themselves. For our family, early fall became the ideal time to spend free weekends exploring the nooks and crannies of the Great Smoky Mountains National Park.

Although Barb and I enjoyed walking and hiking in the Smokies, with two children we enjoyed learning about many of the almost unknown but easily accessible roads into this pristine wilderness. We took immense pleasure in the solitude of these drives and the fact that they forced us—allowed us—to slow down a bit from the fast pace of the medical practice.

During these fall drives, the grandeur of this park captured our hearts. We would stop often just to get out of the car and listen to the sounds of the forest. We would walk with the children down quiet pathways—often seeing turkey or deer, and even on rare occasions a black bear.

It was like entering another world. The ice-cold tumbling streams sparkled crystal clear. Small rounded boulders made great "mountains" for Kate to climb and summit. She was walking better and better in her leg braces but still with a noticeable limp on her bent left leg, and she loved to collect the gorgeously colored leaves carpeting the forest floor. Barb enjoyed the verdant mosses, soft as velvet, while the rich smells of earth and moisture and humus captivated me. The gentle fall breezes blowing through the trees and the mountain laurel enchanted us all, and many times we'd stop along a lonely road to sit and talk—or just sit and listen while the forest talked to us.

The high-elevation road through the Heintooga Ridge and Balsam Mountain area became one of our favorites. I'm not sure which I enjoyed more—the startling vastness of the mountain peaks as we rounded a curve or the sound of Barb's sudden intake of breath and the hush of her voice as she compared these views to favorite memorable scenes from our backpacking days.

One beautiful fall day we drove about nine miles along this road and chose a picturesque picnic area next to a small, rushing mountain stream to spread our blanket for lunch.

We were all alone and for some reason totally silent when I heard it. At first it was hardly noticeable and then more apparent—but we all tilted our heads to listen to a soft symphony of bird sounds. We all easily recognized the soft but clearly enunciated *chick-a-dee-dee-dee, chick-a-dee-dee-dee* of the Carolina chickadee. Kate had learned to mimic the sound to a tee.

As we lay on our backs and looked up to the forest ceiling, we spied them flitting from branch to branch. These aerial acrobats performed their gymnastics, flitting from trunk to trunk, as easily hanging upside down as perched right side up. The children recognized their distinctively patterned black cap and black bib with white cheeks and buff sides.

Then we noticed another chickadee in some of the lower branches. At first I thought it was just the Carolina chickadee. But as we watched, Barb pointed out that these birds seemed larger and their call noticeably different—more rapid and higher pitched. Several came close to us, and we noticed a distinct white streak on the wing. Only later, conferring with Rick, did I come to realize the rarity of what we had seen. The larger chickadees were called black-capped chickadees. Usually found farther north, they could on occasion be found in the lower Appalachian Mountains—but rarely in the same habitat as the Carolina chickadee.

Kate gasped and pointed to the nearby trunk of a massive tree. We all smiled as we watched a small bird climbing down the tree headfirst! It had a black cap over a white face; small, black, beady eyes; and a beak that was both longer and sharper than that of a chickadee. Its tail looked stubbier than that of the chickadee, and its white breast contained no black bib. *Aha*, I thought to myself, *it's a nuthatch*—one of the few birds in the eastern United States that go down a tree headfirst. The children giggled as they watched this one—a white-breasted nuthatch—almost woodpeckerish in behavior, tapping the wood in search of food, but totally upside down.

$\mathscr{S}$cott had dozed off and Kate walked away to do some exploring. We knew that with her braces and limp she couldn't get too far away. We also knew that this "exploring time" was an important part of her growth and development.

I sighed and lay my head back on Barb's lap. "Honey," she asked, "what do you think we should do for our anniversary?"

Even though I had been wrapped up in the intricate plans for our celebration, I had forgotten to talk with Barb about them. I knew I would need to be careful. "Well, I'm planning a surprise."

"Oh, Walt," Barb sighed. "You *know* how I hate surprises."

I smiled. "I think you'll like this one."

"This one what?"

"Well, we're going to take a trip."

"Where?"

"I can't say."

"You mean you *won't* say?"

I laughed. "Okay, I *won't* say."

"Will you at least let me know what to pack?"

"It's a deal!"

"And what about the kids?" she asked.

"I'm working on a plan. It'll all work out just fine."

"Is Rick involved?"

"Well, he knows some of the basics—after all, he's got to cover the practice while we're gone."

Barb sighed, seemingly acquiescing to my secret planning process. "As long as Rick is comfortable with it all, I guess I will be."

I smiled and sunk into my thoughts about the anniversary plans and the children. I hadn't really thought about the fact that we'd be leaving them for almost two weeks—something we had never done.

"What are you thinking about, Walt?" Barb asked.

"Guess I'm just worried about Kate."

"In what way?"

"Oh, don't get me wrong. I couldn't be happier that she's ambulatory. And her vocabulary is growing every day. For a kid who was supposed to never walk or talk, it's just amazing."

"Miraculous, I'd say."

I chuckled. "You're right, honey." I paused to gather my thoughts.

"What's wrong?"

"I guess I'm just concerned about her contractures."

"Contractures?"

"Yes. Her hemiplegia on her left side is making her leg and arm muscles a bit spastic, and that's causing her joints to be less supple. Her left knee and ankle are contracted, and when she walks, it makes her leg look bent."

"Do you think it's getting worse?" Barb sounded anxious.

"It's just subtle for now. But I think it's likely to worsen over time."

"What do you mean?"

"At worst, it could mean that Kate will have more and more trouble walking, even in the braces."

"What should we do?"

"I think at some time we need to make a trip back to Duke, honey. They're doing some amazing surgery these days. As I understand it, if you wait too long, the surgery is less likely to be successful."

"What will the surgery do?"

"It'll lengthen the tendons. You see, the muscle spasticity will never go away. But lengthening the tendons will allow her little joints to maintain normal or near-normal range of motion. In fact, I wonder if it wouldn't allow her to learn to walk with no braces at all."

"You're kidding me!" Barb exclaimed.

I smiled. "No, I'm not."

We heard the sound of Kate's laughter as she returned to our picnic site. When she arrived back, Barb lifted Scott into her lap, while I took off Kate's braces and rubbed her legs. Kate always enjoyed massages. As I massaged her legs, I showed Barb how Kate's left hip, knee, and ankle all had less range of motion than her right. Barb silently nodded.

What I didn't share that day was another growing concern. I knew that children with profound brain damage were at increased risk for anesthetic problems. Sometimes their little brains would react very negatively to the medicines used to put them to sleep. The surgical risk was greater for them—even the risk of death from anesthesia.

I wondered whether I had made a mistake. If I hadn't mentioned the possibility of surgery, it was unlikely anyone caring for Kate would have thought of it—because it was fairly new technology. With no surgery, there would be no anesthetic risk. But with surgery, Kate would likely be able to ambulate better and have an increased chance for a better future with more opportunity. I just wasn't sure which road to take. *No matter,* I thought. *No need to decide today.*

We finally packed up from our banquet and followed the one-way, one-lane, graveled Balsam Mountain Road, which wound several more miles through the wilderness before depositing us onto the eastern edge of the Cherokee Indian reservation.

For me, these magical weekends provided large measures of memory-making time, and they nurtured my budding realization that, more than the material things made possible by a sixty-hour week or a second income, children need generous amounts of time with each of their parents on a regular basis. As we drove home that day, I discovered I felt richly refreshed. I wasn't sure what the future held for Kate. I wasn't even sure how many years we'd have her. But on that special trip into the mountains, I determined I would make my relationship with my wife and my children a priority.

Today, over twenty-five years later, I am grateful for the smorgasbord of pictures and sounds in my memory that resulted from that decision. This mental scrapbook continues to bring me great joy and satisfaction—despite some very difficult turns in the road of life.

part two

FALL

chapter eleven

CHICKEN POPS

It was the end of the office day. Mitch was on call and had been called to the hospital to see an emergency. Ray had taken the day off, and I was finishing up the day's paperwork when Helen, in her usual dour manner, approached me with two charts in hand. I did not sense that good news was arriving.

"Mitch just called. He's in OR and wonders if you'd make a home visit for him."

Without waiting for an answer, she gently tossed the charts in my direction and continued. "It's the Nichols twins up Toot Holler. The mom, Sarah, thinks the kids have what she calls 'chicken pops.' They're thinking of having a 'pox party' and just want Dr. Mitchell to confirm the diagnosis. But since he's busy and you're not, perhaps you'd help him out."

I was a bit disquieted by both her rather rude approach and her insinuations that a difficult afternoon in the office was less busy and less important than an afternoon in OR. Quite frankly, I preferred the time in OR to office time any day. The patients who were asleep could not groan, grouse, grumble, or gripe. In addition, the surgical patients almost always got better. You weren't rushed in OR, and you felt the luxury of completing one task at a time. In the office, you usually had several patients waiting to be seen, charts and phone calls between every visit, prescriptions to sign, and Helen.

"Why would I make a home visit for chicken pox?" I inquired. "Can't they just run over here to the office?"

Helen looked at me like I had a chicken sitting on my head. "And why would I want to have kids with chicken pox in my waiting room? Why would I want everyone in the waiting room exposed? Don't you know that chicken pox can lead to shingles? I don't know about *you*, Dr. Larimore, but I don't want my patients exposed against their will."

"Helen," I tried to reason, "first of all, we're through seeing patients. There's no one in the waiting room. Secondly, if there were someone in the waiting room, couldn't we just let the Nichols family come in the back door?"

She cocked her head at me and scowled. I was sure there was a bit of color rising in her cheeks but couldn't be certain. She applied her facial makeup fairly heavily—especially the blush.

"Dr. Mitchell says that the pox virus, just like the measles or mumps virus, can spread through the air and can be blown across an entire exam room with one deep breath or sneeze. He never allows that to happen in *his* office. Why, there's just no telling how long those nasty viruses will stay in the air."

She drew herself up, obviously proud to be teaching what she still considered me to be—the newcomer.

I thought I might try to bring Helen's medical knowledge into the twentieth century, but before I could speak, she continued. "Besides, all the doctors in town make home calls for such sicknesses. It's just the way it's done. And Dr. Mitchell is expecting you to do this for him—since he's doing other important things."

She turned to leave.

"Helen . . ."

She whipped around, fists clinched. *Whoa!* I thought to myself. *Is she going to slug me, or what?*

"Helen, I was just wondering."

"Wondering *what*?" she hissed through pursed lips.

I thought, *If I didn't know she was menopausal, I'd swear she was in the throes of PMS.* Fortunately, I thought it better not to mention these musings but instead asked, "Where's Toot Holler? I haven't a clue."

She relaxed for a moment, sensing she had won the encounter. I think I may even have seen a trace of a smile.

"Well, when you leave the office, just head up the Road to Nowhere. The first right is Toot Holler Road. At the gap, just as you start heading down into Deep Creek Valley, you'll see a small dirt road on your left. Their house is up about a half a mile. At the end of that road is where Dr. Eldridge lives. He's one of our two town dentists. But he's been here the longest."

"Yes, yes, I've gotten to know him at the football games. He's the PA announcer at the stadium for all the home games. Nice fellow."

She turned to leave. I finished my chart work and then grabbed my trusty black bag.

━━

I turned off the Road to Nowhere onto a narrower and slightly winding road that initially passed small home sites and then a farm or two. As the road ascended toward the gap, trees began to enclose the road. At the gap, I slowed down and began the descent toward Deep Creek Valley.

Two old rusty mailboxes marked the driveway, each looking equally tenuous in its attachment. "Nichols" was painted on the side of one and "Eldridge" on the side of the other.

The one-way dirt road was bordered on one side by a steep embankment and covered with thick rhododendron bushes. The other side had an even steeper falloff to a small bubbling stream. My windows were open, and immediately upon entering the rhododendron thicket, I felt the air temperature drop ten degrees. I drove slowly, absorbing the smells of moist clay and listening to the rushing brook.

The Nicholses' house, located just off the road in its own tiny little hollow, appeared clean and nicely kept. I parked my Toyota and walked up to the screen door. A voice called out from inside. "Come on in. It's open."

Inside I found a beautiful young lady sitting on a quilt laid out on the living room floor, playing with two of the cutest young girls you could imagine. Toys and blocks were scattered across the room. The two-year-olds crawled busily from toy to toy—squealing and giggling.

"Hi, I'm Sarah Nichols," she said, bounding to her feet and holding an outstretched hand. "You must be Dr. Larimore."

She was lovely, wearing a denim long-sleeve shirt with the sleeves partially rolled up. Her hair was pulled back. "I am. I am indeed," I replied.

She pointed to the sofa, indicating I was to have a seat. "Some tea?"

"No, I'm just fine. Tell me about the girls."

"Well, they're as fit as fiddles. Pregnancy, labor, and delivery were uncomplicated. I've been breast-feeding them. Their only doctor visits have been for immunizations and checkups."

"Does Dr. Mitchell do their checkups?"

She wrinkled her nose. "No way! I take them to Dr. Hasselbring, the pediatrician over in Sylva."

"Why?" I asked, almost dumbfounded.

"Well, the girls were born over there, and Dr. Hasselbring has been their doctor from the moment they were born. Besides, Dr. Mitchell doesn't really care for kids anymore."

I was confused. "Then why didn't you call Dr. Hasselbring about this? Why did you call Dr. Mitchell?"

"Oh, *any* doctor could handle this. It's not really that complicated."

She turned to keep an eye on one of the girls, who was starting to crawl off the quilt. *And you think child checkups and immunizations are complex?* I thought to myself. Suddenly I was feeling very used. She turned back to me and smiled—a smile that could warm any developing cynical spirit.

"I can imagine if I was you I'd be pretty miffed about this call."

I thought, *You're right about that!* But I kept my thoughts to myself.

"Well, I had heard you were in town and actually called to see if you might be willing to come up. Helen said I would have to see Dr. Mitchell, since he was on call. I said okay—but I was disappointed. Anyway, she called back and said that Dr. Mitchell was doing something really important but that you were available and would come up. I thought that was sweet."

"Tell me a bit about what's going on." I was still a bit miffed, but my miffedness was softening.

"About a week ago I took the girls to a pox party at a friend's house."

"Excuse me," I interjected. "A pox party. What's that?" I had honestly never heard of such a thing.

She cocked her head. "Well, Dr. Hasselbring told me that if any of the neighbor kids ever came down with chicken pox, we could take the girls over to play and see if they would get them. Dr. Hasselbring said it's better for them to get the pox when they're young—then they'll be immune for life. She also told me the incubation was seven to fourteen days and if the kids did start to break out, to get a doctor to look at them to be sure it was the pox, and if it was, then we could hold our own pox party for other small kids to come to."

Well, I must admit I had never heard of such a thing, but it did make sense—after all, the chicken pox vaccine was still a decade and a half away from being available. Feeling I was being one-upped by a neighboring town's baby doctor, I decided to take control. We doctors do that by talking, not listening. "Have the girls had any fever?"

"No sir, they haven't. And they've been acting just as normal as can be. Well, maybe a tad irritable."

"Any cough, or are any of the lesions draining pus?"

"No."

"Mind if I take a look?"

"I'd like that!"

The girls had the classic chicken pox lesions on their cheeks, trunk, and arms—little dewdrops on a slightly red and raised base. The older lesions were a bit bigger, the newer ones very small. This was classic for the pox. I checked the kids' ears and mouths, which were normal, and listened to their breath sounds—again normal.

"Sarah, this looks like classic chicken pox. If you keep the girls a bit cooler, the rash will be less severe. You can use calamine lotion on the wet lesions to help dry them out and over-the-counter hydrocortisone cream on the dry lesions to keep them from itching so much. Oatmeal baths in cool water can be fun and soothing for the kids. And let them drink lots of fluids."

She looked impressed.

I continued. "If there's any fever, feel free to give them some baby Tylenol." In those days we were just learning of the potential for Reye's syndrome in kids under seventeen years of age who take aspirin.

"Tell the moms of any kids who come to the pox party that, just as Dr. Hasselbring said, it may take their kids seven to fourteen days to break out. The lesions can last up to a week but are only contagious until they crust over."

She sat, raptly listening to my mini-lecture. It wasn't over. "If the kids develop a bad cough, a high fever, or a fever you can't control, get them checked by a doctor right away. Also, if any of the lesions look like they're getting infected, I should take a look."

This was fun. I was sure the other doctor hadn't given her this much useful information. I was in my element. "Last but not least, if any of the moms who are coming to the pox party haven't had chicken pox or don't remember having the pox, and they might be pregnant, don't allow them to come or bring their kids."

"Why not?" She wrinkled her nose up again.

"Chicken pox in pregnancy can be really bad for the mom and her unborn baby. No sense taking any chances we don't need to take. Well, that should about do it. I'll be on my way. My best to Mr. Nichols, whom I hope to meet someday."

Her eyes widened. "Oh, I'm glad you mentioned Peter. We own a tubing center—it's near the Deep Creek entrance to the national park. Let me get you some free passes." She stood and walked over to a bookshelf and picked up the passes, which she handed to me. "We hope you and your family will come and grab a tube and enjoy the creek sometime."

I took the passes and thanked her for the courtesy. As I stepped to the door to leave, she asked, "Do I owe you anything?"

I opened the door and turned to reply. "Nope. I'll have Sarah Crisp, one of our office staff, send out a bill at the end of the month. Will that be okay?"

"You bet. And by the way, thanks for all the information. It's really helpful."

"You're welcome. Have a good day."

I enjoyed the drive back to the hospital. Dusk gathered around the car as I drove, and the cool air and the sounds of crickets singing wafted through the open windows. I took my foot off the accelerator. *Time to slow down,* I thought to myself. I felt suddenly blessed.

Most doctors don't make home visits anymore. Certainly I could drive to the Nicholses' house more easily than this mom could drive her sick twins to the office. Yes, it took me a bit more time, but then I would have missed this delectable drive and delicious evening. It couldn't have been a more enjoyable or affable experience for me. I decided I could not afford to not make more home visits.

I smiled as I thought I'd probably see the Nichols girls in the office sometime. After all, that drive to Sylva is a really long one. And I thought I should take Sarah up on her offer to tube Deep Creek, but maybe I'd wait until next summer—when the weather and water would be a bit warmer.

chapter twelve

SWAIN COUNTY FOOTBALL

Ever since my first football season in Bryson City, I, like most county residents, was looking forward to the fall.

The previous year had been my first as the on-the-field team physician for the Swain County Maroon Devils. This year would be Rick's first.

The previous year's team had won its second Smoky Mountain Conference championship in as many years, played in three state play-off games, and brought their win-loss record in the new stadium to fifty-nine wins and only thirteen losses. The spring practices had gone very well, as had the end-of-summer, two-a-day practices. The team, the coaches, and the fans were ready for another season. I was too. Unfortunately, it would turn out to be one of the worst seasons of that decade—primarily because of one injury.

After seeing the last patient of the afternoon on Friday, I drove to the house to eat a quick supper and change into my "game uniform"—coach's cleats, maroon pants, and a white golf shirt. Then I drove up to the temple of local football—Swain County Stadium.

For a small town, this stadium was magnificent. I suspect there are junior colleges that would lust for such an arena. It was carved into the side of a small mountain. The visitors' metal bleachers could hold nearly a thousand fans, but the concrete home stands, running from the 25-yard line on the north to the 25-yard line on the south and climbing over thirty rows high, could easily seat 2,500 fans—with another two thousand or so being accommodated on the adjoining hillside. At the peak of the stadium was a spacious press box. At the north end of the stadium was a two-story field house—more fitting for a small college than a high school.

I parked in one of the two parking spaces reserved for Rick and me, the team doctors, and then walked toward the immaculate field. I felt remarkably at home. As I walked around the field, I saw two of the Maroon Devils' most loyal fans, Preston Tuttle and Joe Benny Shuler.

"Hey, Doc. How ya doin'?" Preston was a large man with a friendly smile. He stuck out his hand to give mine a shaking. "You remember Joe Benny?"

"Hi, Mr. Tuttle. Of course I remember Mr. Shuler. He brings me my mail every day."

"Preston's fine with me, Doc, if it's the same to you."

"Okay, Preston. Walt works for me."

"Sounds good to me, Doc." Preston couldn't bring himself to call me Walt. And he never did.

Preston asked, "Joe Benny, this young doctor still keepin' your mailbag full?"

Joe Benny chuckled. "Preston, Doc here gets a mess of medical magazines. 'Bout breaks my back sometimes."

I laughed. "Just keeping you in shape, Joe Benny. And, Preston, your boys looked good in spring and summer practice. Scott's shaping up as a fine tight end. I think he'll have a super senior year. How's he feeling about his little brother being on the team with him?"

"Aw, Doc. He's plum tickled. Scott and Ritchie are awfully close. Jest like Joe Benny's kids."

"Yeah, that's true," agreed Joe Benny. "Heath and Benjie are good boys—and they're good friends. I reckon one day Heath will start for the Maroon Devils at quarterback, and his little brother will be catching all the balls he throws."

"Heck with the Maroon Devils!" Preston noted. "I can see Heath throwing the ball for the University of Tennessee."

"Now wouldn't that be sweet!" exclaimed Joe Benny, a smile reaching from ear to ear.

Preston's prediction was truer than he ever could have imagined. Heath and Benjie would later star at Swain County High School, long after I would leave the town. I would do their youth league physicals and enjoy watching them play and seeing their daddy take obvious pride in their development. Both would play college ball at the University of Tennessee. Heath would become a Heisman Trophy candidate and then play professional football with the Washington Redskins. But that was far in the future.

Preston looked back at me. "Hey, Doc. My wife, Dean, is gonna interview with you—if'n y'all ever git that new office built. She'd love to be your new office manager. She's had experience doin' that, and she'd be mighty fine. Knows just about everyone there is to know and can run a business just fine."

"We'll be interviewing at the start of the new year. But it wouldn't hurt to have her bring a résumé by Dr. Mitchell's office. Okay?"

"I'll do it. You can be sure."

"Best make my rounds, gentlemen. Good to see you both."

It was already getting dark, but the state-of-the-art stadium lights illuminated the field like day. And for a die-hard football fan, there's nothing quite like the feeling of walking out onto the cool turf on a crisp autumn evening. The crowds gathering in the stands, the smoke from the grills at the hamburger stands, the band warming up. I drank in the sights.

As I walked onto the field, a thousand memories flooded my soul and my arms looked like gooseflesh. My dad and I would go to LSU games together in Baton Rouge, where opponents had nicknamed the stadium "Death Valley." I not only can still name the heroes of my youth but also can remember most of their jersey numbers and some of their most outstanding plays. There, too, games were almost always played at night—and the turf was and always has been thick and luscious.

I felt at home. The kids from both teams were already on the field warming up. What had surprised me during my first fall in Bryson City—the visitor and home stands nearly at capacity a full hour before the game—was no longer a surprise. Some fans were even beginning to stake claim on the grassy mountainside. And all along the chain-link fence around the field the men were two to three rows deep.

I dropped off my medical kit in the locker room, as was my habit, and made my way through the crowd on the track in front of the home stands.

The way to the press box was a small asphalt road from one end of the stadium up and behind the box. I climbed the steep slope and made my way inside. Before each game I went up to visit with Gary Ayers, the morning DJ for WBHN, our local radio station; Bob Eldridge, one of our two local dentists and the stadium announcer; and Pete Lawson, the editor of the local paper, the *Smoky Mountain Times*. They never failed to give me a hard time about something. That night they were in a mood to kid me about my infamous first "home delivery."

It started with Gary. "Your bovine patient still kicking?" he asked, adding, "Good thing you didn't have to do calf CPR."

"Yeah," piped in Pete, "that would have been a mooooving story for my readers." They all rolled in laughter. I blushed, then chuckled along with them.

On the way back down to the field, I passed Preston and Joe Benny, who were guarding their spots on the fence at about the 40-yard line on the home side. This was just far enough down to avoid having their view blocked by the players on the sidelines, yet close enough to yell any needed encouragement to particular coaches or kids.

When I got to the sideline, Rick was there.

"Well, welcome to your first home game, partner!"

"I knew the stadium was big; I just had no idea it was this big. I'm not sure we had this many folks for a game at my college." Rick had attended the University of Delaware for his undergraduate work. "And I can't believe the other doctors wouldn't want to be here on the sideline."

"Me either. But I'm glad they don't. Let's go check in with Coach Dietz."

He had no medical concerns to report to us about any of the kids but asked, as he did before every game, "You got some Tums in your medical kit?"

"I do."

"Keep 'em handy for me?"

"Will do, Coach."

As he walked away, I noticed Rick looking at the other team.

"Man, Walt, look at the size of their boys compared to ours!"

"Rick, Coach Dietz is fond of saying, 'It's not the size of the man in the fight but the size of the fight in the man.' I suspect our boys will do just fine."

After warm-ups were complete, the teams retreated to their locker rooms. Each coach had his kids in a small group, reviewing last-minute details and asking and answering questions. Each kid had been taught how to "scout" his opposing players during warm-ups and would share his observations on any apparent injuries. Several of the junior varsity coaches who had scouted the opponent in previous games and during warm-ups would go from group to group to share their surveillance findings.

A referee entered the room. "Coach, I'll need your captains in two minutes."

"Okay," Coach Dietz responded. Then he clapped his hands, and the entire locker room grew silent as each boy looked at their coach as he walked among them. "Men, we've all worked like crazy to prepare for tonight. There're lots of folks who've spent their hard-earned money to come to see you. They want to see you do your best. I know you will."

He paused to spit out some dip in a cup he was carrying.

"Seniors, this here's your last home opener. You've never lost to these boys, and they've come here to give you a whippin'. I tell ya right now, that's what they're here to do. If'n they beat ya, their season is a success and they'll have braggin' rights till next year."

He was quiet for a full half minute as he walked slowly among his boys, looking into the eyes of each one. Then he continued. "If'n ya let 'em whip ya, they'll be talkin' down about Swain County—you can bet on that."

He walked back through the assembled team to the front door. "Men, this stadium's your house. You don't let these folks down. You don't let your parents down. Most of all, you don't let yourselves down. This is your house. Get out there and let's defend it."

The team erupted to its feet and moved toward the door—a surging, chanting, testosterone-laden mass.

"What a speech!" Rick shouted to me. I smiled and thought, *Classic Boyce Dietz. No wonder these kids and his assistant coaches love him!*

The team tore through the paper banner, fire extinguishers went off, the band played the fight song, and the stands erupted. I thought I could feel the ground trembling—the sound was deafening. Rick and I walked toward the field. "Welcome to Swain County Football!" I shouted. He smiled and patted me on the back. Together we jogged onto the field.

At halftime the score was tied. The halftime sermon was even more intense and motivational than the pregame speech.

The third quarter was scoreless. The team and the crowd seemed to be waning. Their size and strength seemed to be wearing down our little guys.

Gary Lackey was our new quarterback for the year—a lanky fellow who, aside from tight end Derek Robinson, was the tallest player on the team. He could really throw the ball, but there wasn't a lot of muscle on his bones. When he would run and get hit, I would wince. After one hit, Rick bent over to me and commented, "I hope they don't break him!"

But then, in one horrible play, they almost did.

chapter thirteen

HOSPITAL POLITICS

Like many quarterbacks, Gary hated to run the ball. Quarterbacks are made to throw the ball. Most of them don't like to hit or be hit.

As the fourth quarter began, we had the ball, and thankfully Gary had not needed to run much. But as our offensive line began to tire, with each ensuing play the defense began to get closer and closer to him.

On one particular play, Gary was forced out of the pocket and took off running toward our sidelines. As he began to cut up the field, two defenders simultaneously hit him low and hard. One grabbed Gary by the ankles and the other hit him at the knees. I saw his right knee snap in at a dangerous angle. As he collapsed and hit the ground, I could hear him scream.

A collective groan went up from the crowd, which then became suddenly silent. By instinct, I was sprinting out to Gary, followed closely by Coach Dietz and Rick. I was certain the medial collateral ligament of his knee was severely stretched and maybe even torn. Certainly a dislocated kneecap or a fracture was possible. By the time we got to his side, he was writhing on the ground, with the exception of his right leg, which he was holding very still. Gary was moaning in pain.

As I knelt at his side, I said, "Gary, this is Dr. Larimore. What are you feeling?"

"Doc, I think my leg's broken. I can't move it."

Rick was squatting next to me. Our eyes met, and he nodded, indicating I should proceed. My three years of training and experience as a sideline physician for the Duke football team during my residency taught me that the easiest time to examine an injured joint is on the field immediately after the injury. Waiting even a few moments to get the athlete to the sideline can risk the formation of joint fluid, swelling, or muscle spasms, making an exam more difficult.

"Gary, I'm going to do a quick exam. Just stay on your back and take some deep breaths in and out." My hands quickly palpated the knee and surrounding tissues. He was most tender over the middle of the inside of the knee—although my fingers could feel the medial collateral ligament, and it felt intact. It was not completely torn! A quick check of the cruciate ligaments showed they were intact. The lateral collateral ligament was fine, as was the patella and the thigh and calf muscles. With his leg extended, I took my fist and struck the bottom of his shoe. He did not grimace. If he had a fracture, that maneuver should have hurt. I was delighted it did not!

Then I gently flexed the injured knee and put stress on the medial collateral ligament, the tissue band that ran across the inside of the knee joint. He threw back his head, gritting his teeth in pain and moaning as I did the test. At the same time, the joint opened up ever so slightly. Immediately I knew the diagnosis. Had it been a mild, first-degree sprain, the test would have hurt but the joint line would not have opened up. Had it been a severe, third-degree sprain, or a completely torn ligament, it would likely not have hurt but would have even more easily and widely opened up.

"Rick, it feels like a second-degree MCL sprain—but not a bad one. His ACL and PCL are okay. I can't tell about the meniscus, but I suspect it's fine." I looked up at the coach. "Boyce, we'll need a couple of the linemen to help get him off the field. I don't

want any weight on this knee. He'll be out the rest of the game."
I could see the coach's disappointment. He and I knew that the
backup quarterback was young and had no game experience.

On the sideline, I placed ice and an Ace wrap on Gary's knee.
His mom and dad came down to the sideline, and I told them,
"He's stretched and partially torn a ligament in his knee. I'd like
to take him to the hospital for an X-ray—just to be sure the ligament's not torn off the bone."

I sat down by Gary. "Son, let's go ahead and get to the hospital."

"Doc, can't I stay till the end of the game?"

"Gary, it's almost over. The game's well in hand. And I'd like
to get the X-rays before there's too much swelling. Also, if we wait
too long, the traffic may hold us up."

He nodded.

Rick looked at me. "Why don't you go with him. I'll let Coach
Dietz know, and I'll cover the rest of the game and come over to
the hospital later."

"Sounds good, Rick. Thanks."

Don and Billy covered most of the games for Swain County
EMS. They helped me get Gary on a gurney, and we rolled him off
the field. As Gary was loaded into the ambulance, Joe Benny and
Preston were at my side. I explained the injury to them.

"He gonna need surgery?" Preston asked.

"I need to X-ray him to be sure. But I'm fairly certain he
won't."

"Doc," asked Joe Benny, "you mind if'n I let 'em know in the
press box? It'll put folks' minds at ease."

"Sounds good to me, Joe Benny."

He turned to leave, and Preston leaned toward me. "Doc, be
careful."

I looked at him, cocking my head. "About what?"

He looked around suspiciously and then turned back to me.
"Be careful of Doc Mitchell. He'll wanna take this boy to the OR.
If he does, Gary'll be out for the rest of the season."

"Thanks for the warning, Preston. But I've got no reason to recommend any sort of unnecessary surgery. I'll tell you that for sure."

"Just be careful, son." He patted my arm and left.

I hopped into my car and followed the ambulance to the hospital. Then I had the paramedics take Gary straight into the X-ray room, where Carroll Stevenson met me. I explained my findings, and before I could tell him what I wanted, he said, "Got it. I'll get you plain films with obliques. I presume you'll want stress views?"

I was impressed with Carroll's knowledge. This type of X-ray was the standard of care back then—the days before MRI scanners, which is the test of choice now for these types of injuries.

As Carroll was taking the X-rays, I was remembering his involvement in one of my most unusual veterinary events. I had sent a patient with severe flank pain for an X-ray exam called an IVP (intravenous pyelogram). The radiopaque dye injected into a vein is excreted by the kidneys, and over the course of an hour or so it allows the doctor to "see" a shadow of the kidneys and the ureters, with X-rays of the abdomen taken every ten to fifteen minutes.

My patient was in the middle of her IVP when Carroll came into the room. "Margaret," he told her, "I need to have you take a seat in the waiting room for a minute." Although she was in great pain, he helped her off the table, placed a second hospital gown over her back, and escorted her out of the X-ray room.

As she was escorted from the room, Dr. Mitchell was carrying one of his injured hunting dogs into the room to be X-rayed. Now, I'd be the first to say that no harm was done to the human patient—other than a tad bit of inconvenience—but it certainly was reflective of the medical politics and the veterinary care provided in our little country hospital.

After Carroll took the X-rays, and while I was waiting for Gary's films to develop, Don and Billy took Gary back to ER. Louise would get the paperwork in order and re-ice the knee. She would help Gary get out of his uniform and also escort Gary's parents into his cubicle when they arrived with his clothes.

As Carroll put the films on the viewing box, I carefully looked at them with him.

"No avulsion fractures," he observed. I agreed.

"Best of all," I added, "these stress films show virtually no distraction." If the ligament was torn, the X-rays taken under stress would have shown a separation, or distraction, of the edges of the tibia and femur—an opening up of the joint that wouldn't occur with an intact ligament.

"You think it's just a first-degree strain?" Carroll asked.

"Nope. When I examined him on the field, the joint opened up a bit. So I'm pretty sure it's a very mild second-degree strain. But I'm also worried about the meniscus."

"Want to get a CT scan when the truck's here Tuesday?"

"Nope. I don't like the CT for soft tissues around the knee. I think I'd like to recommend he get scoped."

Carroll looked at me with a funny expression. "Mitch usually takes these cases to OR."

I was quiet for a moment, looking at the films and hearing Preston's warning still ringing in my ears.

"I know. But if we open him up surgically, he's out for the season. A good sports orthopedist can do an arthroscopy and get a good look at the cartilage and ligaments, repair any damage, and get out quicker than we ever could. Furthermore, if the damage is as minimal as I think it is, we've got a good chance of getting Gary back on the field in the not-too-distant future."

It was Carroll's turn to be quiet for a moment. Then, in a whisper, he said, "Mitch doesn't like us referring out things we can do here."

I knew I needed to be very careful—with both what I said and did. I paused and then nodded. "Carroll, how about we let the parents decide?"

Carroll smiled and nodded his head. "Sounds good."

I picked up the phone and called the emergency room. Louise answered, and I asked her to find out who was on call for the Sylva Orthopaedic Associates in Sylva. I had met the two docs who cared for the Western Carolina University athletes, and I was impressed with their skill and judgment. "When you get the on-call doctor, let me know."

I continued to look at the films until the call came in. It was Cliff Faull, M.D., an orthopedist who had trained at the Bowman Gray School of Medicine. I explained the case. Cliff agreed to see Gary on Monday morning at the hospital in Sylva. "Have him come see me without having had food or fluids after midnight. I might be able to scope him Monday morning, if that's okay with you."

"That sounds great, Cliff."

I hung up the phone and went over to ER. I found Gary and his parents and explained the results of the X-ray and the various treatment options. After a few minutes of discussion, they decided to take Gary home and see Dr. Faull on Monday.

I had Louise show them how to keep the knee iced and wrapped in an Ace wrap. She also fitted Gary with a knee splint and crutches. I also had her dispense some pain pills. Louise had Gary's parents pull their car next to the ER entrance, and before long, they had him loaded into the backseat of the car.

I walked out with them, and when Louise took the wheelchair back inside, I had a quick powwow with Gary's parents. I told them I sensed that the community standard was open surgery. I reassured them that I thought they were making the right decision but that I needed *them* to make the decision.

Mr. Lackey looked away quietly for a moment and then turned back toward me. His jaw seemed set. "Dr. Larimore, we want what's best for our son. If there's a way to get him back on the field this season safely, we want to do it. I know you're taking a professional risk to send us to Sylva, and I want you to know I appreciate what you're doing for him. And if anyone asks, you tell them this was *our* decision. If Dr. Mitchell or anyone else has a problem, you have them call me."

We shook hands, and I turned to go back into the ER. About halfway to the door, I heard Gary's mom. "Dr. Larimore . . ."

I turned to face her. She had misty eyes, and her lips whispered, "Thank you."

I nodded my head, sheepishly waved good-bye, and went inside. As I sat filling out the paperwork, Louise walked up to me and was quiet. I looked up at her. "You talk to Dr. Mitchell about this?"

"About what?" I inquired.

"About sendin' that boy to Sylva?"

"Why should I?" I asked, turning toward her as I stopped writing.

"Well, well. Number one, Dr. Mitchell don't like us referrin' folks to Sylva. And, number two, he does a lot of knee surgery right here."

I was detecting a theme here—from Preston to Carroll to Louise. "I understand your concern," I began.

Louise broke in, laughing. "Ain't no concern of mine, Dr. Larimore. I just know how things are done around here."

"I appreciate that, Louise. And you know how very much I've learned about that."

"Uh-huh," she quipped.

I thought, *What I should say is, "Louise, Gary needs arthroscopy. An open procedure would not be in the best interest of anyone but the surgeon. And we don't do arthroscopy here."* But I chickened out. "Louise, Gary's parents were bound and determined to take him to Sylva. You heard me tell them they could have surgery here. They chose otherwise. What are we supposed to do—chain him down?"

She glanced at me and said, "Well, you just be careful," and walked away.

Coach Dietz called the emergency room while I was doing the paperwork. I updated him on what had happened. When I was finished, he was quiet for a moment. Then he said, "Doc, I've had some boys sliced and diced I don't think needed it. What you're doing here is the right thing—for Gary and for the team. I appreciate it. I really do. But you be careful. There's some folks around here who want to carve on folks every chance they get."

"I understand," I said. And I surely was beginning to.

"You know," he drawled, "there's some bobcats 'round here, and they can inflict some harm if they attack."

"Yes sir," I replied, "I'm getting that message loud and clear."

"Thanks, Doc. I appreciate you."

We hung up, and I turned back to finish my paperwork. I was prepared for the possibility of one bobcat attack. I didn't know that on that particular night there would be two.

chapter fourteen

THE BOBCAT ATTACKS

*R*ick arrived at the ER just as I finished the paperwork.

"How'd it go?" he asked.

Louise was milling around, so I whispered, "How 'bout a cup of coffee?"

Rick smiled, and we walked to the lounge and each poured a cup. I explained what had happened and then confessed, "Rick, I feel like I should have just been straightforward with Louise. Cutting that boy's knee open would be malpractice. He doesn't need anything but an arthroscopy. And I suspect he'll be back in uniform in a few short weeks—certainly before the end of the season."

Rick took a sip of his coffee. "Walt, I think you handled it right. I didn't tell you about it, but I had a tourist in ER last week with a Colles' fracture of the wrist. She must have been sixty-five years old. I knew I could reduce the fracture and set the bone and cast it in place. But you and I both know that at her age the fracture site is likely to collapse some after she gets out of the cast. And that would put her at risk for chronic pain and arthritis of her wrist—not to mention not having full range of motion. So I sent her to Asheville for surgery to get her wrist placed in an external fixation device."

"So what's the problem?"

"Well, Louise told me I shouldn't have done that. I stood up to her and told her in no uncertain terms that I was doing what I thought was best for the patient. I still think that's true. But she must have told Mitch, and on Monday I got chewed out at the office."

"You're kidding! Why?"

"Well, he feels we should handle everything we can in Swain County. He said one of the problems with Dr. Nordling was that he sent everything out—and that was harmful to the hospital and the community. So if we want to start sending stuff to other hospitals, we should go practice in those hospitals."

"Wow! Maybe that's why he does so many types of surgery that aren't normally done at a hospital this size."

"Could be. But I'll tell you this. I think you handled it just right. If we let the patients know their options, then we can let *them* decide. We're not *sending* them anywhere—they're taking themselves where they want to go."

"You don't think we should just tell it like it is and face him head-on?"

Rick smiled. "It makes me think of the Bible verse 'We should be as wise and shrewd as snakes and as innocent as doves.' That principle applies to us right now. I think until we're a bit more established here—maybe after we're in our own office—we should be very careful about referrals and how we do them."

We sat quietly for a moment, and then the door of the lounge opened—without a knock—and in flew Mitch. He didn't even say hello but glared down at me. "You sent that boy to Sylva? Are you stupid?"

I looked at Rick and then at Mitch. He seemed really irritated! Before I could answer, he continued. "Don't you know I take care of the surgical injuries of our football team right here in town? There was no need to go send 'im off!"

"I didn't," I replied.

"You didn't? Then where is he?"

"Went home with his parents."

"Went home? That boy needs surgery. From the stands it looked to me like he has at least a second-degree MCL tear, maybe a third-degree tear—and no doubt he tore part of the meniscus. I take care of those types of injuries right here. What are you trying to do?"

"Mitch, he didn't have a third-degree sprain. In fact, I don't even think it was a second-degree—or maybe barely a second. And with no joint effusion, I doubt he had meniscal involvement. But either way, I *know* you do surgery here for these injuries. And I like to care for our patients here in town—just like you do. I told the parents that—and Louise heard me, so you can check with her if you want. But Gary's parents wanted Cliff Faull in Sylva to see him. What was I supposed to do?"

"Keep him here until I could evaluate him and talk to the parents."

I felt myself getting irritated but could see Rick's eyes telling me, *Be careful!* I took a deep breath. "Mitch, I've got their home phone number. Why don't you call them? I'm sure they'll be glad to hear your opinion. If they decide on surgery here, that's fine with me. In fact, if that's what *they* decide, I'd love to scrub in with you."

He thought for a moment and then seemed to calm down. "No, that probably won't be necessary." Then he turned and left.

"Wow!" I commented to Rick.

"How'd that make you feel?" he asked.

"Like I was attacked by a bobcat."

Rick laughed. "I experienced the same thing Monday. But *I* had to go it alone." He laughed again and then took the last swig of his coffee. "Thanks for the coffee, partner. I need to get on up to the inn. Want to come by?"

"No," I replied. "I've got a lovely lady and two beautiful children I need to see. How about a rain check?"

"Any time, partner. Oh, by the way, how are your anniversary plans coming along?"

I smiled, as Rick was now an accomplice. "Sally Jenkins helped me order all the furniture. It will all be shipped to her house. She and R.P. are putting it in their garage. While Barb and I are at Disney World and then on the cruise, she's having our bedroom repainted and the old carpet torn out and replaced with a new color she's chosen. Then she's making new drapes that she'll hang."

"Wow. Barb's gonna really be surprised. I'll be available that night if you need me to treat her for shock!" We both laughed.

After Rick left, I sat and thought for a few moments. I was feeling bad about having misled Louise and Mitch. I wondered if I shouldn't have stood up to them. What they wanted to do was, in my opinion, just plain wrong. I just wasn't sure I had been as courageous or forthright as I should have been. Had I been wise or shrewd? Or had I just plain been a coward?

And then I thought about Rahab, the Canaanite prostitute who had lied to the Jericho men who were seeking the two Israelite spies she was hiding. Yet her lie saved the lives of the two men. She had, it seemed to me, done the right thing. *So*, I thought to myself, *maybe there is a place for righteous deception, eh?*

But was I just rationalizing? I didn't know, but I continued to wrestle with those thoughts until I finally fell asleep that night.

———

Suddenly the phone rang. "Dr. Larimore, get over to ER, stat!" I recognized Louise's voice, but before I could say anything, she hung up.

I quickly hopped out of bed and slipped into the scrubs and clogs I kept near the bed when I was on call. Barb, as was her habit, didn't move. I put on a light winter coat and tried to leave as quietly as possible and then ran to ER. It was a crisp, cool Sunday morning. Our home was just across the street from the hospital, so I was there in a few minutes.

When I arrived in the emergency room, Louise and Carroll were helping a patient get from a wheelchair to a gurney. I could see that his shirt and pants were covered with blood and his right arm was covered in a bloody bandage.

As I ran to the gurney, I could see it was Randy Childs.

"What happened?"

"Doc, you won't believe it."

"Try me."

"Like I said, Doc, you won't believe it."

Carroll cut off Randy's bloody clothes while Louise carefully removed his blood-soaked bandage. He had several gashes on his forearm. All were actively oozing, but none were spurting.

By now, Maxine and Vernel, two of my favorite nurses, had run to ER from the nurses' station. Maxine was taking vital signs, and Vernel was setting up a laceration tray.

"You want me to scrub the arm?" Vernel asked.

"You bet." I turned to Randy, who looked white. "Randy, did you lose much blood?"

"I'm not sure, Doc. I don't think so."

"Maxine, call the lab."

"I'm here." I turned to see Betty Carlson, the head of the lab.

"Betty, what are you doing here early on a Sunday morning?"

"Just like you, Dr. Larimore. I'm pulling my shifts."

"Aw, you just like getting those big bucks." I smiled at Betty. She ran a great lab. We had access to almost any of the tests we needed—and for a forty-bed hospital, that was almost unheard of.

As the team worked, I gloved and turned my attention to the wounds. "These don't look life threatening, Randy. Thank the Lord!" I drew up a large syringe of lidocaine and began to numb the wounds. Then after they were numb I took a Betadine sponge and began scrubbing the wounds. They looked like surgical wounds—the edges of the lacerations were not torn or bruised. When only Louise and I were left to tend to him, I began suturing the wounds and asked, "Randy, can you tell me what happened tonight?"

"Doc, like I told you, you won't believe it."

"Try me."

"I was attacked by a bobcat."

I looked at Louise, who was smiling. For a moment I wondered, *Am I being taken for a ride here?* I decided to follow the road, wherever it would take me. "Well, tell me about it."

"After the game last night, Bob Eldridge and I took off in my Jeep up into the mountains. We got a place we like to hunt."

"Where's that?" As soon as I asked I knew I shouldn't have.

"Doc, you know a man don't talk about where he hunts."

"Sorry."

"Anyway, we got up there by midnight and turned in for a short sleep. Got up 'bout 4:00 a.m. and then hiked out into the woods."

"What were you hunting for?"

"Turkey. I was sittin' with my back against a large poplar tree. I was facin' one way, and Bob was against the same tree facin' the other way. Then, just at first light, I began with my turkey callin'."

"So did you get attacked by a wild band of turkeys?" I asked, trying not to laugh.

"That ain't funny, Doc."

I tried to stop snickering but couldn't.

"Nope, I really was attacked by a bobcat."

If I had not been so shocked, I might have thought, *So was I!* I stopped sewing to look at him. He seemed serious.

"Yep, I was doing my gobblin' when I heard a noise near me. I thought maybe it was a big ole gobbler I had called in—when all of a sudden, just as I gobbled again, this big ole bobcat sprung over a rock with his fangs and claws ready to grab him a big ole gobbler. Only instead of a big turkey, he found me. Well, in midair he screeched, and I screamed. We both commenced to scare the dickens out of each other. I threw my hands up in front of my face, and he was clawin' the air to turn and get out of there. I reckon he clawed me as he turned to run—and he got me good."

I was quiet for a moment. "You're serious, aren't you?"

"I'm as serious as a heart attack, Doc." he replied. "Ain't nothin' I've ever experienced been as frightnin' as that bobcat attack. I don't recommend it. If you can avoid the fury of one of them things, it's worth doin', I tell ya!"

I nodded in agreement and thought, *True, indeed!*

chapter fifteen

DUNGEONS AND APPLES

Increasingly, my off weekends would be disturbed by patients who, when they couldn't find me or Rick covering ER, would just walk over to our houses. My initial response when I'd see a patient walking up the driveway was to hide in a back room.

I mentioned this to Mitch one day, and he laughed. "Walt, don't be stupid!" He smiled and then continued. "If you let folks do this to you and you don't complain about it, you're actually teaching them their behavior is all right. You gotta either leave town when you're off—get you a farm to escape to, like Gay and I have—or you gotta tell folks you're not available. Period. Just be up-front with 'em. Or you can do both. That's what I recommend."

I found applying his advice difficult, but I was committed to try. Barb, however, had no problem meeting folks at the door or on the driveway and telling them our family and off time were private. Period.

Over time, the interruptions became fewer and fewer. A few people left the practice, but most understood. Nevertheless, we still enjoyed leaving town on weekends. We especially loved driving around and exploring western North Carolina and eastern Tennessee. Our weekend trips allowed us not only to get away from the practice of medicine but also to spend quality and quantity time with our children.

I particularly loved our trips during the fall. Besides the wonderful colors that blanketed the mountains, it was the time of year we enjoyed visiting the orchards in our region. And our favorite was Barber Orchards between Bryson City and Asheville—not far from Waynesville.

The first time we pulled into the spacious lot in front of the Barber Orchards fruit stand, I was drawn to a sign just above and to the left of the front door:

An Apple a Day
Keeps the Doctor Away

On that particular day the store buzzed with activity. I presumed it was just because it was a Sunday afternoon, but later I learned this was a daily phenomenon—with great numbers of customers returning annually, like the swallows to San Juan Capistrano.

We finally found a place to park. I had to hold Kate's hand more tightly, as the contractures in her left leg were worsening and her walking was becoming increasingly difficult—even while using the braces. As we entered the store, Kate's eyes widened, as did mine. The array of goodies was tantalizing—a nearly endless variety of apples interspersed among patches of pumpkins and a group of gourds.

The staff typically offered samples for customers to taste. Besides the common varieties, like Granny Smith and the Red and Golden Delicious, there were many others, like Gala, Sundowner, Rome Beauty, Stayman, Ginger Gold, Honeycrisp, and Braeburn. That day we sampled apple varieties we had never even heard of, much less tasted. I really liked the Ginger Gold, which had a cream-colored flesh and was mildly sweet. It looked similar to a Golden Delicious but with an orange blush. Scott liked the look and the taste of the Gala apple—which had a distinctive red- and yellow-striped, heart-shaped appearance. The salesclerk told us they were an excellent snack for kids.

Kate and Barb were not nearly as interested in the fruit as Scott and I were. Instead, they sauntered over to the baked goods—

where the variety was staggering. At least a dozen freshly baked pies beckoned—including strawberry-apple and apple-rhubarb. But the most fabulous aroma was wafting up from the apple muffins and apple cakes. By the time Scott and I arrived at their side, we found Barb and Kate chomping down on a warm apple turnover and sipping warm apple cider.

We sat on a bench next to an older man and watched the locals and tourists circulating around the shelves of gifts, jams, and jellies—and the myriad of bags and crates containing the apples. Barb picked up Scott. "Tell ya what. Scoot and I will head over to look at the cookbooks. Okay?"

"Okay with me!" I replied as she left Kate and me working on our turnovers. The old man next to us leaned over to Kate. "Nice set of braces you got there."

I looked at him in astonishment—I didn't consider it to be a very polite comment. Nevertheless, my stare didn't dissuade him.

"I used to wear braces like that on my left foot," he said, more to Kate than me.

"You did?" Kate asked.

"Yep. It was after my stroke. My foot got a bit spastic. But my brace was metal—not a fancy plastic like yours."

I smiled as I saw this old man connecting with my daughter.

"But I don't have to wear a brace no more," he added.

"Why not, mister?"

"Had me some surgery. Now my foot's 'bout as good as new."

"Really?"

"Yep. You might want to ask a doctor 'bout it. I hear they do it on kids all the time."

Kate looked up at me. "Daddy, I'd like to have my foot fixed."

I nodded. She didn't know I had been thinking about it for months now.

"Where ya from?" asked the man.

"Bryson City, North Carolina," replied Kate.

The old man nodded and smiled. "You been in the jail there?"

It was Kate's turn to smile. "No sir. I've never been arrested. I'm too young!"

The old-timer threw back his head and laughed out loud. I couldn't help but smile. After he stopped chuckling, he leaned over to her. "Well, that's good, sweet thing. That's the only jail I ever knew of where you could actually be buried under it."

"Really!" Kate exclaimed and looked at me.

Kate looked back at the old-timer. He appeared to be in deep thought as he rubbed his whiskers. "Well, it was some time back. I believe it was before the turn of the last century that they dug what they called the dungeon. It was a room dug below the Swain County jail. I never seen it, but my grandpappy did. He said it was a log room within a log room—with stones filling the space in between. The only entrance to the room was in its ceiling, and it was a locked trapdoor from the floor above it."

"How'd they get the prisoners in and out?" I asked.

"Well, I believe they'd put a ladder down through the hole. And if the dungeon was occupied, there was another log room under the front outside stairs of the courthouse. Them stairs led up to the upstairs courtroom—which was used as a court, a schoolroom, a place for social gatherings, and as a church on Sundays."

"I've heard about the church services held there," I commented.

"Well, that wasn't all. They had them a second log room what locals called the cage. It was just outside the courthouse and could be observed by anyone what was walkin' or drivin' by. They used it for what they called misdemeanants. And my grandpappy told me the courthouse over there was the first building in Swain County to get water from the first public water supply system."

I smiled. "That so?"

"You bet. And since they didn't have no pipes back then, the water was carried down a series of Black Gum logs, which are naturally hollow, ya know, all joined together, end to end. This wooden aqueduct carried water from a spring up the hill from the courthouse, and not too long after that the system was extended to other buildings in Bryson."

"You know more about Bryson City than I do!" quipped my admiring daughter.

He reached over to stroke her head and smiled. "What's yer name, sweetheart?"

"Katherine Lee Larimore."

He appeared taken aback and was quiet for a moment. "I had me a little girl name of Kate. And she was 'bout near as purty as you."

Innocently, Kate asked, "What happened to her?"

The old man's eyes suddenly filled with tears. "She went on to glory when she was only a bit older than you. That was many years ago. But I still long for her powerfully. I miss her hugs, I'll tell you that."

Without even thinking, Kate struggled to stand up. She balanced herself against his knee as she turned to face him. "I give good hugs, mister. They're mighty good for a sad heart."

The old man looked at me, his lip trembling. I nodded. Slowly he leaned forward as my little girl hugged his neck. And then, ever so slowly, I watched his hands rise up to hug her back. They hugged for a full minute, and then he released her. I could see the tears running down his cheeks—and I felt mine filling my eyes.

Kate turned to me. She was smiling from ear to ear.

The old man pulled a handkerchief out of the front of his overalls and blew his nose. He seemed embarrassed. "Forgive me," he whispered, talking to no one in particular as Kate sat back on the bench.

Then the old man slowly stood up and began to walk away. After shuffling a few steps, he turned around. "Thank you, Miss Katherine Lee Larimore, for my hug. I will *never* forget it." Then he turned to leave.

We sat together, finishing our turnovers. I wondered whether Kate had, in some small way, opened up this old man's dungeon and let in some light and fresh air. After all, she had a very precious way of doing just that!

chapter sixteen

A Tale of
Two Surgeons

I didn't arrive at Mitch's farm until late afternoon. Earlier in the week we had crossed paths during morning rounds at the hospital. "Walt," he muttered, not even looking up from the chart he was scribbling on, "you on call this weekend?"

"No sir, I'm not."

"You in town?"

Now my suspicions were aroused. The older physicians very seldom took vacation. It just wasn't part of who they were. Therefore, they were critical of Rick and me both being willing to take time away from town and seeming to enjoy doing so. I believe it was Dr. Mathieson who once asked me, "You really enjoy taking time off, don't you?"

We did. So with a furrowed brow I responded to Mitch. "I *am* in town this weekend." Then I smiled and continued. "Couldn't think of any place I'd rather be."

He looked up and sarcastically replied, "Yeah," and continued his scribbling. When done, he even more quickly scribbled his signature and closed the chart, placing it back in the rolling chart rack.

"Well, I'm gonna be up at the farm this weekend and wondered if you'd want to come up and go fishin' with me."

Dumbfounded, I paused for a moment and then said, "I think I'd like to. Let me check with Barb, and I'll let you know."

⟶

I think that would be nice," Barb told me when I asked her about going fishing that weekend. "Nancy and I were planning to take the kids and go shopping in Dillsboro. You go ahead."

So I let Mitch know I'd be there. To tell you the truth, I was looking forward to being with him away from the office.

Mitch had two farms. One was his dairy farm on the banks of the Tuckaseigee River just south of town. The other was a smaller farm up Johnson Branch. It was the latter farm I was traveling to that particular Saturday afternoon.

The farm was mostly wooded with a small amount of pastureland that contained a beautiful pond. Just above the pond was a small cabin. Most folks in town didn't know about this farm—and for Mitch it was his place to go to escape.

When I pulled up to the cabin, I could see his pickup truck parked around the back of the cabin. I thought this was probably his way of keeping folks who traveled the road—and who might recognize his truck—from knowing he was there.

I got out of the car and walked around the cabin. I could see Mitch sitting on a log on the shore of the pond.

"Hey, Mitch!" I yelled.

"Hello, Walt!" he exclaimed as he turned around. "Come sit a spell. Won't be time to fish until the sun is down a bit more."

I sat on a second log bench next to his. I took a deep breath as we sat in silence. I took in the trees, just beginning to change colors, and the air beginning to get a bit nippy as evening fell.

"This is such a peaceful place," I finally observed, breaking the silence.

"I've always loved it. Just don't have enough time to get up here."

I nodded.

"Walt, seems like you're gettin' settled here. Folks seem to be takin' a likin' to ya."

"I'm grateful for that, Mitch. You and Ray have made us feel welcome."

Mitch smiled. "You remember the first night you were on call? You remember Shitake Sam?"

It was my turn to smile. "Yep. He broke his ankle, and I wanted to take him to OR. Louise wanted me to put him in a skintight cast. I had never heard of such a thing and thought she was nuts. She had me call you, and you set me straight."

"Worked out, didn't it?" Mitch chuckled.

"Yes sir. It did. But I tell you, I wasn't sure it would."

"You know, Walt, there's one form of medicine—I call it the medicine most doctors practice. That's what you were taught in school. Then there's medicine as it used to be practiced. Now, I tell you, most of the old medicine needs to flow into history. We've got better ways now. But some of it's still good, even if most docs have forgotten it. There are things I learned as a doctor in the Army I still use today—no one's come up with any better technique. But most young surgeons don't have a clue how to do it this way. I think that's a shame."

Mitch took a long sip out of a cup of ice water sitting by his side. "I didn't offer you anything to drink. Can I get you something?"

"No sir, I'm just fine."

Mitch sat back. "Then," he continued, "then there's medicine as it will be practiced."

I wondered where he was going with this discussion.

"There's so much yet to be discovered. New ways of doing things. New approaches. New techniques." He took another swig of water.

"Walt, don't be satisfied just to do things the way they taught you at Duke. Keep your thinkin' cap on. Look for new ways to do old things. If you do, practicin' medicine will never be boring. And it'll be a lot more satisfying."

I thought there might be some truth in what he was saying, but I was still bothered by the potential risk of this approach.

"Mitch, couldn't folks be hurt if we just experiment on them?"

"Yep, it could happen. But folks can be hurt if we don't experiment when it's called for."

"How do you tell the difference?"

He sighed and looked up to the sky. "Ever hear of Francis Moore?"

I thought for a moment. "I think so. Wasn't he one of the first transplant surgeons in this country?"

Mitch smiled. "He was. But before Francis Moore was a famous surgeon, he was a young doctor, just like you. And he, like you, had a fabulous mentor." Mitch chuckled.

"And who might my fabulous mentor be?" I laughed.

"I'm too humble to mention my name." Mitch chuckled. "Anyway, during his fourth year of surgical training, Dr. Moore was forced to try an experiment that changed the way we care for burns."

"What happened?"

"Well, it all started with a fire in a packed nightclub in Boston in the early 1940s—1942, I believe. Because of the fabrics on the wall and ceiling, the fire engulfed the building before many folks could get out. Hundreds died in the flames. Of the over two hundred who were rescued, many were severely burned. About half were taken to one hospital, and the other half were transported to another—where Dr. Moore and his mentor, a crusty old doc by the name of Oliver Cope, were on duty."

"Ah," I commented, "I can identify with having a crusty old mentor."

"Not funny," Mitch noted as I laughed.

He continued. "Dozens of the most severely burned patients taken to their ER at Massachusetts General Hospital died quickly. Many died quickly from shock or trauma. Many others died from asphyxiation. Either their lungs were fatally damaged or their windpipes were burned and slowly swelled until the patients' throats were completely closed. Moore and Cope gave the patients injections of morphine for comfort and turned their attention to the three or four dozen severely burned patients they thought might have a chance."

Mitch took another sip of his drink and continued. "Walt, they had a choice. They could use the standard burn care of the day, or they could think of something new. Fortunately for their patients, they did the latter."

I remembered back to my first job as a medical student in the burn unit at Charity Hospital in New Orleans. I could remember giving the severely burned patients a large injection of pain medicine and then lowering their severely burned bodies into a tank of warm water to debride their blisters and dead skin. It was torturous for the patients and miserable for me. After the session, we'd cover the burns with a soothing, cool, antibiotic burn cream.

In spite of the awfulness of this treatment, it was necessary to inflict pain to cut away the dead skin, because those who survive the shock and trauma of the burn have a very high risk of developing infection. God designed our skin to keep out infectious bacteria and viruses. And when that skin is broken or maimed, the gate is open for these germs to invade our body, set up shop, and kill us from sepsis. So I was *very* interested in this medical history lesson.

"What was the standard treatment back then?" I asked.

"It was dreadful. The blisters and dead skin would be cut away first. Then tannic acid would be very, very slowly poured onto the burns."

"Tannic acid? You've gotta be kidding me! The pain would be horrible!"

Mitch nodded. "It was. In fact, the process was excruciating. It would take at least five or six people just to hold the patient down and slowly pour on the acid. It was horrible—and sometimes fatal."

"That seems incredibly cruel to me."

"Well, it was the standard therapy then. And burns had been cared for that way for years."

"Didn't someone question whether or not it was right?"

Mitch smiled. "Your first night on call, when you saw Shitake Sam with that trimalleolar fracture of the ankle, you didn't question whether or not to go to OR, did you?"

I felt the color rising in my cheeks.

"No sir."

"Why not?"

Now it was my turn to be quiet for a moment. "I don't know. That's just the way I had been taught. In residency there's not a lot of reward to be inventive. You're just expected to do it the way you've been taught."

"Exactly, Walt. By its very nature, medicine and her physicians are conservative. A good doctor is taught to abandon established techniques and medicines and procedures only with a great deal of reluctance."

"Isn't that good?"

"You bet it is! If you try something new and it's the wrong decision, someone can get hurt or killed. I think that's why most doctors are reluctant to try new things until there's pretty good evidence that the potential benefits strongly outweigh the risks."

"So what'd they do that was so different?"

Mitch laughed. "Well, it may shock you, but all they did was cover the burns with sterile petroleum jelly and then apply sterile gauze."

I was stunned. "That's all?"

"Well, back then, an approach like that was revolutionary—but necessary. Using this technique a single doctor and nurse could treat people by themselves—and very quickly, I might add. Furthermore, it was much more comfortable for the patients."

"How did their idea work?"

"Well, good and bad. The bad was that the senior physician, Oliver Cope, was initially criticized—and heavily—by both the press and others in the surgical brotherhood. To them this treatment seemed foolish."

"Mitch, where'd Cope get the idea?"

"Well, that's the neat part of the story. The attack on Pearl Harbor took place about a year before the Boston fire. Medical investigators had found that most of the post-attack deaths at Pearl Harbor were not from trauma or blast injuries but from burns. Because the tannic acid method was the treatment used at Pearl Harbor, and just because it was so labor intensive, it took days after the attack to complete the initial care of all the burned men. Many, many men died as they waited for treatment for their burns. When Oliver Cope heard of the Pearl Harbor tragedy, he envisioned a treatment that would be quicker, less labor intensive, and less painful. The question in his mind was whether it would be as effective."

Mitch looked out over the pond as he slowly took a sip of ice water.

"And how'd he go about that?" I asked.

"Well, prior to the fire in Boston, his experience with the idea was very limited. He had only tried it on two humans—one of them himself after an accidental burn. However, he had experimented with animals in the lab and found that blisters protected by the petroleum jelly and gauze stayed sterile."

"Well, what's the end of the story? How'd it work out?"

"Well, about two-thirds of the initial survivors at Boston City Hospital lived, while at Massachusetts General Hospital, where Cope and Moore worked, *all* of the initial survivors stayed alive."

"I bet that was an encouragement."

Mitch laughed. "Especially to those sent to MGH! And this experience is what launched Moore's career. You see, he wasn't a better surgeon than his colleagues—in fact, he was said to have been only average. He wasn't even a scholar. But he was willing to innovate and create and think. And because of that, he became one of the most important surgeons of his era."

"How so?"

"In many ways. When he was the chair of surgery at Harvard— I believe, the youngest in their history—he led some daring experiments that paved the way for organ transplants, heart valve surgery, and even hormonal treatment for breast cancer."

"Sounds like an interesting guy."

"Yep. But lost in the bins of history."

"What ever happened to him?"

"Well, he's still goin'. I think I'd like to meet him one day."

I smiled and nodded.

"But," Mitch continued, "my point is that I don't want you to be limited by your training. No doubt they worked overtime at Duke to train you well. But the professors at Duke don't know everything. There are lots of facts they've forgotten—like skintight casts—and lots yet to learn."

Mitch paused to take a sip of water. "Walt, I want you to be like Francis Moore—willing to do anything, even unconventional things, to help a patient, to save those others consider beyond saving. I want you to always be cautious about the costs of caution. A dose of caution is wise, no doubt. But too much of it can harm your patients. It's only when a doctor is willing to try anything to help his patients that he can find something new to do for them. And sometimes it'll be like walking on hot coals—it's not easy, and not everyone's willing to try. But if you keep your patients' best interests at heart, I think your skin will be thick enough to handle the heat. And the rewards of doing what's right, even when it's not easy, are among the sweet things that make our profession so satisfying."

After that, we just sat back and listened to the sounds of the evening. Mitch took in a long, deep breath.

"Walt, summer and fall in these mountains have a sound all their own. Ever since I was a little boy, I've loved the evening sounds in these hills. But my favorite musician is that little ole tree frog."

As I listened more carefully, I could discern a variety of voices in the evening choir. There were flutelike trills and melodious whistles. Once in a while, there was even a bell-like sound.

"Other than when they come up on the side of the house or I see them on a window, I hear them much more often than I see them. And their voices are a lot bigger than they are."

As I listened to the increasingly animated concerto coming from around the house and tried to stay focused on the lecture about woodland amphibians, I found myself feeling more and more comfortable.

Mitch was a great teacher. I'd had professors who knew more, but I'd never had a professor who knew more and could practice it better. There were medical schools that would have benefited from his energy and expertise. He could have trained and influenced untold students and residents. But here he was in Bryson City—his hometown—caring for his people.

There are tens of thousands of physicians just like Mitch spread throughout the small towns of America. They too could have become academic icons like Francis Moore but chose instead a different calling—a quieter road.

Their choice was no less important than Dr. Moore's—and certainly no less effective.

And here I was with my own private professor. It was a luxurious situation I found myself in that evening. And it dawned on me that my mentor and colleague was now inviting me to become his friend.

chapter seventeen

TANNED FEETS

Susannah Truitt, the first patient of the afternoon, was a forty-six-year-old woman who looked much older than her confessed age.

Mitch said this was a common observation—especially in the "old days." He had recently told me, "A woman in these woods had a difficult life. It aged a woman faster than a man."

Susannah had come from hardy mountain stock—reliable, hardworking, self-sufficient, and honest folks who would do about anything they could before asking for help. Thus, many of the medical problems we took care of were fairly well developed when they presented.

However, Susannah's problem was of a more minor nature. She had a case of bronchitis that was "movin' down in the chest," and she was worried—now that she "had the fever"—that a case of "the walkin' pneumonia" might not be too far behind.

Although pneumonia was incredibly easy to treat, given the advent of modern antibiotics, the older locals remembered the days when one out of three adults and most children with pneumonia would die. Because of this memory, even the thought of pneumonia would strike fear into most folks. So we tended to see upper respiratory infections even more frequently than our big-city colleagues.

What intrigued me about Susannah was not her medical case—the diagnosis and treatment were fairly straightforward. The chest X-ray showed no pneumonia, so I diagnosed pneumonitis and wrote a prescription for an inexpensive antibiotic. But looking at her sandal-clad feet, I saw something that piqued my interest. The toes, the soles, and the sides of the feet—about an inch up—were a dark yellow-orange color. It almost looked as though she had been stomping on some carrots. Yet the rest of the skin looked normal.

"Susannah, did a new pair of shoes stain your feet?" I asked.

She gave me a half-toothless smile and then let out a full-barreled laugh. "Why, naw. I tanned ma feets."

"You what?"

"I done tanned ma feets."

She went on to explain that she had been born with a condition that had been passed down on her mama's side of the family—sweaty feet. Not only did her feet sweat incessantly—even in winter—but also the constant sweating would cause her feet and shoes to smell and lead to frequent foot infections. So her family had picked up a "tanning the feet" technique from Bryson City's original doctor, Dr. West, in the 1880s.

She described it to me, and the technique sounded as simple as it was ingenious—and made simpler with the advent of tea bags: Just boil six tea bags in a teakettle of water. Allow them to steep overnight as the water cooled. Put approximately one inch of the tea solution into a container large enough to soak the feet. Soak the feet in the tea solution for fifteen to twenty minutes twice daily for three days. The tannic acid in the solution discolors the soles and apparently causes the sweat glands of the feet to go into hibernation.

I smiled to myself at the ingenuity and planned to store this "mountain trick" for future use—and, as it would turn out, publication in the *American Family Physician* journal over ten years later.

Nevertheless, for obvious reasons, I do not recommend this technique for sweaty palms.

—

$\mathcal{T}$he real surprise of this appointment came near the end of the visit. As I handed Susannah a prescription, she gave me a funny look.

"What?" I asked, smiling.

"Oh, nothing," she said, looking down.

But I sensed she had something to say. So I just sat back quietly. After nearly a minute of waiting, she looked up at me. "Some of the ladies in my community tell me it's wrong to come over here to you."

"Really?"

"Yep. They say I should just wait for their spell to work."

"Spell?" I asked. I tried not to show the astonishment I was feeling.

She looked away for a moment and then explained. "A few years ago I was frustrated. My husband was havin' an affair. I went to my pastor, but he told me to just submit and to pray for my husband. But I couldn't. So I left him and moved out. My family and my church all shunned me. As far as they were concerned, I was at fault." She lowered her head, and tears started to flow down her cheeks. I handed her a box of tissue. She pulled one out, wiped her face, and then blew her nose.

"My girlfriend came over. She seemed to be the only one who understood my side. She invited me to meet some other women at her home for dinner. I went, and I liked this group. They understood me. They accepted me."

She blew her nose again. "Before I knew it, Dr. Larimore, I had become a good witch. At first the whole thing seemed so good. But then I began to see more and more bad things." She paused.

"Like what?"

Her eyes widened. "Oh, I couldn't tell you, Doctor. If I did . . ." She looked away, unable to finish her statement.

"Susannah," I asked, "is this group a Wicca group?"

She nodded. "The girls were so nice to me. And I liked all the mystery surrounding it. Then the leader—she called herself a priestess—took me under her wings. She told me it was all white magic, and that's all I was interested in. But after a few months, I began to get deeper and deeper into darkness and black magic."

She was quiet for a moment. I thought about my discussion with Mitch. I remembered his words: "Walt, I want you to be willing to do anything, even unconventional things, to help a patient." Although I hadn't been trained in any sort of spiritual counseling, and although combining medicine and spiritual interventions was considered by many to be out-of-bounds at best and unethical at worst, I knew I was being called at this moment to be, as Mitch said, "unconventional."

"Susannah," I began, "I don't know a lot about this religion. But I do know that the Bible teaches it is wrong—even dangerous—to fool around on the dark side."

She smiled. "I didn't really expect to come to the doctor and get preached to."

She did not appear to be angry, so I continued. "Oh, I don't mean to sound like a preacher. But as a physician, I *am* interested in your health. And I wonder if this might not be dangerous for your health."

She looked down at her lap as she told me a story. "About two weeks ago I was lyin' awake in my bedroom. It was a warm evening, but my room became ice-cold. Then a freezing breeze blew in through my windows. Doc, I began to feel scared. I curled up in a ball, and then I seen 'im."

"What?" I asked.

"A dark figure just circled over my bed. He was laughing at me. I started chanting some of the spells I had learned. But it only made things worse. The laughter grew, and I tried to scream, but nothing came out. I felt like my breath was being sucked out of me. And then I knew it."

Susannah looked pale and began to tremble.

"What?" I asked again.

"I knew I was going to die. I knew it. And then, all of a sudden, I remembered back to a Vacation Bible School when I was a kid. I remembered what the teacher told me about Jesus—about how he loved me and wanted me to spend eternity with him in heaven. Doc, I hadn't thought about that in decades. But at that instant I called out to Jesus Christ to save me from this evil in my room."

Then Susannah looked up at me. "Doc, I know this sounds crazy. I know it do. But the darkness was gone in a flash. And then my bedroom was warm again."

"Susannah," I asked, "are you still a member of that group?"
She silently nodded.
"It sounds like you know you need to get out, eh?"
She nodded again.

"I know a pastor in Robbinsville who is a good man. He and his wife know the Bible and how to apply it in everyday life. Susannah, their church is a church of truth and love—not judgment and legalism. So here's what I'd like to do. Besides giving you a prescription for an antibiotic for your infection, I'd like to give you another prescription."

As I wrote on the prescription pad, Susannah looked on curiously.

"Here it is!" I tore it off and handed it to her.

She read it and then smiled. "I'll fill it!" she declared as she stood to leave.

$\sim$

The pastor called the office later that week. "Dr. Larimore," he began, "thanks for referring Susannah to me. However, I've got to tell you, I've never been asked to fill a faith prescription before." He laughed.

"Well, Pastor, I've never written one before. So it's a first for both of us."

"I was glad I could read your handwriting. You had written for her to call me and to begin reading her Bible every day. You even wrote some verses for her to memorize. I wanted to let you know she's done them all."

I was pleased. "How's she doing?" I asked.

"She's been hurt by the church before. But I'm hoping she'll be able to fall in love again with the Lord. In his sight she's precious, and I suspect he has an incredible plan for her. Her story is an amazing one."

"I suspect that's true for all of us."

"True enough," he concurred. "Well, if there's any way we can help you fill more of those faith prescriptions, you let me know. Our spiritual pharmacy is open twenty-four hours a day."

———

Mitch had told me, "If you keep your patients' best interests at heart, I think your skin will be thick enough to handle the heat. And the rewards of doing what's right, even if it's not easy, are among the sweet things that make our profession so satisfying."

I smiled as I thought about the day just before falling asleep. It had been a satisfying day indeed. But as much as I had been pleased by practicing something new and unconventional—at least to me—even more I prayed that my Father was pleased. Somehow I sensed he was.

chapter eighteen

WISE COUNSEL

*L*ike most married couples, we always considered our wedding anniversary to be a special day. And in November we would celebrate our tenth anniversary. The planning for that special week was going exceptionally well. The furniture was at Sally's—as were the airline tickets and confirmations for all of our reservations. My accomplices, Rick and Sally, had been able to keep a secret—which, I was learning, was a rare talent in Bryson City!

One evening, with Dorinda taking care of the kids, Barb and I went up to the Hemlock Inn for dinner. John and Ella Jo Shell would invite us to join their guests for dinner several times a year. Their dining hall was always packed. Each of the seven tables had eight chairs around it. John greeted each arrival at the door and directed them to their assigned table. Seating and eating were strictly family style—with John arranging and rearranging the inn's guests at each meal, guaranteeing a variety of conversation with people from all over the country.

John and Ella Jo always took pleasure in sprinkling "locals" in with their guests—and we enjoyed being considered locals. As guests gathered at the tables that evening, the servers brought out large platters and bowls filled with fried chicken, green beans with ham hocks, ham that could easily be cut with a fork, creamy potatoes with brown and sawmill gravies, candied carrots, and a basketful of steaming-hot yeast rolls with local clover and wildflower honey butter and an assortment of homemade toppings and jams. At the ping of a small bell, John said grace, and then we all enjoyed a delectable dinner and fabulous fellowship.

An elderly man sitting next to us leaned over to Barb and inquired, "You young people here for your honeymoon?"

Barb and I laughed, and he looked a bit surprised.

"We *were* newlyweds," Barb responded.

"*Were?*" the man's wife asked.

"Yes," I answered, "but that was ten years ago!"

"Ah," she commented, "you must have married very young. And ten years? Can that be true?"

"You're so kind," Barb remarked. "And the truth is, we're leaving on our anniversary trip next weekend."

"Where are you going?"

Barb turned to look at me and smiled. "You'll have to ask *him*. He hasn't told me just yet."

"Don't you think you should?" the man asked me.

I nodded. "Okay, I will."

Barb looked at me with surprise. "You will?"

"Yep," I answered. "After all, I've got to tell you sometime. And we need to pack the right stuff, don't we?"

Barb chuckled. "You're finally learning!"

I looked at our dinner companions. "What she's referring to is the fact that I didn't tell her where we were going on our honeymoon, and she wasn't able to pack exactly what she needed."

"So where *are* you taking her?" the woman asked.

"Well, first we're going back to our honeymoon hotel—the Polynesian Resort at Disney World. I've talked to the manager, and they've scheduled us to stay in the very same room in which we spent our honeymoon."

"Oh, that's sweet!" the woman exclaimed.

Barb looked surprised. She had let it be known that Walt Disney World would *not* have been her top choice for a honeymoon location in the first place.

"That's not all," I explained. I looked around. By now, all of our tablemates were listening to the conversation. "Then we fly to Miami to catch a cruise ship for a seven-day Caribbean cruise."

A small round of applause broke out at the table, and Barb smiled.

"Now you're talking!" the woman exclaimed.

"You *are* educable!" Barb added, smiling.

Peals of laughter echoed around the table.

After dinner, Barb and I walked outside to sit on the deck of the inn overlooking the Alarka Mountains. This particular night we had to wear light coats, as the evening air was cool. So we just sat beside each other, gently rocking in the rocking chairs and listening to the evening sounds as we viewed the spectacular vista.

"A penny for your thoughts," Barb whispered.

"I was just thinking about our marriage—especially over the last three years."

Barb reached out to take my hand. "It hasn't been easy, has it?"

I shook my head. "Barb, besides being a single parent or losing a child to death, I'm not sure there's greater stress on a marriage than raising a child with a disability. And you've done such a marvelous job."

"We've come a long way, Walt. I'm pleased with that. But raising a strong-willed boy isn't easy either."

I laughed.

"What's so funny about that?"

"I was just thinking about the evening I found you nearly at the end of your rope."

"You could tell?"

"You bet I could!"

"How?"

"Well, besides the fact that you were nearly in tears at the kitchen sink, there were the two wooden spoons—one stuck in each back pocket of your jeans. I could tell it hadn't been a good day—for you or for Scott!"

Barb laughed. "I think Scripture saved his life that day."

"Really? Which one?"

"Exodus 20, verse 13."

"Got me!" I confessed. "What does that verse say?"

"Seems to me it's a key verse in parenting."

"You've still got me stumped, honey."

Barb chuckled. "It says, 'You shall not murder.'"

We laughed and then rocked a bit more. My admiration for her as a woman, a wife, and a mother continued to grow. My thoughts raced back to when Barb and I met. We were in kindergarten—at five years of age. We each had three siblings and professional moms who set aside their careers when we were young to devote energy and love to raise us. Our parents practiced strict discipline and had high expectations for us. We were required to eat breakfast and supper with the family. We took vacations together and developed family holiday traditions. Not only were our parents committed to us; our extended families—aunts, uncles, cousins, and grandparents—encouraged, nurtured, admonished, supported, loved, and protected us as well.

We truly were blessed to have been raised in nurturing families—and to have parents who were committed to each other for life. The word *divorce* was never in their vocabulary. No matter how tough things might be, staying together as a family was a high priority. These commitments to family and marriage provided a strong model and foundation for Barb and me.

Barb took a deep breath. "As I think back over the last few years, I'm convinced that without the support of our neighbors, the Bible, and prayer, I wouldn't have made it."

She squeezed my hand and continued. "I've never really asked you, Walt. What caused you to hang on during those dark days?"

I felt my eyes misting. My wife's faith in God had been *so* much stronger than mine during those years. I thought for a moment. "Well, I think our neighbors *were* crucial. They gave us so much love and really helped us. Of course, our church and pastor were crucial. And most of all, Barb, I think your prayers were essential."

Barb nodded.

"But there was something else," I added.

"What's that?"

"A memory from a long time ago."

"Tell me about it," Barb implored.

"Well, the year before my grandfather died, he sat me down in his backyard one day to talk. We sipped sweet tea and rocked in our chairs as he admired his yard and garden. 'Walt,' he began, 'when you decide to get married, I want you to remember one thing.'"

"What was it?" Barb asked.

"He told me that the part of the wedding vow that says 'till death do we part' means divorce is not an option. He told me that a marriage vow is intended to be a lifelong vow—one I'd be making to you, your parents, my parents, and the church. 'But most important of all,' he said, 'you're making a sacred vow to God.' He told me not to make it if I didn't mean it."

"You've never told me that."

"I know. In fact, I think I chose to forgot his advice in those difficult months after Kate was born. I was so angry about her disability that it wiped out any conscious memory of his advice. So I credit our church, our wonderful neighbors, and one incredible wife for keeping our marriage from ending up on the rocks that destroy so many other marriages."

I looked at Barb and could see tears streaking down her cheeks. I let go of her hand to reach into my pocket, and I handed her my handkerchief. She wiped her tears and then sat back and began to rock again. I knew she wanted to sit in silence for a moment.

I returned to my rocking and could see the new moon rising above the crest of the mountains across the valley. The longer we lived together, the more I came to appreciate the incredible woman I had married. I had determined to make her tenth anniversary special indeed and had, in fact, been preparing for it for ten years thanks to another piece of advice from my grandfather—a romantic at heart—who'd been a Pullman conductor for the Illinois

Central Railway's trains that ran from Chicago to New Orleans. Once, when Barb and I were visiting my grandmother, she showed us a shoe box full of romantic letters he had written her. He would write them on the train and mail them from the various stops along the way.

Barb interrupted my thoughts. "Walt, I thought you might take me to dinner and a romantic weekend in Asheville or to a quiet mountain bed-and-breakfast. But a cruise? How'd you make all the arrangements without me suspecting a thing?"

"R.P. and Sally did a lot of the work. Rick helped with strategy."

"That dirty dog!"

"Who?"

"Rick, that's who!"

"Why?"

"A few months ago he was quizzing me about our honeymoon. I told him I'd like to go back to Disney World one day, but that I'd prefer to go on a cruise. He told you, didn't he?"

I laughed.

"So where'd you get the money, Walt? We don't have that much, do we?"

"Well, there was another piece of advice my granddad gave me as we sat in his backyard that day."

"What's that?"

"He asked me if I wanted another tip. Of course, I told him I did. So he told me to start saving—the day I got married. He told me to save a little every month. To save for my tenth, twenty-fifth, and fiftieth anniversaries. He told me to look forward to them. To aim for them."

"So have you?"

"Indeed, *we* have! And that account is going to cover the costs of a great trip."

Barb suddenly stopped rocking, sat up, and looked at me. "What are we going to do with the kids?"

I chuckled. "Got it covered. We'll drive to the Asheville airport. You and the kids have tickets to Baton Rouge. You'll spend a couple of days with your mom and dad, leave the kids with the grandparents, and then fly to Orlando to meet me."

"What are you going to be doing?"

"I've been asked to speak at the Family Medicine Residency Program. Then I'll go down to Kissimmee to visit John and Cleta Hartman. I'll meet you at the airport in Orlando when you arrive, and then we're off in a limousine to the honeymoon hotel."

"I can't wait to start packing. I already know what I'm going to take. This is going to be so much fun!" Barb exclaimed.

I nodded, smiling, because Barb didn't even know the best part. She didn't have a clue about what would be happening in our house while we were away.

chapter nineteen

An Anniversary
to Remember

As Barb and I enjoyed our incredible second honeymoon, including a trip to Walt Disney World and a Caribbean cruise more romantic and restful than we could have imagined—climbing Dunn's River Falls in Jamaica with a private guide, snorkeling in the Caribbean, shopping in Cancun—Sally Jenkins was hard at work coordinating the makeover of our bedroom.

The hand-carved, solid-wood furniture was set in place. The new sheets, pillows, shams, and comforter Sally had helped me pick out adorned the bed. The room glowed with a fresh coat of paint, brand-new carpet, and window coverings—compliments of the hospital after Sally had R.P. convince them to spring for that part of the makeover.

The time came to head home, and Sally had everything prepared. She had made the bed, put chocolates on the pillows, turned the lights on to a low and romantic intensity, and placed fresh flowers by the bed and in the bathroom. Even better, Sally arranged for Kate and Scott to spend one additional night with Nancy Cunningham—so that we could enjoy one last day (and evening) in our new, secluded boudoir.

We had promised ourselves an entire day after returning just to unpack and rest. In so many previous vacations, we had rushed back and then dashed back to work the very next day. This always frustrated Barb and would end up aggravating me. So we had learned to arrive back from vacations on Saturday—giving us a day of rest before returning to work.

As we parked our little yellow Toyota by the garage, I told Barb I'd come back to get our luggage. Arm in arm, we walked up to our little green house. I unlocked the door, opened it, and then gently lifted Barb into my arms.

"Just what in the world do you think you're doing?" she asked, laughing.

"I'm taking you across the threshold into our honeymoon cottage."

She laughed. "You're silly. We've just been on a honeymoon."

I carried her into the dining room and gently put her down. I turned her toward me and looked at her beautiful face. "Honey, we did have a wonderful trip, but it's not over. Today is just the continuation of your second honeymoon. Today we begin the rest of our marriage. Close your eyes."

She looked quizzically at me. "For what?"

I smiled. "Just close your eyes."

She did. I grasped her hands in mine and led her toward the bedroom. Once we were at the door, I let go of her hands. "Keep your eyes closed," I cajoled.

Then I walked behind her and held her shoulders as I directed her toward the door to our bedroom. The view that met my eyes was so stunning I almost gasped. I whispered in Barb's ear, "Open your eyes."

It was Barb's turn to gasp as she clasped her hand to her mouth. She turned to look at me, her eyes as wide as saucers, and then turned back to the room. Slowly she stepped into the bedroom and began to walk around, combining gasps and laughs with each new discovery.

She was shocked—and terribly pleased.

It was the most perfect ending to a perfect anniversary.

And it was the beginning of a deepening and a new maturity in our married life. However, our new bedroom carpet almost resulted in the end of Scott's life.

﹁

That next Monday morning, I was seeing a patient in the office when Helen knocked on the door. "Dr. Larimore, I need to see you. Now!"

I excused myself and met her in the hall. "What is it?"

"Barb just called. There's an emergency at home. She needs you up there now. Rick's going to cover your patients—there's only two left."

"Helen, what's going on?"

"I don't know. Just go. Now!"

I could think of any number of horrible things that might have happened. My only solace was remembering a similar incident in residency—when Barb called me home to view Kate's first steps. Nevertheless, I ran out of the office, jumped in the car, and raced up the back of Hospital Hill and into our driveway. There were no ambulances there. I leaped out of the car and ran to the house.

There was no one in the kitchen or dining room. I heard a noise in the living room and ran in. Barb was on the sofa, sobbing. Kate and Scott were sitting silently on the floor.

"Mommy is *very* sad!" Kate announced. I walked over to the couch and sat by Barb. Her sobbing worsened, and she threw herself into my arms. I held her tightly.

"What's the matter?" I asked Barb. She could only sob. She tried to talk but could not. "Barb, tell me what's wrong!"

She stood and took my hand. We walked out of the living room across the dining room, heading toward the bedroom. I was confused. Everything looked and smelled fine. No fire. No water leak.

Then Barb pointed to the floor. There, outside our bathroom, on her new baby-blue carpet, was displayed the most beautiful little childlike drawings you could imagine—on the carpet—in bright red lipstick.

Through quivering lips, Barb tried to explain. "Scott Bonham got into my lipstick, and he's ruined the carpet. He's ruined my bedroom." I knew she was angry—she only used Scott's middle name when she was. She began to sob. "He's ruined my life!"

My spirit smiled on the inside, but I knew an external smile would be deadly. I just pulled her close and held her tight.

When she quit sobbing, we sat in the dining room. I gave Barb my handkerchief, and she blew her nose. "I'm so sorry to call you. I know I interrupted your time with patients."

I leaned forward and held her hands. "Honey, you are more important to me than anyone. I want you to feel free to call me anytime. When you need me, I need to be here."

She leaned forward and gave me a hug.

"Honey," I began, "it won't be a problem to fix this."

Her lips quivered. "I don't think it will wash out."

"No problem."

She looked at me with a look of surprise.

"What do you mean?"

"Even if a professional carpet cleaner can't get it out, that section can be removed and replaced. And the way they do it these days, you won't even be able to find the seam."

She smiled, and we hugged.

"I guess it's not the end of the world," Barb sighed.

"He's just a little boy," I commented.

Barb smiled. "And *so* different from Kate."

"Let's go spend some time with the kids."

❧

That night before we went to bed, Barb and I had a long talk about being parents. We talked about the ups and the downs. We discussed how hard a job it is and how much time and effort it takes. We talked about the differences between boys and girls. We discussed how much each of our children needed our love and encouragement, our teaching and affirmation—in short, how much they need us to be their coaches and cheerleaders.

We spoke about the sacrifices parents had to make—ours included—and when all was said and done, we concluded that it's the most important and gratifying job in the world.

After our bedtime prayers, Barb went to sleep—but I could not.

I ended up on our bench, with a coat protecting me from the autumn evening chill. For some reason, I found myself thinking about my relationship with my Father in heaven. I was glad that when I goofed up, he was there to love me and forgive me. I suspected there were lives I had hurt and expectations I had not met, yet he loved me and cared about and for me through it all. I hoped that as I grew and matured as his child, he would be pleased with the son I was becoming. I wanted to be more and more like him, because I knew that Scott, like any normal boy, would want to be like his father—me.

part three

WINTER

chapter twenty

MRS. BLACK FOX

*L*ouise called me at the house during the height of a fierce winter snowstorm. The flurries were thick and heavy, and there were already at least twelve inches on top of the picnic table outside our dining room window.

Louise's voice sounded pressured. "Dr. Larimore, you need to get over to the birthing suite stat." Then she hung up.

I quickly rolled out of bed, pulled on my scrubs, a heavy coat, and my snow boots and trudged through the snow down our driveway. The going got easier when I got to the road between our home and the hospital, because the road had been cleared of snow by the county crews. It was usually one of the first roads cleared in the county.

The back door to the hospital was just across the street from our little green house, and within minutes I was in the labor area. Maxine met me outside one of the birthing rooms.

"Hi, Dr. Larimore," she said almost lackadaisically.

"Louise called and said to get over here stat!" I exclaimed.

Maxine was writing on the chart. "Oh, she says that to all the docs. Gets them over here quicker than usual—especially during a snowstorm."

I was a bit annoyed but made a note to discuss this with Louise later. "What's up?"

Maxine continued to write as she gave me the patient's story. "A twenty-two-year-old woman from Cherokee was just sent over. She's due next week. It's her first baby, and her prenatal care was unremarkable, other than obesity and type 2 diabetes—controlled with diet. She's shaped like a bowling ball, short and round. Her great-grandmother, one of the tribal matriarchs, is with her. One bossy woman, if you ask me!"

I hadn't, but I continued to listen as I took off my coat and sat down.

Maxine continued. "The patient's nearly completely dilated, just a rim of anterior cervix. Membranes are intact. Her vital signs are normal, and the baby's heart rate is fine. She's ready to meet you, but I'm not so sure about her great-grandmother."

"What's wrong?"

"I don't think she likes men."

I smiled at Maxine. "Gives you all something in common," I kidded.

Maxine looked over her glasses and the chart to glare at me. "One day God's gonna send us some nice doctors to work with!"

I laughed and walked over to the sink to wash my hands. Then we walked into the patient's room.

Maxine made the introduction. "Sylvia, this is Dr. Larimore."

Sylvia was lying on her side and just nodded.

"Dr. Larimore, this is Sylvia's great-grandmother, Mrs. Black Fox."

I looked at Maxine to see if she was kidding. Apparently she was not. The ancient woman sitting on the other side of the bed looked to be ninety years old. Her face was wrinkled like a prune, and her disposition seemed to match. She spoke in a husky voice. "Men not good in labor. Sylvia needs midwife."

I smiled, thinking to myself, *Me too!* But I refrained and just nodded in the direction of the antique woman. "During this storm, I'm afraid I'm all that's available. Sorry." I smiled at her, but she didn't smile back. Then I looked at the patient. "Sylvia, do you mind if I do a quick exam?"

Sylvia nodded her consent, but Mrs. Black Fox rather harshly commented, "Cherokee midwives tell by looking and listening. No need to touch."

I looked across the bed at the matriarch, but she looked away—apparently disgusted with me or males or both. I did a quick external exam of the mom's abdomen. All was fine, except that the baby seemed quite large to me. *This baby must weigh nine or ten pounds!* I thought to myself. I really wondered if Sylvia's diabetes had been controlled—diabetics with less than optimal care tend to have oversized babies.

I nodded to Maxine, and she had Sylvia lie on her back. I put on a sterile glove, and Maxine squeezed some warm lubricating jelly onto my pointer and middle finger. I began my internal exam, relating my findings to Sylvia, Maxine, and Mrs. Black Fox. "Sylvia, your cervix is completely dilated and the baby is already heading down the birth canal. The baby's head is in a good position, but I'd like to rupture your membranes, if that's okay."

Mrs. Black Fox obviously didn't think so. She turned to glare at me as she snarled, "Cherokee midwives never rupture water bag. It let in bad spirits." She turned her head away again.

"Sylvia, it's your call."

Sylvia didn't answer. I was quiet for a moment. "Sylvia, what do you want to do?"

She was quiet. Suddenly I realized I was putting her in the terrible position of having to choose between a doctor she didn't know—a male one at that—and her great-grandmother's authority in the tribe. "Tell you what, Sylvia. I think your great-grandmother is right. I certainly do not have to rupture the membranes. Okay?"

Sylvia, for the first time, both smiled and nodded.

Within just a few contractions, the baby's head was down the birth canal and was beginning to separate her labia with each contraction. Like many Cherokee women, Sylvia was quiet during the contractions—barely breathing more heavily, or perhaps furrowing her brow when the pain was at its peak.

"Maxine, let's set up to have a baby."

As Maxine prepared to convert the birthing suite's labor bed into a birthing bed, I stepped into the hall to scrub my hands. When I entered the room, Sylvia was in position for delivery. I put on a sterile gown and gloves and turned to my patient as she began to push.

"Mrs. Black Fox," I said, "if you'd like to come stand by Sylvia, you're welcome."

She glared at me. I took that as a *Thanks, but no thanks, Buster!*

Louise, having been called by Maxine, joined us in the room, turned on the warmer above the baby crib, and began to prepare the layette for the baby. At the next contraction, Maxine helped Sylvia sit up and coached her pushing. Slowly the baby's head began to appear.

During this stage of the delivery, I would usually just watch—hands off. The Designer of all design—the Master Physician himself—usually did not need help at this point. This moment just before birth was for me one of the most miraculous of all. Those who believed that life just evolved and was only the product of time and chance could not have seen the delivery of a newborn or examined a just delivered little baby. To me, both the delivery itself and the newborn baby were creations of the highest order.

As Sylvia pushed, the water bag began to emerge, and then it suddenly ruptured. The clear fluid looked completely normal. Then the head began to come into view. *Looks kinda big,* I thought—not realizing this would be the first sign of the disaster to come.

As more and more of the head appeared, I realized, *This is going to be one big baby!*

Gently I reached out, as was my routine, to help the head remain flexed. If the baby's neck extends during this stage of the delivery, a larger diameter of the skull presents and can damage the woman's sensitive tissues. Helping it remain flexed prevents tears and also the need for the birth attendant to make a cut—known as an episiotomy.

Just then the head slipped out. At this moment, I reached for the suction bulb, so as to clean the nose and mouth of secretions just prior to delivering the baby. However, to my horror, no sooner had the head slipped out than the baby was sucked back in, pulling the head tight against the perineum. *Shoulder dystocia!* I thought.

Shoulder dystocia can lead to an emergency in the birthing process. We can see it at the delivery of very large babies. The head will come out, but one of the shoulders hangs up just behind the pubic bone—giving the appearance of someone inside the woman pulling the baby back inside.

Although I had cared for shoulder dystocia many times in my training, it was always frightening to see it. Nevertheless, I'd been well trained in managing this problem—so, despite my initial concern, I began to walk through the step-by-step management.

The first step was to let the nurses know what was going on—and I always did this by talking to the patient. "Sylvia, the baby is very large, and its shoulder is wedged behind your pelvic bone. I'm going to ask Maxine and Louise to help me."

Many doctors will instinctively start pulling down on the baby's head to attempt to dislodge it, but this can be very dangerous, as it can stretch, damage, or even tear the nerves in the neck that go to the arm and leave the baby with a broken collarbone or even a nerve palsy—not something I wanted for this baby. I felt the first beads of sweat breaking out on my brow.

I quickly filled a syringe with lidocaine and rapidly numbed Sylvia's perineum. I then took a pair of scissors and cut a generous episiotomy—hoping it would give me much more room to work and to deliver this child. Then I inserted and quickly removed a small catheter to be sure Sylvia's bladder was empty. It was.

By the time I had finished these procedures, Maxine was at Sylvia's right side, and I directed Louise to her left. As Louise was getting in position, Mrs. Black Fox commented, "Cherokee midwives don't have this problem because they don't let woman get in bed." Years later, studies would actually provide proof for Mrs. Black Fox's observation—nevertheless, I did have the problem, whether Sylvia was in bed or not.

"Ladies, with the next contraction, I want you to pull Sylvia's thighs up toward her chest and out." This movement, called the McRobert's maneuver, helped open up the diameter of the pelvic outlet and would often work all by itself to allow the baby to be delivered. We tried this procedure through several contractions, with no success at all. Thankfully, the baby's heartbeat indicated that there was no distress—yet.

Then I tried to rotate the baby's shoulders to a position that was not directly behind the pubic bone. First I tried one way and then the other. Several attempts failed. I was beginning to feel panicked.

The baby's head was getting more purple, and the sweat on my brow fell into my left eye. I dabbed it with my shoulder as Mrs. Black Fox commented, calmly and almost coldly, "Are you going to kill my great-great-grandchild?"

I looked at her. She was now standing behind Louise and appeared coolly composed. I was not so calm—I was feeling deeply afraid—and I did not answer her as I gently placed my right hand behind the baby's head and tried once again to rotate the baby's shoulders one way and then the other. There was no movement at all. *This baby is really stuck!* I thought to myself.

"Maxine, get the fetal monitor. Now! Louise, let's get Sylvia to roll over and get on her hands and knees."

"All fours?" Louise asked.

"Like a dog?" asked Mrs. Black Fox. "No midwife would do that!"

I didn't have time to explain—but in actuality midwives had taught me this age-old trick. Many times having a woman push while in this position would dislodge the baby's shoulder and allow a safe and rapid delivery.

As Louise and I helped Sylvia get in position, Maxine returned with the fetal monitor. I attached a small clip to the baby's purplish head. Maxine turned it on, and I felt sick. The baby's pulse was less than seventy beats per minute, indicating that the baby was now distressed.

Mrs. Black Fox was standing near Sylvia's head. She almost growled. "Doctor, the baby is not breathing."

"That's okay, Mrs. Black Fox. The baby is getting oxygen from the placenta via the umbilical cord. But I need to work quickly to get this little one out."

To my chagrin and mounting terror, the change in position made no difference.

"Louise, let's get Sylvia on her left side." My training by midwives in England when I had been a Queen's Fellow in Nottingham gave me one more technique to try. But if this failed, I'd need surgical help, and I'd need it fast.

"Maxine, call the surgeon on call, and let's get ready for a stat C-section."

She looked at me as if I had two heads—after all, the baby's head was already out. "Move it!" I commanded.

"Dr. Mitchell's on call. I'll page him." She immediately left.

As Sylvia was getting on her left side, I could hear the fetal heart tones slowing.

"Getting close to sixty per minute!" Louise commented.

I knew this heart rate was getting dangerously low. "Louise, hold her upper leg for me."

I moved behind the patient. "Sylvia," I told the patient, "I'm going to try again to rotate your baby. While I'm doing this, please don't push. Okay?" She nodded as I looked into the eyes of Mrs. Black Fox. I could see in her eyes what I was feeling in my heart—the fear of an impending death. She slowly raised her head, closed her eyes, and began an ancient chant.

As she chanted, I inserted my hand behind the baby's head and tried one last desperate time to rotate the baby.

As I did so, Mrs. Black Fox chanted, and I prayed.

chapter twenty-one

THE LITTLEST CHEROKEE

$\mathcal{T}$he heart rate dropped, as did my hope of saving this baby. Mrs. Black Fox's haunting chants only increased my anxiety as the sweat ran profusely down my brow. Louise dabbed my brow as I helped Sylvia onto her back.

The side-lying position had failed. Now I had no choice. I had to try to push the baby's head back up the birth canal. I had never done this before, and I'd only seen it done once by one of my senior residents while on an obstetrics rotation at Charity Hospital in New Orleans during my medical school days. By pushing the head back into the birth canal, it would make the baby easier to remove with an emergency Cesarean birth.

Please hurry, Mitch! I thought.

Maxine quickly entered the room. "Mitch is coming! I've got the other nurses setting up the OR. Are you ready to transport her to the operating room?"

"Give me a minute, Maxine." I turned back to my patient. "Sylvia, your baby is stuck and isn't coming out. I'm going to try to push the baby's head back into the birth canal, and then we're going to rush you to the operating room for a C-section. We have to operate to save your baby!"

Sylvia nodded and then began weeping. Her great-grandmother's chanting only increased in volume—as did my sweating and heart rate.

I slowly flexed the baby's head and was surprised at how easily the head actually slid back into the birth canal. I was just getting ready to ask Maxine to help me transport Sylvia to the surgical suite when Dr. Mitchell burst through the door. Although it was obvious from the sweat on his brow and his mussed-up hair that he had rushed here from bed, his demeanor, as always, was calm and unruffled.

To my utter surprise, he began to gown and glove. I walked over to him and leaned toward him. "Mitch, what are you doing? We're getting ready to move her to OR for a stat C-section."

Mitch looked at the patient and then turned his back to her. Leaning toward me, he whispered, "Walt, our anesthetists are both snowed in and can't get here. County crews won't be able to get Kim, who's the closest, here for at least an hour. Bacon's out of town, and other than me and our anesthetists, he's the only one who can administer anesthesia. I'm going to have to show you an old-fashioned and very primitive way to get this baby out. Just go with me on this one, okay?"

I was shocked at what he had just told me and began to feel nauseous. I had never had a baby under my care die before. Although I had no idea what he had in mind, I had no choice but to trust him.

We both turned toward the baby. "Louise," Mitch commanded, "hand Walt a Foley catheter; Maxine, get me a disposable scalpel with a #15 blade, will you?"

When Louise handed me the catheter, I gently slid it up the urethra and into the bladder. We could both see that the small trickle of urine was clear—indicating no trauma to the bladder.

I turned to see Mitch filling another syringe with lidocaine. The heart rate of the baby was slowing down. "Thirty beats per minute," Maxine whispered—clearly concerned.

I knew we didn't have much time. Apparently, so did Mrs. Black Fox, who now sat on the floor by the bed and began to weep out loud as she continued to chant.

What is he doing? I wondered as Mrs. Black Fox's wails grew in intensity.

"Walt," Mitch whispered, "you're going to have to cut apart the symphysis of the pubic bone."

"What?" I whispered back. I had never heard of such a thing. I had, of course, heard of the symphysis pubis, the ligamentous connection of the right and left pelvic bone—right above and behind the clitoris.

"Symphysiotomy," Mitch explained. "I've not done one in a lot of years. Learned it in the Army. It's only used in life-and-death situations. And, son, that's what we've got here!"

I'm sure I looked shocked, but he continued. "Here, take this #15 blade scalpel while I numb things up." He talked as he took the syringe and needle and began to inject the lidocaine into the soft tissues overlying the pubic bone. "The catheter is in the urethra, so palpate carefully to avoid the clitoris and urethra at all cost. Feel for the pubic bone and gently advance the scalpel to the symphysis."

As I took the scalpel, his experienced hands guided mine. I palpated the pubic bone. "Walt," he continued to whisper, "as you know, there's ligamentous tissue at the junction of the pelvic bones—right here in the middle. At the end of pregnancy, the ligament is pretty soft. You're going to cut it. But go slow! Once the knife separates the front part of the ligaments, the rest will separate like butter. You won't have to apply much pressure."

I advanced the knife and watched it easily separate the vaginal skin. I could feel the blade moving toward the bone and then lie just on top of the symphysis.

"Slowly and carefully advance the knife," Mitch instructed. "Hurry, Walt!" he coached.

"Twenty beats per minute!" Maxine exclaimed.

Mrs. Black Fox's wails continued. "My great-great-grandbaby is dying!" she wailed. She had no idea how right she was. Sylvia was just staring at the ceiling, apparently in shock.

As I slowly advanced the scalpel, the ligament parted, and then almost instantly the pelvic bone opened up—feeling as if it popped apart. I froze for an instant, but Mitch kept coaching. "Slowly and carefully remove the knife."

I did.

"Now, Sylvia," Mitch commanded, "push out this baby. Now! Walt, reach down and rotate the baby's shoulders. Quickly now!"

Miraculously, Sylvia seemed to wake up and push. As she did, the baby's head almost immediately delivered. I quickly reached down and tried to rotate the baby's shoulders. To my delight, the baby quickly rotated, and I was able to fairly easily deliver the baby.

Mitch had the cord clamps ready. He clamped the cord as I cut it. "Take the baby, and I'll finish here!" he commanded.

I hastily took the purple, lifeless body to the baby warmer. As Louise vigorously dried the baby, I suctioned out its mouth and nose.

As Louise palpated the stump of the umbilical cord, she said, "The heart rate is thirty per minute."

The baby was not breathing.

"Bag and mask," I instructed. Louise handed them to me, and I applied the respirator mask to the baby's face, gently hyperextended the neck, and began to compress the ambu-bag, forcing oxygen into the baby's lungs.

Lord, I silently prayed, *this is your child, and so am I! Help us both!*

I looked down at the genitals for the first time. *Save her!* I silently pleaded.

In the background I could no longer hear Mrs. Black Fox's wails. I looked to my side and was shocked to see the ancient woman standing beside me. She was staring at the baby and softly chanting a prayer as tears streaked down both cheeks and dripped off her aged jaw. As I bagged the baby, both of our prayers intertwined.

I looked back at the baby and to my delight could see her pinking up.

"Sixty beats per minute!" Louise exclaimed.

The little girl coughed and then began to breathe and cry at the same moment. I removed the mask, and Louise held oxygen over her nose. "Over a hundred beats per minute!" she exclaimed.

As the littlest Cherokee began to cry, so did her great-great-grandmother. And, I must admit, so did I! I've never so enjoyed the hot tears that streaked down my face and absorbed into my mask.

I looked at the old woman, and she looked at me—each looking at the other through grateful eyes filled with tears. She smiled up at me. "You were an answer to my prayers!" she whispered.

It may have been the most wonderful compliment of my career. But I could not take credit.

"Mrs. Black Fox, we both need to thank the Lord."

"And don't forget to thank Dr. Mitchell," came Mitch's soft voice from behind us.

Mrs. Black Fox, Louise, and I all laughed—as our laughter mingled with the newborn's cries and floated up toward heaven.

I wondered if I had not just been treated to one of the sounds of heaven—the sound of life. It was the sweetest sound I had heard that winter—or, for that matter, the entire year.

chapter twenty-two

CHRISTMAS FIRSTS

The week before Christmas, I saw Ella Jo Shell for a routine office visit. Ella Jo and her husband, John, were the proprietors of the Hemlock Inn and had become a major source of referrals to our practice. Therefore, I wasn't surprised when Ella Jo said, "Before you run off to your next patient, I need to tell you about Evan."

I cocked my head. "Evan?"

"He's become a good friend. He's an older man—I'd guess sixty or so—and he and his partner own a shop in a nearby town."

"I bet Barb's been there, but I don't think I ever have."

"Well, it's a great shop. I like browsing around there."

"Who's his partner? Do I know her?"

Ella Jo smiled. "I would guess not. Evan's partner is actually a guy whose name is Richard."

"A *guy?*"

"Yep. Where they live they're pretty well accepted—although I'm not so sure they'd be well accepted over here in Swain County."

I nodded.

Ella Jo continued. "Anyway, Evan is concerned about his health. He's been losing some weight and has some funny-looking moles developing on his legs. He asked me to look at them. Walt, I've never seen anything like it. They look like purplish lumps. Can you think of any sorts of special rashes that occur in homosexuals?"

Frankly, I had never cared for a homosexual—at least none that I knew of—through all of my training in the 1970s.

"Other than the sexually transmitted diseases, I don't think I know of any."

I was quiet for a second, developing in my mind what doctors call differential diagnoses—a list of possible diagnoses. Usually I would try to think of the most common diagnosis or diagnoses that would fit the history and exam (and any tests that had been ordered). But at the same time I'd been taught to always think of the worst possible diagnoses—so that I wouldn't miss something bad in its earliest stages. In Evan's case the worst diagnosis I could think of was some form of cancer. For internal cancers to cause fatigue and an unexpected loss of weight, as well as changes in the skin, was not unusual.

"Walt, I told Evan he should get a skin biopsy—for safety's sake—just to be sure it's not some sort of melanoma or something like that. Anyway, I told him about you and Rick. I think he's willing to come over here for an evaluation, if you're willing to see him."

"Ella Jo, I think it's a compliment that he's willing to come over here. Seems like most folks from their town get their care in Sylva or Waynesville—many even travel to Asheville."

"Yep. But it seems like folks are more willing to stay here for their care. And I think that's good."

I agreed. We finished our visit, and I asked her to wish her family a Merry Christmas from Barb and me.

The morning before Christmas, I was on call for our practice. After I had finished seeing patients for the morning in the office, I was dictating charts when the phone rang. It was Louise from ER.

I greeted her with, "Hi, Louie!" when I picked up the phone.

"Dr. Larimore, don't you start with no 'Hi, Louie' to me. You need to learn to respect your elders!" I grinned as she continued without a breath between sentences. "In the meantime, I've got a patient here with a pretty bad pneumonia. He's got a temperature of 102, a productive cough, a low white blood cell count, shortness of breath, and a low oxygen level."

She paused for a breath and then lowered her voice. "Dr. Larimore, he's an older white man, and he's all skin and bones. He looks cachectic, and I bet he's got 'im a bad cancer. I'll begin writin' up some ICU admission orders for him."

She sighed and then continued. "The respiratory therapist is down here, and I've got him on oxygen."

As Louise paused to take a breath, I couldn't resist the temptation. "Louise, why is the RT on oxygen? Is he sick also?"

Louise didn't reply. I was sure she was trying to process what I was saying, so I struck while the striking was good. "Oh my goodness. Is some plague sweeping over the hospital? The county? Oh dear, Louise! Should I come work at your side, risking life and limb? Or should I flee for my life to Franklin or parts asunder? And if I do come, do you and I need to be on prophylactic oxygen ourselves? And, Louise, what if the hospital runs out of oxygen? Then what? Oh dearie me!"

I paused to chuckle. However, Louise apparently did not share my sense of humor. "Dr. Larimore, you ain't funny one bit. This man's sick, and you best be givin' me some ICU orders."

I agreed and gave Louise the admission orders. I wanted him cultured up and started on high-dose antibiotics. "Does he have family?" She and I both knew this case probably did represent some sort of end-stage cancer.

"Not that I know of. Just a friend who brought him in."

Loners were not at all unusual in the mountains, and loners who came to the doctor only after their disease process was pretty far along were very common. You see, to most of the mountain people, the hospital was a scary place. They would tell me that they knew people—friends and neighbors—who would come to the hospital only to die. The result was that, instead of coming in early in the disease process when treatment and sometimes a cure were at least possible, the locals would often wait to come in until it was too late for us to help them. "I'll be up to see him just as soon as I'm done with my patients. That okay?"

"Sounds good, Dr. Larimore. I'll let you know if you need to get here any quicker. And ..." Louise paused.

"And what?" I inquired.

"And you can leave your smarty-pants side down there in that office before you come here to *my* ER!" Before I could respond, she hung up.

⚬

*W*hen I arrived at the hospital, I paused in the lobby to look at the Christmas decorations. The tree was actually a live tree from Greg Shuler's Christmas tree farm. The lobby, strung with beautiful lights and freshly cut evergreen garland, smelled exhilarating— it looked like a scene from a Christmas card.

I thought for a moment of how hospitals were places of death, without a doubt, but also places of new birth and healing. In a very real sense, the events most of us celebrated at Christmas—the birth of the Christ child—and then on Good Friday and Easter— Jesus' death and burial—were represented in my day-to-day life in the hospital caring for patients. *No wonder,* I thought, *God calls himself the Great Physician.* I suspected that today I'd have to tell an old man of his impending death. I had no idea of the birth that would occur.

I passed through the lobby and went first to the X-ray suite. Carroll was there. He found the patient's films and put them on the viewing box. "Looks like an atypical pneumonia, Walt."

I nodded. Carroll was as good at reading films as any radiologist I knew.

"I went ahead and did tomograms of the hilum," he commented.

I nodded again, as Carroll was thinking just what I was—this pneumonia was probably caused by a cancer. The tomographic X-ray allowed us to look at the area between the lungs—in this case, for lumps of cancer. Carroll replaced the plain films with the tomograms. "But I don't see any cancer. Maybe it's a small-cell carcinoma."

I smiled to myself. Small-cell cancer of the lung was a name that described a deadly type of cancer—but in no way did the name imply that it didn't form masses that could be seen.

"Thanks, Carroll. I'd best go take a look at the patient."

"He's interesting, Doc, I'll tell you that."

Aren't they all? I wondered to myself.

"Hi, Peggy!" I called out as I entered the nurses' station. Peggy had been at the hospital for many years. She led the choir at the Presbyterian church when she wasn't working at the hospital. She was married to Joe Ashley, a longtime ranger at the national park.

"Hi, Dr. Larimore. Here to see the new admit in ICU?"

"Yep." Our ICU was really just a former four-bed ward located close to the nurses' station and converted into the place where we cared for our sickest patients.

"You gonna tell him what he's got?"

"Guess I'd better figure out what it is first, don't you think?"

Peggy smiled to herself. It wasn't unusual for the nurses to know what was going on far before the doctors did, and in this case, Peggy, like Carroll, strongly suspected cancer. She handed me the chart. The name on the front was Evan Thomas. *Could this be the Evan that Ella Jo was talking about?* I thought to myself.

As I entered the room, the patient looked worse than I could have imagined. He was fairly emaciated. The oxygen had normalized his color, but instantly I knew this was a very sick man. Another man was sitting by Evan's bedside. As I entered, he stood.

"Hi, I'm Dr. Larimore. I'm the doctor on call today."

"I couldn't be more delighted!" the man exclaimed. "My name's Richard White. Evan and I know about you and your partner, Dr. Pyeritz. Ella Jo Shell often visits our shop and has told us so much about you both. We were hoping either you or he would be willing to care for us."

"Richard, Evan, it's good to meet you." I turned my attention to Evan, taking a complete history and then doing a complete physical. When I was through, I pulled up a chair. I always felt it was better to communicate face-to-face, and sitting with patients helped me accomplish that.

"Evan, I think you know you've got pneumonia."

He nodded.

"But it's not a typical pneumonia. It's atypical. Given your weight loss and fatigue, I've gotta be honest with you." I paused for a moment.

Evan reached out and took Richard's hand. He looked fleetingly at his partner and then back to me. "Is it cancer?"

I nodded. "To tell you the truth, that's my guess. We would need to do tests to be sure. But that's what I suspect."

"Is it treatable?"

"It depends on the type. But my guess is that it's probably already widespread. So we'll just have to see."

"When can we start?"

"Well, let's get the infection under control, and then we'll talk about getting started." I was quiet and let them absorb the information. When it was clear they didn't have any more questions, I left the room.

The next morning was Christmas, and I made early-morning rounds—well before Kate and Scott would wake up to celebrate Christmas. I found Evan alone but awake. I greeted him and sat on the bed. His breathing was labored and shallow.

"Evan, how are you feeling?"

"Not so good, Doc. Didn't sleep well."

"Seems you're breathing harder than last night. I'd better get Carroll to take another X-ray."

"He's already been here—along with Betty the Vampire."

I smiled at his reference to Betty Carlson, the director of our laboratory. "Let me go take a look at it and let you know what I see, okay? Anything else I can do?"

"Doc, I've been told you're a man of faith. I've also been told you're a very good doctor. But I've got to tell you, I was worried about coming over here to see you."

"Why's that?"

Evan didn't answer for a moment. Then he looked deeply into my eyes. "Doc, lots of Bible-thumpers call people like me evil and nasty things. I was worried you might think the same."

Now it was my turn to be quiet for a moment. I was trying to think about how to respond to this man's honesty and transparency. It was an unnerving moment for me. But, cautiously, I continued.

"Evan, my faith teaches me that the most important thing in life is a personal relationship with God. Everything else pales in comparison to that. And I found that when I began that relationship with God, he was fully able and willing to guide me into doing and thinking the right things. So the real issue isn't what I think or what you think, but what *he* thinks."

Evan smiled, and I saw tears forming in his eyes. "When I was a kid, church was important to me. I really enjoyed going—but never did I enjoy it more than on Christmas Eve. But when I grew up I just grew away from it. Do you think your God would even want a relationship with me?"

For a moment I thought about the Bible verse "Always be prepared to give an answer to everyone who asks you to give the reason for the hope that you have. But do this with gentleness and respect." I was pleased Evan felt comfortable enough to ask. But I'd always been taught in medical school that it was unethical to discuss religion with patients. However, Evan *had* asked—in essence, he had given me permission to share with him. So I decided to proceed—albeit carefully and *very* uncomfortably. Spiritual discussions were simply not something I had been trained to provide in the medical environment, but I'd begun to carefully incorporate them into my practice during my first year in Bryson City. Furthermore, a still, small whisper was encouraging me to harvest this opportunity to share an intimate part of myself with a very, very sick patient.

"Evan, I *know* God wants to have a relationship with you. My understanding of the Bible is that it tells us that God loves each of us. Actually, he loves us so much that he sent his only Son, Jesus, not just to be born in a manger but to live a perfect life for us as an example and then to die a torturous death for us—for all of our wrongdoing. Evan, if you're willing to believe that, God's willing to begin that relationship with you—today—but only if you want to."

Evan looked out the window of the ICU. The daylight was just starting. For just a moment, I was concerned he might have been upset, but instead he turned back to me and whispered, "It would be a good day to start."

I was quiet. The tears began to flow down his face, and he sniffled. I reached out and took his hand. He gave my hand a squeeze and then looked back at me. "Doc, I've done a lot of wrong things. Guess you thumpers would call me a pretty bad sinner, huh?" He smiled as he wiped his tears with his free hand.

I smiled back at him. "Evan, that puts you and me in the same exact crowd."

He cocked his head and looked at me. "Dr. Larimore, are you . . . ? Are you like me?"

"I am."

"You *are*?" he asked.

"Yes, but let me explain. The Bible explains that the sexually immoral and idolaters and adulterers and homosexuals will not inherit the kingdom of God. But, Evan, it also says in the same verse that the greedy and slanderers and swindlers won't either."

Evan was quiet in his thoughts, so I continued. "You're a homosexual. And I'm greedy and a slanderer. I've been far more selfish than I should have been, and I'm certainly guilty of gossiping more than I should. So, according to the Bible, you and I are in the same exact crowd."

Evan smiled and squeezed my hand. I felt an acute sense that God was gently leading my thoughts and words.

"Evan, the Bible describes many names for Jesus. My favorite is that he was known as a friend of sinners. All he requires from us, if we want to have a personal relationship with him—if we want to be his friend—is for us simply to admit that we've missed the mark, that we've sinned and done wrong."

"I guess I would qualify."

"Me too, Evan." I paused to let him think for a moment.

"I think I'd like to be his friend. That would be nice—especially on Christmas Day," Evan whispered between labored breaths. "How do I start?"

Dear Lord, I thought, *what do I say now?* Then I had an over-shadowing and extremely comforting sense that God had been at work in Evan's life for a long time. His spiritual journey and awakening had started long before today. I wasn't exactly sure who had been involved in his life up to this point, but I was sure God now had a small part for me to play in Evan's story.

"Actually, Evan, it's pretty easy. You just talk to God—what we thumpers call prayer." We smiled, and I continued. "Just let God know you're ready—invite him into a relationship with you, into your heart, and he'll come in. First you have to realize that you've done wrong. Then you have to be willing to trust him with your life and your choices."

Evan nodded and closed his eyes. "Lord," he whispered, "I begin."

It was the shortest and sweetest prayer I had ever heard. He looked up at me and smiled. We were both silent—sitting together after a conversation we had begun as doctor and patient and concluded as spiritual brothers.

"Evan, the Bible says that when we admit to God our wrongdoing—just agree with him that we've missed the mark— he will instantly and eternally forgive our sins. And based on that forgiveness, he's willing to become your friend and your Lord and to reserve a room for you in heaven."

The tears were still flowing down his cheeks. He nodded.

"Evan, the Bible says that when we receive Jesus, when we believe in his name, he gives us the right to become children of God, not like when we're born physically but when we're born spiritually—of God."

Evan nodded, tears still running down his cheeks.

"So, my friend, if you're a child of God and I'm a child of God, then what does that make us?"

He thought a moment and then smiled. "Brothers?" he whispered.

I smiled and nodded.

"I've never had a hug from a brother," he said quietly.

I slowly pulled him up and felt his arms encircle my shoulders. He was very, very weak, but his hug was very, very real. After we hugged, I eased him back down.

"Would you like to see a pastor today to talk a bit more about this?"

He smiled, nodded, and squeezed my hand. We were quiet for a moment as I thought about our extraordinary encounter. I hadn't been trained to incorporate spirituality into my medical practice, and despite my initial discomfort, my time with Evan had seemed so spontaneous and sincere. Once Evan gave me permission to share all of who I was as his physician, it had seemed natural.

"Evan, I need to go check that X-ray, okay?"

I went to the X-ray reading room, and on my way back to ICU, I saw one of the RTs running toward the unit. I walked quickly into ICU and arrived just in time to see Evan surrounded by nurses and in the process of being intubated by the RT.

"What happened?"

"He just had a respiratory arrest. BP has bottomed out. Bradycardia. Okay to get him on a ventilator?"

I nodded my assent and went to work.

But from there, things went downhill fairly quickly. Evan's pneumonia quickly evolved into ARDS—a severe form of respiratory disease that is very difficult to treat—and then he went into kidney and liver failure. He died late that afternoon.

—◆—

The autopsy report confirmed the pneumonia but blamed it on a bacterium I'd never treated before—*Pneumocystis carinii*. The report also confirmed multi-organ failure and a form of cancer—Kaposi's sarcoma—but said the cancer was confined only to his skin. I could only assume, with what I knew then, that this unusual infection had overwhelmed his immune system and caused his death.

I called Richard's shop to give him the results, but the number had been disconnected. I then called Richard's home—but, once again, the number had been disconnected. Ella Jo told me she heard that Richard had closed the shop soon after Evan's death and left the area. I was never able to find him, but I wondered if he didn't know, even then, that Evan's death had in some way been related to their relationship.

For Evan had *not* died of cancer. Nor would such a mild bacterium have overwhelmed an intact immune system. I now know he died of a disease that was then unnamed—HIV/AIDS.

So Evan was my first patient with this horrible disease. But he was also the first patient with whom I shared my personal faith so forthrightly—and the first to so openly ask me to do so. Looking back over a long career in family medicine, Evan's case and his decision to give his life to Christ represented one of the high points.

But what his autopsy did not show, and could not show, was that Evan died a new man—spiritually. He had become a friend of God. He had been born as a son of God on the day we celebrated the birth of the Son of God. And his life truly began the morning of the day it ended.

I know I'll see him again one day. I hope he'll give me—his brother in the Lord—another hug.

chapter twenty-three

THE SILVER TORPEDO

On January 1 Greg Shuler came to pick me up at 5:00 a.m. We were off to Graham County in his old ramshackle truck to look for a very special fish.

According to Greg, there were two lakes near Robbinsville that were home to the steelhead trout—a species found much more commonly out West than in the East. However, according to Greg, there were only a few lakes east of the Mississippi that harbored this large silver trout. And once a year, in late December or early January, they would leave the depths of these two mountain lakes to migrate up the streams that feed the lakes to spawn the next generation.

"Son," promised Greg, "this is some of the sweetest fishin' known to man. The steelhead is rated one of the top five sport fish in North America because of the hard fight they put up. The difficulties of landin' a hooked steelhead in a swift, rocky river in winter are legendary."

We stopped in Robbinsville at a café. It was already packed with men—hunters and fishermen—smoking and drinking strong, black coffee. Greg was not a man of many words, but I had grown to like him and dearly enjoyed our time fishing together. He knew these mountains, and, more important, he knew their people.

As we ate a hearty breakfast of scrambled eggs with country-smoked bacon and ham surrounded by grits and biscuits smothered in butter, he shared a bit of his family's history. His great-grandfather had come into the area on the back of a wagon, and his family set up a farm west of Almond. His grandfather and father had been born on that farm.

Greg's voice slowed measurably as he told of the government coming in and taking over the farm, clear-cutting the land around the barn and home place as the men in the family took both buildings apart, board by board. The lumber and all of their belongings were loaded onto a flatcar and hauled via rail over to Bryson City to be reassembled on what would become the new home site—where Barb and I purchased our live Christmas trees every year we lived in Bryson City. Then the valley was flooded to become Lake Fontana.

"My daddy still tells the story of when he were a young'un, how he done sat on the back of that train when it pulled out. He were lookin' back at the valley that would become the lake. All them trees done been cut back. The river were flowin' through this terrible scar in them woods. Daddy just whittled on a stick as the train pulled out. He said all his dreams were left behind in that there valley." Greg took a sip of coffee, his eyes looking away to another time, another place.

"He's ne'er been well since then. Has to git his medicines at the VA hospital in Asheville. But don't git no carin' there. Just gits prescriptions." Greg emptied his mug. "He done left his dreams and his heart in that valley." We rose to leave. There was laughter echoing off the walls of the café—but it wasn't Greg Shuler's.

We drove west from the town and then up a long dirt road, finally pulling off the road as far as we could get. Greg turned off the truck, and we hopped out into the predawn silence. The air was cold and so fresh it almost burned in my lungs. Up the valley,

I could hear the hoot of a great horned owl. Light was just breaking as Greg opened the back of the truck.

"I ne'er asked 'cha, Doc. You done got a fishin' license?"

I smiled, thinking back to the first time I had gone fishing in this area. Don Grissom, one of the EMTs, had taken me fishing in the national park without a license. He told me I didn't need one—which is true—but only if a law enforcement official doesn't ask to see it!

"Yep," I responded. "I purchased a lifetime license."

Greg looked aghast. "A lifetime license? Why?"

"Well, two reasons. One, you've paid for it after only five years. And the way the state's running up the prices, it could pay off even quicker."

"What's the second reason?"

"Well, Greg, I hope to live in this area my entire life."

Greg nodded. "Folks around here gonna look on that real good, Doc. None of them docs what came here before you done ever bought a lifetime fishin' license. That's the shore 'nuff truth!"

He pulled out two small rods and a tackle box. "Doc, them trout are swimmin' upstream to spawn. They ain't thinkin' of eatin', just thinking of spawnin'. So we gotta use somethun wit color on it—what to attract 'em." The lures he pulled out were called rooster tails—colorful yellow lures with a petticoat of brightly colored rubber bands. As the morning light was brightening, we started upstream along a small rushing creek. At each hole we'd stop to fish the hole. "Doc, they just won't bite in the shallow rapids. 'Bout the only place to git 'em to bite is in the holes. They pause to rest a bit."

Greg was working ahead of me as we circled along the edge of a wide, deep hole just off the road. I flicked the yellow lure across the hole. As I quickly reeled in the lure, I first saw it out of the corner of my eye—a glimmer deep in the water as the fish rolled on her side to eyeball the lure—exposing her silver side to the reflection of the light. She rolled back, exposing her dark top and erasing the glimmer deep in the hole. I didn't see her mad rush to the surface, the strong flicks of her huge tail, the puff of the sandy bottom, as she exploded off the bottom of the hole—instinctively pursuing a prey she wasn't hungry for.

My next memory, occurring in an instant, was seeing a silver torpedo racing toward the surface—a mouth as large as a #10 can, expanding even wider as the lure was sucked in. In my shock, and not yet registering what was happening, I barely heard Greg's frantic warning as he watched the drama unfolding. "Don't set the hook! Let her do it!"

However, I instinctively pulled the rod up as fast and hard as I could, setting the hook of the lure but also causing the torpedo to whip around 180 degrees as she erupted out of the water in an explosion of splash, violently shaking her head and body—throwing all of her strength and energy into her escape—and snapping the delicate line in an instant.

I fell backwards onto the shore as the torpedo shot to the bottom of the hole.

Greg was running up to me. "Oh my goodness. That was a monster! A monster! Oh man! You didn't nary need to set that hook. That monster'd a done it for ya. Oh man!" He collapsed by me—speechless.

I was feeling nauseated. That was the biggest fish I had seen in these hills.

"How big was she?" I asked.

"Musta been narly two feet long. That were a monster."

I sighed.

He laughed. "Well, there's more of 'em. Let's git goin'."

We stood to leave. I turned to look at the woods, and then I heard Greg let out a whistle. "Looky there, Doc! Looky there!"

I turned back toward the hole, and my eyes, I'm sure, widened like saucers. At the downstream end of the hole, almost upside down, was the torpedo, swimming slowly toward the shore—until she lodged herself in the sand of the shallow water.

I ran down and gently lifted the huge fish out of the water and onto the shore—with no fight—not even a flicker of muscle movement. She was sleek, shiny silver, and slippery—a real beauty.

Greg and I stared in disbelief at the huge fish. He leaned forward and opened her jaws.

"There it is. Looky there, Doc!" Greg was pointing at the lure lodged in the top of her mouth. "That lure done lodged in her brain. That's why she was actin' that way. Just swimmin' till she's dead. Ne'er seen nothin' like this."

Nor had I.

Back at the Shuler place, we cleaned our catch—several nice-size brown and steelhead trout, but none like the trout with the lure still in the roof of her mouth. Greg's pappy came down to look her over. He didn't say a word but just lifted her and looked her over. Then he smiled, and then laughed—and continued to laugh.

We joined in with him. Laughter's like that—almost like when you see someone yawn—you just can't help but join in!

As we cleaned the fish and split up the fillets, Greg's pappy sat back and whittled. At one point, he stopped and sighed. I turned toward him. He smiled and began to whittle again, then muttered, "I'm a proud of my boys. You'uns done good."

I paused to look at him and smiled.

My boys, he had said. My boys.

chapter twenty-four

ANOTHER NEW YEAR'S CATCH

*B*y early afternoon, I was pulling into the driveway.

Barb quickly came out of the house. "Walt, get over to labor and delivery! They need you right now!"

"Okay. Can you get the fish out of the cooler and put them in the refrigerator?"

I ran down the driveway, across the road, and into the side entrance of the hospital. It seemed quiet as I quickly walked toward our two-bed labor area. I could hear the moaning as I approached. Peggy stepped out into the hall as I walked up.

"Oh good, glad you're here, Dr. Larimore. Cherokee Hospital sent this lady over to us. She's visiting family in the area and went into labor. This is her third baby. No prenatal problems, and her labor's been quick. They usually send their babies over to Sylva, but one of the new docs at Cherokee Hospital sent her here since we're closer. She's completely dilated. We'll be having a baby soon."

"Where's Rick? He's on call, isn't he?"

"Oh yes. He's over in OR with Mitch. Said he could break away if needed, but asked if we'd call you when you came in to back him up."

Now I understood. "Let me go change."

I walked to the OR to change into scrubs and then stuck my head in the room. Rick and Mitch were deep into the abdomen of a very obese patient. Kim, the anesthetist, was sitting at the patient's head, and she waved to me.

"Why aren't you guys out playing golf?" I asked.

Mitch looked up. "Why pay money to hit a golf ball and then spend a morning trying to find it when someone will pay you to find a golf ball in them?"

"What are you talking about?" I asked.

Rick turned to me. "Look here. This woman swallowed a golf ball, and Mitch found it." At that moment Rick reached into the abdomen and pulled out a golf ball–sized gallstone. "Just found this in her gallbladder."

"And it's not the only one," added Mitch.

"How many?"

Mitch, without pausing, spelled "F-O-R-E!"

He and Rick laughed. Kim's eyes were smiling as she shook her head.

"Rick, while you all are having fun, I'm going to go babysit your OB patient."

"Sounds good, Walt. Thanks!"

I turned to leave when Mitch chimed in, "Walt, this'll be our first delivery here in the hospital this year. Hope everything comes out okay."

I smiled.

When Rick entered the delivery room, the patient was prepped and draped, and I was scrubbed and coaching, "Just one more push. Slow and easy. You're doing fine."

Peggy and the woman's husband were helping her sit up as she pushed. Rick walked over to Peggy's side. I looked at him. "Want to switch places?" I asked.

"Nope. Looks like you're doing fine. Mind if I observe?"

"James and Patty," I said to our laboring guests, "this is my partner, Dr. Pyeritz. Mind if he sits in for this little one's arrival?"

They nodded their consent. Another contraction began as Peggy and James helped Patty sit up and begin her final push. I gently applied pressure to support Patty's perineum. "Gentle, Patty, gentle. Here comes your precious one."

The head slowly slid over the perineum. As the nose exited, I picked up a suction bulb to clean out the nostrils and the mouth. The baby reacted instinctively.

"Patty," I softly instructed, "one more push and you'll be able to hug your baby."

Patty began her push. I gently applied pressure to the head as I worked a shoulder past the labia. "We're almost there. Gently keep pushing. Gentle."

As she pushed, I instinctively positioned my left hand around the back of the baby's neck as the anterior shoulder delivery was quickly followed by the posterior shoulder, and then the entire baby quickly flipped out of her mom and onto my left forearm.

As I suctioned out the baby's nose and mouth, the father smiled and the mother beamed. I looked down at the little one in my arms, and there she was—sleek, shiny, and slippery—a real beauty.

Rick and I stared at the beautiful baby. Peggy spoke next. "Looky there, Doc. The first baby of the New Year in Swain County!"

After the delivery, Peggy turned the lights down, and we let the mom and dad spend some time bonding with their new family member. We talked softly—about their family and their dreams. During the time after each delivery, families typically open up in ways they rarely do otherwise—granting those attending their birth a special glimpse into their souls.

After some bonding time, Rick, James, and I walked behind Peggy, who was carrying the baby to our small newborn nursery. We watched her measure, weigh, and clean our "catch."

While we were watching, Mitch came down to look her over. He didn't say a word. He just bent down and slowly lifted her, carefully looking her over. Then, while holding her up, he smiled—and then laughed, and continued to laugh. We joined him.

Then Mitch placed the little one back in the crib and turned to us. I thought for sure I saw his eyes getting misty. He nodded at us—then turned and left.

"I think he's happy for us," Rick commented.

"He's happy for Bryson City," Peggy whispered.

On this special New Year's Day in Bryson City, two beautiful creations were delivered from their watery place of conception. Both were twenty-one inches long, and both weighed about eight pounds. One gave great joy to me at the end of her life—the other gave great joy to me and others at the beginning of hers.

I have pictures of both, which I still pull out from time to time. I still smile as I remember.

chapter twenty-five

TURNED TABLES

The morning dawned crisp and cold. I bounded out of bed and headed to the children's bedroom for my favorite morning ritual—to give Kate and Scott what I called their "cock-a-doodle-doo."

I would sit on the side of the bed of each child and softly sing, "Cock-a-doodle-doo, I love you; cock-a-doodle-doo, I love you; cock-a-doodle-doo, I love you—cock-a-doodle-doo."

Once Scott was awake, he'd be completely awake, and I'd lift him out of his crib and carry him to our bedroom to play with his mom in bed. Then I'd head back to the kids' bedroom. Kate would awaken more slowly, but as she'd begin to wake up, always with a smile on her face, she'd stretch her arms above her head as I would give her a vigorous rubdown across her chest and tummy.

Then I'd help her with a series of stretches. I'd massage her spastic muscles and slowly flex and extend her joints through their range of motion. But even with the massages and therapy, I noticed that Kate's contractures were worsening.

That morning, as I rubbed her spastic muscles, I came to the realization that the constant spasticity was slowly and steadily pulling in such a way that her joints were increasingly losing their mobility.

As a dad, I didn't want to subject Kate to any more pain. I knew the recovery from surgery would be challenging and potentially

painful. I knew the therapy she'd need would be tedious and difficult. I felt myself once again asking God, *Why Kate?* And in my pity
I also thought, *Why me?*

As I rubbed her legs, my mind turned to Rachel Bell—a little
girl I had treated that week.

Her father and mother didn't like or trust doctors very much.
Their farm, located far up an isolated valley near town, was fairly
self-sufficient. Other than an occasional trip to town to sell fruits
and vegetables at Shuler's Produce Stand and to pick up staple
goods, they kept pretty much to themselves. Having met David
Bell at the market and taken a liking to him and his family, I had
invited him to bring the kids in for well-child checkups. He just
smiled and said, "If'n they ever need a doctor, we'll call. Don't see
no reason to waste good money when I can see they're all doin'
fine."

"David," I protested, "the county will pick up the costs of the
visit and any immunizations. It shouldn't cost you a cent."

"Well then, Doc," he continued, "don't see no reason to waste
good time bringin' the children into town to see you when I can
see they're doin' just fine."

I knew that arguing about finding problems early would be
lost on this mountain man. But I also sensed if he needed any help,
he'd call.

The call came one Saturday afternoon. Louise phoned the
house to tell Barb that I needed to come over to the emergency room
to see a child who'd had an accident. Once I was there, I saw David
sitting beside the gurney. Next to him, his little Rachel moaned in
pain, her arm in a homemade sling. I greeted David and then slowly
removed the sling. Rachel's elbow was obviously deformed. I
quickly checked her radial pulse and the sensation in her fingers.
Thankfully, there was no sign of nerve or artery damage.

"She fell off the roof of a shed," David explained. "Tried to
catch herself but done broke her arm. Figured if it healed like this,
she'd be crippled. Doc, I don't want my daughter crippled. Can
you fix her?"

"X-rays are already done," Louise told me.

"Let me look at the films, David."

After viewing the films, I returned to ER with good news. "David, there's no fracture. Rachel has only dislocated her elbow. I can fix it fairly easily, and all things being equal, she should heal just fine."

After I numbed a patch of skin behind the elbow with an ice cube, Louise discreetly slipped me a syringe of lidocaine so Rachel wouldn't see it. I slowly inserted the needle through the ice-numbed skin and then injected lidocaine, painlessly sliding the needle toward her elbow joint. When the needle penetrated the joint lining, I felt a tiny, almost imperceptible pop, and then I aspirated a bit of yellowish joint fluid. This was a very good sign—as bloody joint fluid could indicate a small fracture not seen on the X-ray. I emptied the lidocaine into the joint and then withdrew the needle. Rachel never even knew she had received a shot.

I stood up and walked to her side. "Rachel, I need to tug on your arm a bit. It shouldn't hurt much, and it will make your elbow feel a lot better."

Her eyes filled with tears as she looked over to her father. He gently reached over to take her left hand. "Honey, you can trust Doc. I do. This may hurt a bit. But Doc'll make you better." He smiled at her, and I could see her anxiety melt away. "You keep your eyes on mine, honey. Okay?"

She nodded her assent as she continued to look at her pa. I gently positioned my hands and then quickly pulled down on her forearm and relocated the elbow with an audible pop. Rachel shrieked, more from surprise than pain, but kept her eyes on her father.

"We're done!" I pronounced as I gently flexed and extended her elbow. "Good as new!"

After taking post-reduction X-rays and finding them normal, I placed an Ace bandage on the elbow, gave David some written care instructions, and arranged Rachel's arm in a sling.

As they stood to leave the ER, David shook my hand. "Thanks, Doc. It ain't easy for me to bring one of my kids to the hospital. I was sure she done broke her arm. I knew it would hurt powerful bad to set it. But I knew there was no other way for her to get fixed. Thanks, Doc."

Suddenly I was transported back to Kate's room as she said, "Thanks, Dad." I smiled at my little girl as I continued to exercise her contracted left knee and ankle. Without knowing it, David had given me a blessing and taught me a lesson. The trust he placed in me would be the kind of trust I would need to place in Kate's doctor. As was true for Rachel, I now *knew* Kate would not get better without an orthopedic intervention.

Then a silent whisper entered my mind. *I didn't tell you the trip would be comfortable. But I did promise to walk every step with you!* It wasn't an audible voice but a still, gentle voice that was unmistakable.

At that moment I knew we would need to return to Duke. And I knew Kate would need to go through surgery. I knew the tables would be turning. For this case, I would not be the doctor; I'd be just the father of a patient. It would likely not be comfortable—for me or for Kate—but I now knew it was necessary for her and for her parents.

———

Arriving back at Duke was like a reunion. Kate's therapists were all there to see her—and, more important, to hug and kiss her. Barb and I were also delighted to see them.

When all the tests were done, we had a visit with Dr. Bob Fitch, who was Kate's pediatric orthopedist at the Lennox Baker Cerebral Palsy Hospital. He confirmed our expectations: Kate would need surgery—and not just a single incision but perhaps up to a half dozen—to lengthen tendons around her left hip, knee, ankle, and foot.

Dr. Fitch explained that the recovery would be slow and would require her to be in a cast and a wheelchair for four to six weeks and undergo intensive physical therapy. He spent a great deal of time with us, explaining the other options and then the risks, benefits, and costs of each option—including *not* doing surgery.

He carefully answered our questions and encouraged us to take time to talk about what we had learned and to pray about what to do. He also offered the names of several colleagues at other medical universities from whom we could obtain a second or even a third opinion.

We knew we didn't need another opinion. It was time for me to practice what I had preached. I needed to place the same kind of trust in Kate's doctor that I was asking my patients to place in me.

chapter twenty-six

DOCTOR DAD

The day before Kate's surgery, we drove from Bryson City back to Duke and checked into the hospital late that afternoon. Kate's room was in the hospital's newest addition called Duke North.

A nurse met us in the admitting office and had Kate hop into a small wheelchair. Barb and I walked behind, holding hands as I held Scott in my other arm, and we were escorted up to the pediatric ward.

I was petrified. Now, I was a doctor. I was supposed to know the drill. But I was also a parent, and the thought of my little girl having to go into surgery was very uncomfortable. I knew the pain she was going to experience, and I felt helpless.

The nurse turned to go into a room, and Scott, Barb, and I were left for a moment in the hall together. Thoughts and emotions flooded my mind. I longed to trade places with Kate. Were we making the right decision? What if Kate had a negative reaction to the anesthesia—or what if she didn't wake up afterward?

I felt my eyes filling with tears. Barb gave my hand a squeeze and whispered, "She'll be okay, Walt. I know it!"

We had been married long enough that I knew to appreciate and trust Barb's intuition. I had also been a doctor long enough to grow to understand and value a mother's intuition. I let go of her hand to turn and face her and gratefully accepted her confident hug.

Then we turned to follow Kate into her room. We entered the room, surprised to find it painted in festive colors and child-sized, with the exception of a chair and bed for one parent. *One parent!* I thought. *That means only one of us will stay with her tonight.* I decided it'd be best not to think about it right then.

The afternoon was a blur. Lab technicians came in to draw blood, take a chest X-ray, and do an EKG. Kate's physical, speech, and occupational therapists all came by for a visit. It was good to see old friends who loved us and our daughter.

The surgeon and an anesthesiologist both came by to visit. The visit from the latter was the most worrisome. Bill Brown, M.D., and his wife, CeCe, were our friends when we were residents together. When he came by the room, we first caught up on all that had happened since we had finished residency as Scott napped in the guest bed. As Barb and I shared stories about our life and times in Bryson City, he laughed. "You should write a book sometime!"

We all laughed. *That will never happen!* I thought.

Bill looked at Kate and commented, "Kate, you'll be our first case in the morning. You're our number one!"

Kate's eyes got big, and she looked at me. "Daddy, did you hear that?" Her chest seemed to puff up just a bit. "I'm number one!"

We all laughed, and then Bill nodded at the doorway. "Let's step out for a second, okay?"

We followed him into the hall. He seemed very serious. "Barb and Walt, there's a concern I need to share with you."

Barb and I quickly exchanged apprehensive glances. "What is it?" Barb asked.

"With Kate's brain damage, I just don't know how she'll respond to the anesthetic. I'll try to give her no more than absolutely necessary, but she could react in ways we can't predict."

"Such as?" I asked.

Bill looked down for a moment and then at me. "Walt, one risk is seizure activity—during or after surgery. But my biggest concern is that she might not wake up."

"What!" My voice was a whisper.

"It's highly unlikely—and very rare. But cases have been reported in children like Kate where they react to the anesthetic in such a way that we lose them on the table. I don't want to alarm you unnecessarily—just because this is so very, very rare. But I want you to be prepared for all possibilities."

"What's the risk?" I asked.

"I'm not sure I can say," Bill explained, "but I would think the odds are very, very low."

We were all quiet for a moment. Bill continued. "I'll need to include the risk of death on the consent form you sign. I'll let you all talk about this. This *is* elective surgery. If for any reason you want to cancel the surgery, I'll certainly understand—and I'm sure Dr. Fitch would also."

We thanked Bill, and he left. We walked back into the room and were alone with Kate and Scott. Scott had awakened from his nap, and he and Kate played together on her bed.

"What do you think?" I asked Barb.

She smiled at me. "I think we can dramatically reduce Kate's risk!"

"How so?" I inquired.

"We'll just pray her through this—you and I!"

She smiled and reached out to take my hands in hers. Then Barb prayed an ever-so-brief prayer—for Kate and for us. When she was through, we both had tears rolling down our cheeks. Barb's strong faith had held our family together from the shock we had first felt at the time of Kate's diagnosis—and now this same faith was overflowing into my life.

We then distracted ourselves by playing with our children.

One of the anesthetists came by to take Kate and one parent on a tour of the operating room. I was glad Barb let me go with Kate while she stayed with Scott. As the anesthetist wheeled Kate in a wheelchair, I walked alongside and held her hand.

These days, taking children to visit the operating room well before surgery is a standard procedure. However, in those days it was a fairly new idea. Anesthetists believed that orienting children to the pre-op area, the OR, the anesthesia machines and masks, and the post-op area would relieve their anxiety. I shared that belief—and this tour confirmed my conviction.

As we went from room to room, Kate's eyes widened again and again in amazement. "Daddy, look at that!" she'd exclaim. I'd just smile and squeeze her hand. The anesthetist had Kate practice breathing into the anesthesia mask—which Kate obediently did.

"It stinks!" she whispered to me as we rolled toward the recovery room. I was struck with the contrast of her matter-of-fact observation and fascination with the very object of my fear for her. As she smiled again, I found myself admiring her simple trust—and wondering if I could trust like that.

As we finished our tour in the recovery room, the anesthetist asked Kate and me if we had any questions—which we didn't. Then she looked at me. "Dr. Larimore, I know you and your wife are people of faith." I wasn't sure how she knew. Was it something I had said? She continued. "So am I. And so are a lot of my colleagues. If you want, I can put Kate's name on our prayer list so there will be folks praying for her during her surgery tomorrow. Will that be okay?"

Before I could answer, Kate blurted out, "Of course that will be okay!"

We all laughed.

Then she bent over and looked at Kate. "Would you like me to pray for you right now?"

"Can we?" asked Kate.

"If it's okay with your dad."

Kate looked up at me, and I nodded.

The anesthetist took Kate's hands, and they bowed their heads. "Dear God, I want to thank you for allowing me to meet Kate. I know the hospital can be a big, scary place. So I ask you to give Kate lots of new friends here. I ask that she might get a good night's sleep. And I ask for wisdom for her doctors and peace for her parents. And lastly, Lord, I ask for a quick recovery for my new friend Kate. Amen."

She looked up at Kate and smiled, and they gave each other a big hug. Then she stood and began to wheel Kate away. "Come on, we need to get Kate back before the ward nurses think we got lost."

On the way back to the ward, I followed this wonderful woman, thinking how she had just given Kate and me a most precious and valuable gift. *It's one thing to get good care,* I thought, *but it's something else to be cared for!*

———

The four of us had dinner together, and then I lay in bed with my little girl, watching an evening TV show. Scott sat in his mother's lap. We were all quiet and just enjoyed being together. Even Scott seemed to sense this was a special event in our family's life.

Finally a nurse came in. "I've got to shoo you boys out. It's time for Kate and her mom to get some rest."

"Come on, Scoot. Time for us boys to go have some fun!" He lifted his arms, and I reached down to pick him up.

Barb would stay with Kate, and Scott and I would stay with Walter and Gertrude Eakes—just across the street from where we used to live. Kate looked at her little brother and then commanded, "Get over here, Scoot! Give me a hug and a kiss!" Her brother happily complied.

Kate then looked up at me. Our eyes met, and both of us immediately teared up. I sat beside her and gave her a long, hard hug. She hugged back, and I could feel her soft sobs. I whispered in her ear, "Father, give my little girl a good night's rest. Give her peaceful sleep. I pray this in Jesus' name. Amen."

I heard her whisper, "Amen."

Then I whispered back, "I love you, Kate."

I held her tight, and she hugged me for a long time.

As we separated, I could see the moist stains on her cheeks. She was crying and smiling at the same time.

We all hugged one last time, and then Scott and I left.

As we walked out of the hospital and across the street toward the parking garage, we turned to look up at the hospital tower. We counted up the floors until we found Kate's room. There in the window were Kate and Barb. We all waved at each other.

I've never felt so helpless or powerless, and yet—because of the precious prayers of a wonderful wife and a compassionate anesthetist—so full of hope.

The next morning, I left Scott with Gertrude and Walter Eakes. They had been our across-the-street neighbors when I was in my residency at Duke, and they had agreed to allow us to stay at their house and to be with Scott when necessary.

I arrived in Kate's room and was surprised to find that the orderlies were already there and were placing her on the gurney.

"Daddy!" my little girl exclaimed when she saw me. I nearly leaped across the room and into her arms.

"I was so afraid you wouldn't get here in time. I needed a hug!"

And I sure gave her one! With my head next to hers, I whispered a prayer. "Father, I ask you to protect my little girl. Give her doctors wisdom and skill. Bring her back soon. In Jesus' name I pray. Amen."

She hugged me tight and whispered. "Thank you, Daddy. I love you!"

"I love you, precious!"

Then she looked into my eyes. "Daddy, I saw the sunrise this morning."

I couldn't help but wonder if it might be her last. Hot tears began to tumble down my face. But Kate, in many ways more spiritually sensitive than I could ever be, looked up at me and emphatically stated, "It was just the first of the rest of the sunrises in my life. Only soon, I'm going to be able to walk, or even run, at sunrise."

I smiled and hugged her again. Then Kate whispered to me, "Daddy, I think I'm a little scared."

"Me too, darling," I whispered back.

As we released our hug, I could feel the tears rolling down my face. Kate smiled up at me. "Don't worry, Daddy. Dr. Fitch does this surgery every day. I'll be back soon!"

And then, in what seemed an instant, she was gone. Barb and I stood quietly in our thoughts and fears. I had no idea if I'd ever see her alive again.

For the first few minutes after everyone left, Barb and I sat alone—speechless, each lost in our own thoughts. I was looking across the tree-lined countryside surrounding the hospital when I heard Barb move. She slowly stood and walked over to me. I turned toward her. "Got room for a girl on your lap?"

I smiled, and she sat on my lap, laying her head on my shoulder. She began to gently weep, and I held her close. We didn't say a thing—we just held on and hugged. And cried.

———

I felt someone nudge me from my nap. "Walt, it's Dr. Fitch!" I heard Barb say. I was sitting up and fully awake instantly.

"The surgery went very well," he said calmly as he sat on Kate's bed. "I couldn't be happier. Dr. Brown did a great job with the anesthesia. We only had to do five tendon-lengthening procedures in her foot, ankle, and around the knee. They all turned out as well as I could have hoped for. I've put her in a long-leg cast, and she'll be in the recovery room very soon. As soon as she's stable there, one of you will be able to be with her. When she's awake and alert, she'll be brought back to this room. If all goes well, and I don't see any reason it shouldn't, she should be ready to go home in a few days."

Before we could respond or even say thanks, he was gone. We were left alone. Before we knew it, we had collapsed into each other's arms and melted into sobs of joy and thanksgiving.

Barb left with the nurse to check on Kate. I tried to read but couldn't. I prayed for a bit. I wandered the halls. I pondered the fact that being a patient—or the parent of a patient—was incredibly more difficult than being the doctor of one.

I finally came back to Kate's room, closed the door, and sat by the window, staring out over the trees around the hospital. I bowed my head in prayer and thanked my Father in heaven for protecting our child. I also thanked him for the deep and profound lessons I was learning—as a dad and as a doctor.

***

I was startled back to reality by a knock on the door, followed by a flurry of activity. Kate had arrived and was transferred to her bed. When the gurney was gone, Kate's nurse saw to it that she was comfortable and stable and then left us alone.

As I looked down at Kate, she looked like a little angel. She was sleeping soundly. Barb and I stood silently, arm in arm. My little girl was back, and she was all right. I was flooded with gratitude and thankfulness.

Kate would leave the hospital healthier and with a brighter future. It was likely that her walking would improve and that one day she might even run. *Not bad,* I thought, *for a little girl who never was supposed to talk or walk.*

But *I* would also leave this hospital changed—with a new view of what it means to be a parent and a physician.

I could feel the tears streaking down my cheeks again. This experience had had a powerful impact on me. Seeing this through both the eyes of the patient and the eyes of a parent would forever change me. I knew I would be empathetic with my patients and their loved ones in an entirely new way.

And somehow I suspected that the comfort with which I had been comforted would serve as a foundation from which I could, hopefully, become a doctor who would be able to cure only once in a while but one who could *always* dispense hope and comfort.

It was for me a remarkable realization—that caring for patients medically involves, first and foremost, a great deal of simple and genuine caring.

———

A few days later, we arrived in Kate's room to find her fully awake, dressed, and smiling. Her left leg, encased in a full cast, was covered by the sheets.

"Let's go home!" she exclaimed as we entered. Her little suitcase was packed and ready to go.

A nurse came into the room with a wheelchair. She shared with us Dr. Fitch's instructions. He was in surgery and wouldn't be able to see us before we left. But we knew we'd see him in just a few weeks.

When it was time, I lifted Kate into the wheelchair. She looked at me and asked, "Dad, can Scoot carry my backpack for me?"

I nodded and turned to Scott to explain to him that his sister was going to need special care for the immediate future and that we were all going to have to chip in.

As I handed Scott the small backpack, he grimaced and asked, "How long?"

Kate looked over at him, smiled the prettiest of her smiles, and predicted, "The rest of your life."

As we walked behind Kate toward the nurses' station, Barb commented, "I think Kate just gave Scott one of his first lessons about the women in a man's life."

I chuckled as she squeezed my arm.

We stopped at the nurses' station, and there were hugs and good-byes all around.

Then, before we knew it, we were in the car and heading home.

On the long drive home we talked and sang. And at times we just sat in silence. I was happy to have my little girl with me. She was all right. And we were going home.

chapter twenty-seven

THE PHONE TAP

*L*iving over an hour's drive from the nearest medical center and from high-powered specialists was both an advantage and a distraction.

Certainly, the distance between us and the most specialized level of care gave us the opportunity to do procedures and to care for patients that our family medicine colleagues in the big city could only dream about.

The other side of the coin was that we would not have access to the skills and experience of the subspecialists in times of emergency. We were grateful that our colleagues in the larger cities and the medical centers in North Carolina grew used to this situation and would gladly assist rural physicians by telephone if we had a question or ran into an emergency.

One of the more interesting telephone consultations of my career occurred with a patient Louise called me to the emergency room to see.

He was a forty-year-old man—Bob Shuler—who was in ER with severe hip pain. He had no memory of an injury, but the pain had been building for several days. By the time he came to ER, he couldn't walk on the hip, and moving the hip was extremely painful. His X-rays and routine lab tests were normal, and I was befuddled.

While I was in the X-ray suite looking at the patient's X-rays one more time, Rick walked in.

"Whatcha got, Walt?"

"I don't frankly know, partner."

We looked at the X-rays together as I reviewed the case.

"Mind if I take a look at him?"

"You can bet I don't!" I replied.

After Rick had completed his exam and history, he was equally befuddled.

"Rick, if he was four instead of forty, I'd diagnosis toxic synovitis of the hip."

Rick nodded. We would frequently see young children with sudden pain in the hip and an inability to stand or walk secondary to the pain. If their X-ray and blood work turned out normal, we'd diagnosis a viral infection of the hip and treat it with the tincture of time, Tylenol, and TLC. Invariably the kids would be better in a day or two.

"Tell you what," I thought out loud. "I'll call Bill Garrett."

Rick nodded again. "Good idea."

Bill was an orthopedic surgeon at Duke. I had spent many hours with him, caring for the student athletes at Duke. Knowing how much Bill liked a challenge and how well he understood the dilemma of physicians in rural locations, I knew he wouldn't mind my calling.

When the Duke Medical Center operator located him, we initially caught up on our practices, our wives, our children, and the state of Duke athletics. As was customary whenever we talked, Bill invited me to come back to Durham to join him in working at the Sports Medicine Clinic at Duke. Given the rising status of Duke basketball, I was always tempted to say yes.

After hearing about my patient, Bill sounded more somber. "Walt, I'd be most worried about septic arthritis. A bacterial infection of the hip can present exactly like this. If that's what he's got, your surgeons'll need to get in there surgically and irrigate that hip immediately. If you don't, the hip could be permanently damaged."

"Should I just call the surgeon?" I asked.

"No, Walt. I'd recommend you tap the hip." I knew he was referring to a procedure in which the doctor numbs the skin with lidocaine and then slowly advances a very long needle through the skin and into the hip joint to aspirate some of the hip joint fluid. The fluid is then evaluated in the lab for signs of infection.

I paused for a moment and then protested, "But, Bill, I've never tapped a hip. When I was at Duke, you orthopedic residents did all the hip taps."

"Yeah, I'm really sorry about that. Sometimes our residents want to get all the experience they can at the expense of you guys in primary care. But if you're willing, I can guide you through the procedure over the phone."

I paused again. "Bill, wouldn't it be better to just ship this patient to Asheville?"

"I don't think so, Walt. Think about it. By the time you arrange a transport, get the patient there, have the ER doc see him, have the ER doc call the orthopedist, and then the orthopedic doc drives in and examines the patient and then does the procedure—well, we could be talking another three or four hours. And in that time period, the hip could be permanently damaged."

I took a deep breath. I had never done this procedure, nor had I ever seen it done! And the age-old dictum in medicine was "See one, do one, teach one." I didn't like the sound of "Hear about one while doing one!"

"Just a second, Bill."

I put my hand over the phone. "Rick, have you ever tapped a hip?"

Rick shook his head no.

I tried another route. "You ever seen one done?" I was hoping he'd say yes, and then I could let him do it.

Unfortunately, he again shook his head.

"Bill, I'm willing if you are. Is it very risky?"

"Nope!"

I hoped he wasn't lying.

"Okay, let me get the patient's permission, and then I'll get ready. Rick'll call you back, and you can relay instructions over the phone. Okay with you?"

"No problem. Let me review the supplies you'll need, and then you all call back when you can. I'm available to you anytime."

I hung up and then called Ray—who was the surgeon on call. He had never tapped a hip either, but he was happy for me to try. "Let me know what you find."

———

*R*ick and I returned to the emergency room to talk to the patient. I tried to sound confident, but I'm sure I failed. Even so, Bob agreed to be my first patient for this procedure, which was incredible—especially given the possibility of a permanent hip disability should I goof up.

As Louise and I prepared for the procedure, Rick called Bill from the ER phone. My patient was, thankfully, the only one in ER at the time. Rick was about fifteen feet from me as I scrubbed the front of the patient's groin and placed sterile drapes around the skin overlying his hip.

Rick called out. "Walt, Bill says to feel for the femoral pulse."

The pulse of the femoral artery was easy to palpate, just a couple of inches lateral to the pelvic bone.

"Bill wants to know if you remember the NAVEL acrostic."

I nodded. The inguinal ligament ran from the anterior superior iliac spine—the bone point just above the waist—to the pubic bone. Just below the ligament, from the outside to the inside, were several critical structures—the Nerve, the Artery, the Vein, an Empty space, and then the Lacunar ligament. The first letter of each structure created the acrostic NAVEL.

"Bill says to numb the skin right over the empty space, just medial to the femoral vein. Okay?"

I nodded and then looked at the patient. "I'm going to numb the skin over the hip, okay?"

He nodded, and I quickly anesthetized the skin and underlying tissues with the lidocaine.

"Bill says to use a 22-gauge spinal needle on a 20cc syringe with a Luer lock. Be sure you have several cc's of sterile lidocaine in the syringe."

Louise and I nodded. As she turned to get the needle, I looked down at the patient. "Bob, I'd suggest you turn your head. The needle is very narrow, but it's real long. You won't feel any pain—and if you do, I'll immediately numb it. But the needle can be scary to look at, and if you're looking at it, you might accidentally move. I'll need you to hold absolutely still. If you move even a little bit, the needle might do some damage we wouldn't want. Can you help me out with this?"

He nodded and turned his head.

Rick continued with Dr. Garrett's instructions. "Walt, Bill says to slowly advance the needle, aspirating and injecting lidocaine as you go. When you get to the bone, continue to inject lidocaine to numb the tissue over the bone."

I nodded as Louise handed the needle to me. It was scary looking—and almost six inches long. I attached it to the syringe and drew up several cc's of lidocaine. Then, holding the needle like a pencil, I penetrated the skin and slowly advanced the needle, aspirating (just to be sure I wasn't in a major vessel) and then injecting the anesthetic every few millimeters—until I felt the needle tip finally hit bone.

"I'm there, Rick!"

"He's there, Bill," Rick relayed. As he listened, I waited.

After Bill finished his next instruction, Rick looked back at me. "Bill says to slowly walk the tip of the needle laterally a millimeter at a time. It should easily enter the joint capsule. Okay?"

I nodded and began slowly moving the tip of the needle up and down, "walking" it across the surface of the bone. At one point, the patient moaned. "Sorry, Bob," I apologized, and I injected a bit more lidocaine. "That better?" He nodded—still keeping his face turned away from me.

Suddenly I felt the needle tip sink into a soft space. *This is not bone!* I thought. *It must be the joint lining!* The needle easily advanced into the hip joint space.

Rick called out, "Walt, Bill says when the needle passes through the joint lining, you don't want to go too far in. When you're just underneath the joint lining, inject some lidocaine. It should flow easily into the joint. Then aspirate as much fluid as you can."

"Will the lidocaine that's left in the syringe hurt the sample in any way?" I asked. "Or do I need to aspirate into another sterile syringe?"

Rick repeated the questions and then called out, "Use the same syringe, Walt. Bill says the lidocaine won't affect the specimen, and changing the syringe could cause the needle to move somewhere you wouldn't want it to."

I could see Bob smile, and then he said, "Hey, Doc. Let's not let that needle move where you and I don't want it to—especially when you're so close to my family jewels."

I could hear Louise snicker as I smiled. I looked over to Rick, who was also smiling.

Then I injected the lidocaine. It passed into the joint effortlessly, which was my confirmation that I was in the joint space, since injecting lidocaine into tissue requires much more pressure. Then I watched the syringe as I began to aspirate. A spout of yellow-green pus entered the syringe. It was like striking oil!

"Tell him it's pus!" I exclaimed.

As Rick shared the news with Dr. Garrett, I explained to the patient, "Bob, there's pus in your joint. That means there's an infection there. We're going to have to get you to surgery this evening to clean out the infection. But it should allow us to save your hip joint. Sound okay?"

Bob nodded.

Rick called across the room. "Bill sends his congratulations on a successful tap, Walt. He said it's the first time he's participated in a phone tap."

I laughed. "Tell him thanks, Rick. And ask him to give my love to Janine and the boys."

"Will do," Rick called.

As Rick finished the phone call, I removed the needle from the patient, capped the syringe, and handed it to Louise. "Best get this to Betty in the lab. We'll need cultures with antibiotic sensitivity, as well as a Gram's stain and white count."

"Yes sir," Louise replied as she took the syringe and left for the lab.

I held pressure on Bob's groin for a few minutes and explained to him what would happen in the operating room.

"Dr. Cunningham will make a small incision in your groin and then open up the hip lining. He'll wash out the joint to clean out the infection. He'll leave a drain in for a day or two, so no further pus will accumulate. Bob, it's the pus that causes all the damage in the joint. In the meantime, we'll give you strong antibiotics by vein. And in a day or two, when there's no more drainage, we'll pull the drain, and you'll be able to go home on antibiotics."

Bob nodded.

"Hopefully everything will turn out just fine."

He nodded again and then turned toward me.

"Doc, thanks for doing this. I know it was scary for you. I appreciate it."

I was quiet for a moment. It *had* been scary for me. But I suspect it had been much scarier for Bob. Even so, he had been more cognizant of me than of himself.

And in that, Bob was not unique. Many times across my career, my patients, even when in extremely dangerous medical situations, would often be more concerned about me than themselves.

It's just one of the unique aspects of one of those special relationships that exists between a doctor and his patient.

———

That night, as I sat on the bench behind our home, rather than looking across Deep Creek Valley, as was my habit, I bowed my head and silently prayed. I thanked the Lord for the success of the procedure. I thanked him for Dr. Garrett, Rick, and Louise. Although I had done the procedure, they had made it possible.

And I thanked the Lord for Bob. As a patient, he had given me a very special gift that day. He had helped me realize once again how blessed I was to be a family physician.

I smiled as I thought of the Great Physician and his grace in allowing me to join him in the healing of his children.

I could not imagine a higher calling.

part four

SPRING

chapter twenty-eight

LABOR PAINS

$\mathcal{D}$elivering babies is an art. Of course, there are the technical aspects I learned in my training. But I primarily learned the art of maternity care from "Professor Time," the teaching of maternity care nurses, and the mentoring of experienced physicians and midwives. However, the observations of the midwives and nurses turned out to be among the most helpful to me.

One spring evening I was sitting at the nurses' station with Peggy Ashley. She was knitting, and I was cross-stitching. I had picked up cross-stitching during my long hours on the labor and delivery deck during training—and continued it during my early practice years while attending a labor.

"Doc, have you ever noticed how uncomfortable most husbands are during labor?" Peggy asked.

I laughed. "Peggy, it seems to me the wife is the more uncomfortable of the two!"

She smiled. "That's *not* what I meant. It just seems that most husbands just don't like being in the labor room. Yet if the mom has a female with her, the female seems much more helpful."

I stopped cross-stitching to look at her. "Never noticed."

"Since my early years in labor and delivery, I've noticed that the father of the baby is not nearly as dedicated or helpful to the woman in labor as other women are—such as the mother's mother or sister or pastor's wife. And that's especially true if the woman who's assisting the woman in labor has had a baby herself."

"Why do you think that is?" I asked.

"Not sure," Peggy answered, still knitting. "It's almost like the men find it difficult to maintain confidence and perspective in an environment that's so strange to them. It's like men feel helpless during labor—and I think it's because they're unable to control the process or the outcome. And I've also noticed that as the birth process intensifies, most men seem to become more uncomfortable and pull away from, not toward, their partner. I've come to believe it's because the man is distressed by having to witness his wife's pain and discomfort."

I remembered back to Barb's labor with Kate and the discomfort I felt during the process. *Maybe Peggy's on to something,* I thought.

She continued. "So, early on, I concluded that having a man involved in the birth process is better than nothing. But not much." She laughed, almost to herself. "No offense, Dr. Larimore, but most husbands aren't nearly as helpful and effective to a laboring woman as another female. When a laboring woman's discomfort increases, the supporting women would actually move closer to the laboring woman, while the husband would move back or even leave the birthing suite."

As I thought back on my experiences in labor and delivery, I wondered if I hadn't seen the same thing but just hadn't consciously recognized the phenomenon.

Peggy put down her knitting. "Here's what I've come up with. Over the years, I've observed that the man who attends his wife's delivery generally falls into one of three categories. He is either a coach—one who actively assists his wife and stays very close to her; or he's a teammate—one who takes his lead from others and is there to help when asked; or he's a fan—one who's there just to observe labor and to witness the birth but not help in the process."

I thought to myself, *This does sound accurate. In fact, most of our dads here in Bryson City are just fans.*

Peggy went on. "I used to try to make the men become coaches but usually failed. 'Bout the best I can do is move a fan to a teammate. But what's easier yet is to encourage women to bring women with them to the labor."

"Does that cause problems with the dad?" I asked.

"Nope, not really. The role of a female partner with the laboring woman and the role of the father actually complement each other. In fact, I've noticed that having another woman present seems to take significant pressure off the father—kinda allows him to participate at his own comfort level, leaving him free to come and go as he desires."

Now, a woman being present with a woman in labor was an age-old practice, but it was new to Rick and me—and to the other doctors on staff. Some, we were to learn later, were resistant to this approach. Perhaps it was this refusal to accept what they saw as a "new" approach that would lead to another crisis among the medical staff.

By Valentine's Day, Kate was out of her cast but still in her wheelchair. Her wounds had healed very nicely, and Dr. Fitch couldn't have been happier with the results. He called her his "best patient," which made her incredibly proud of herself.

Once out of the cast, Kate needed to begin therapy. So Barb brought her to Swain County General Hospital for daily physical therapy. After only a couple of weeks, Kate had begun to walk with assistance. By early March, she was walking without assistance.

Barb and I were grateful that the prediction given us when her first CT scan showed so little brain—that she'd probably never walk or talk, and she'd never know the Lord—had been proven wrong on all three counts.

But while Kate was improving, there was good news and bad news at Swain County General Hospital. The good news was that

Rick and I were doing more and more deliveries. We both really enjoyed the privilege of attending birth—with each delivery a reminder of the hope that new life brings to a family and a community. The bad news was to appear shortly in our nursery.

The second baby born that year at the hospital was to another couple who lived in Cherokee. They had been referred to our practice by one of the physicians who served at Cherokee Indian Hospital—where they did not deliver babies—and by Mrs. Black Fox.

Rick and I were excited about this turn of events because prior to this delivery all Cherokee deliveries had been referred to an obstetrician at C. J. Harris Hospital in Sylva.

Rick had attended the birth and then called me to join him in the nursery the next day. "Look at this," he said as I entered our small nursery. I quickly scrubbed my hands, put on a gown, and joined Rick by the baby's crib.

"Cute baby," I commented.

"Sure is," Rick responded. "I think it's because of the doctor who delivered her!"

I chuckled.

"But," Rick commented, sounding suddenly serious, "look under here."

He took off the baby's shirt and diaper, and the problem was obvious. The baby's diaper area and trunk were covered with tiny pustules.

"The baby's vital signs are normal, the CBC is normal, and she's eating like a champ. I don't think this is a systemic infection. But what do you think?"

I thought for a moment. "Do you want to culture the baby?"

"I've cultured the pus from several pustules I ruptured and have done blood and urine cultures. I'm just not sure about whether to do a spinal tap."

"Rick, I think I would. We can't afford to be conservative with little ones like this. And I think I'd cover her with IV antibiotics for at least forty-eight hours—until we get the cultures back."

"I was hoping you wouldn't say that," Rick commented.

"Well, why not call Tom Dill over in Sylva? He's practiced pediatrics for a long time. See what he says."

"Sounds good."

Dr. Dill concurred with my recommendation. And the baby did well. All of the cultures were negative, except for the skin cultures, which were positive for a type of bacteria called staphylococcus. After two days on intravenous antibiotics, the lesions were drying up, and Rick sent the baby home with another week of oral antibiotics.

Then, in the fourth week of January, we had two babies in the nursery with the same problem and the same clinical course.

Nancy Cunningham, Ray's wife, was the RN at the hospital in charge of infectious disease problems. She reviewed all of our obstetrical and nursery policies, procedures, and practices and couldn't identify a problem.

"Be careful," Nancy warned us. "There are nurses whispering that the problem is you two."

"How can that be?" I asked.

"Just be careful," she warned.

❦

The next week we delivered four babies—a new record for one week at the hospital. That was the good news. The bad news was that three of the four came down with the mystery pustulosis. That put Nancy and me on the phone with an infectious disease expert at the North Carolina Department of Health and Human Services. We agreed to send the records of the six infants and their moms to him for review. Our concern was that they might shut down our birthing suites and nursery.

"Could it be our facility?" asked Nancy during the discussion.

"I doubt it," answered the expert. "But I want to initiate a complete investigation. I'll send a team out there. They'll arrive tomorrow night and go over these cases and the hospital with a fine-tooth comb. So far no babies have been hurt. But staph infections can be very dangerous. Something's going on, that's for sure!"

When we hung up, Nancy gave me even more bad news.

"It's Dr. Mathieson."

"What now?" I moaned. I remembered last year when he and Dr. Nordling had, I believed, led a movement to have our hospital privileges revoked.

"He says one of our nurses in the hospital is willing to testify to the medical staff that you and Rick don't use good technique in the birthing suites. They say you all allow too many women in the suite to help the laboring woman, and these women aren't sterile. Whoever this nurse is, she says you all don't always scrub before you examine the babies in the nursery."

"Nancy, that's all a bunch of hogwash. Of course the women aren't sterile! Neither are our nurses. And they don't need to be. And furthermore, our practices in the birthing suites and the nursery are standard of care. This infection isn't coming from us! But it's got to be coming from someone. Staph doesn't live on inanimate surfaces for very long. I bet someone's carrying this germ and spreading it— just like Typhoid Mary. I'd call the culprit 'Staphylococcus Sally' or 'Staph Sam' and begin looking for him or her."

"That may be, Walt, but have you considered that maybe the carrier is you? Maybe even Rick?"

"Well, I'm surely willing to be checked. But everyone else needs to be checked too. That's only fair."

"Let's see what the infectious disease team says. But I've got to tell you, Ray is concerned. And as chief of staff, he'll have to investigate this complaint."

I nodded, and Nancy whispered, "Just keep a heads-up, okay?"

chapter twenty-nine

STAPH AND STAFF

$\mathscr{T}$he mandatory meeting was called by the hospital's administrator, Earl Douthit. All hospital employees and physicians were to attend. Ray and Mitch hadn't let on that they knew about the meeting—and when we asked them, they wouldn't tell us its purpose. We only heard about the meeting at lunchtime the day of the meeting. Reva brought a note to us with the announcement.

"You know anything about this, Walt?" Rick asked, showing me the announcement.

"I don't."

"Do you think they're going to take some action against us?"

I shrugged my shoulders. I just didn't know.

$\mathscr{W}$e joined the crowd in the hospital cafeteria at 6:00 p.m. It was the only room in the hospital large enough to hold everyone.

Rick and I sat near the back, next to Dr. Bacon. I could see the other doctors seated near the front of the room. There were also several members of the hospital board and of the local health department in the room. To my surprise, there was a reporter from the local paper—the *Smoky Mountain Times*.

"Rick, what's a reporter doing here?"

"Beats me."

Harold Bacon bent toward me. "Walt," he asked, "do you know what's going on?"

I wasn't sure if he was pulling my leg or trying to appear innocent. "You don't know?" I asked. I'm sure I must have sounded incredulous. If the dean of the medical community didn't know, then I *was* concerned. "Harold, I don't have a clue. But I wouldn't be surprised if it has something to do with those infected babies."

At just that moment, Earl Douthit entered the room with the chairman of the board of the hospital and a man I didn't recognize. A hush blanketed the room as the three men sat in chairs arranged at the front of the room. They briefly whispered to each other, and then Earl stood.

"I appreciate you all coming on such a short notice. For hospital employees, be sure you indicate this time on your time card. You will be paid for this time."

He cleared his throat and then continued. "You all may be aware that our newborn nursery has had a flurry of cases involving a very serious bacterial infection—a staphylococcal infection."

Earl looked down at the stranger, who nodded, and then returned his attention to us.

"There have been allegations—both from sources internal and external to the hospital—that this infection has come from improper policy or procedure. There have been allegations that our facility is substandard in some sort of way. Unfortunately, even some hospitals in our region have made these regrettable comments to the state."

A murmur crossed the room. Earl was quiet long enough to let it pass.

"There have also been allegations—mostly from local sources—that one or more of our physicians have not or do not practice according to the modern medical standards of care."

I could feel the color burning my cheeks—and my blush must have been made worse by sensing that some who were sitting around us were turning to look at Rick and me.

"These allegations are serious, and because of them, and with the concurrence of the chairman of the board of trustees and the chairman of the medical staff, I asked the North Carolina Department of Health and Human Services to initiate an independent investigation of these matters and report to our board their findings and recommendations. Our board has heard their report and has called you here tonight so that you can hear the report and the actions we will be taking."

Rick leaned over to me and whispered, "You think this is a public lynching?"

I was too bewildered to answer.

Earl continued. "Let me introduce Dr. Melvin Birnbaum. Dr. Birnbaum is an epidemiologist and an infectious disease expert from the Department of Health and Human Services. He sent a team here to perform a complete and thorough investigation of this matter, which they have done. He has traveled all the way from Raleigh to give us their report in person. Dr. Birnbaum."

Earl sat down, and the room remained silent. The physician slowly stood. He was older and much shorter than Earl. His face was round and ruddy—which made his gray mustache look even more authoritative. He buttoned the coat of his three-piece suit and cleared his throat.

"Ladies and gentlemen, and member of the press." He nodded to the reporter. "At the request of the hospital and the local health department director, my team has conducted a comprehensive investigation of this matter. We have reviewed the medical records of the babies and the mothers involved. We have made home visits to each family. We have examined the hospital from top to bottom. We have interviewed the physicians and hospital personnel, and we have performed nasal and skin cultures of all who could have possibly carried this infection."

I nodded, remembering my visit with the team one morning, when they swabbed my nose, throat, and hands and took scrapings from under my fingernails.

The expert continued. "First the good news. In every way this hospital, its employees, and its physicians are to be commended. Both the quality and quantity of care you provide in this rural location are extraordinary. Your board and administration run a first-rate facility that is second to none in its class in this state."

A round of light applause filled the room. Many of the employees were smiling. As the room quieted, he cleared his throat.

"However, there *is* a problem." Our speaker paused for a moment and then continued. "We did find, as we suspected, two individuals who are carriers of this staphylococcus infection. In both cases, these individuals had the bacteria living in—colonizing—their nostrils and under their fingernails."

A murmur wafted across the room, and Rick and I looked at each other. *They wouldn't dare expose us publicly like this, would they?* I wondered. My mind was racing. *How could Ray and Earl turn on us like this? Why didn't they just come to us in private and discuss this?* I continued to face forward as the speaker went on.

"We were able to type the bacteria obtained from these two persons and compare it to each of the babies. All eight cases matched. Furthermore, the bacterium was not carried by any family member or any physician or employee at the health department or Cherokee Indian Hospital—which were the referring entities for each of these cases."

"Here it comes," whispered Rick.

"I know you are curious to know who these two individuals are. But first I must tell you that this situation is not uncommon. Infections in hospitals are usually not spread by equipment or instruments; they are usually spread from person to person. And our team noted—on more occasions than we might like—that physicians and employees of this hospital do not wash their hands. Therefore, we are working with your hospital administrator to be sure that proper hand-washing policies and procedures are instituted."

Dr. Birnbaum paused for a moment. "Now, as to those who actually spread the infection in the first place . . ." He paused, and once again, I sensed those sitting around us looking at us out of the corners of their eyes.

"I won't name either individual. But I will tell you that *none* of your physicians are involved."

In unison, Rick and I let out a huge sigh of relief.

The doctor continued. "One individual worked in the lab, and the other was a nurse. Both had contact with each baby. Both have been treated, and both individuals no longer carry the infection. Naming them would do no good—and we will not do so."

There was a polite round of applause. Rick and I looked at each other and smiled. Harold reached his arm around my back and gave me a hug.

Dr. Birnbaum continued. "Let me say this in conclusion. I would encourage you all to learn from this. Any one of you could have carried and spread this infection, and you never would have known the harm you were causing. So when there is a problem with medical care, don't start pointing fingers, but rather work together. These types of problems are almost never the fault of one single individual. Typically there are problems with the system. In this case, accusations were made against your hospital and against certain physicians here that should not have been made."

He was quiet for a moment to let his words penetrate. Then he continued. "Let me encourage you all to work more closely together in the future. You have far more in common with each other than you have differences. And your small facility will need you all to work together. Swain County Hospital is too important to your town and to your county to break apart because of minor aggravations. Your community and its citizens need you. Our state needs you. Thank you for your attention."

As the doctor sat down, applause slowly crossed the room and then swelled into a standing ovation. Rick and I nodded at each other as we stood—an appreciative and thankful nod indeed.

To this day I don't know who was involved. I *do* know that the nurse who had been the most critical and condescending toward Rick and me left the hospital about that time.

And I do know that after that day, the physicians and staff at the hospital seemed to meld together a little more closely.

Finally we felt we at least had a chance to be part of their team—but we knew we still needed to "be very careful."

chapter thirty

THE RIBBON CUTTING

$\mathcal{D}$uring the fall and winter, our new office building had slowly taken shape. Rick and I tried to get by at least once a day to check on the progress—and we retained a practice management firm out of Asheville to help us with the thousands of details necessary to set up a new practice. They guided us as we interviewed several dozen applicants for jobs in the new office.

We were looking for an office manager, a bookkeeper who could help in the front office, and two nurses—one to work with me and one to work with Rick. The pool of applicants was surprisingly qualified for such a small town, and the decision was much harder than we ever thought it would be, because we wanted to hire not only exceptionally qualified individuals but also folks who were well known and well liked in the community.

It ended up that we hit the ball out of the park with all four selections. Dean Tuttle, Preston's wife, was hired to be our office manager. She had managed other offices, and both she and her husband were locals. Their two boys played football for the Swain County Maroon Devils. Dianna Owle had great bookkeeping experience and had worked in other medical offices. She was married to a local man and had a beautiful baby girl. Beth Arvey was the daughter of the police chief, and Patty Hughes was married to a local fellow. Both were LPNs with both hospital and office experience. Both were young, energetic, and easy to get along with.

We were delighted to be blessed with such a great staff. Mitch and Ray were gracious enough to allow our staff to work alongside their staff for the month prior to our office opening. Although we were as crowded as peas in a pod, our new staff learned so very much from their staff. Rick and I would take our staff to lunch each week just to discuss what we were learning and how we could apply the lessons learned once we got to our new office.

———

*W*hen our new office opened, the hospital hosted an open house. It seemed like the entire town came out to tour the new facility of our practice, which was now called Mountain Family Medicine Center. At first I suspected many were just scoping out the new practice to see if they might want to choose it as their practice. In actuality, the word had gotten out about the food that was to be served.

Ella Jo Shell from the Hemlock Inn, Katherine Collins from the Fryemont Inn, Ruth Adams from the Frye-Randolph House, and Eloise Newman from the Swain County General Hospital cafeteria each outdid themselves in preparing delicacies for our guests.

To our surprise, all the local doctors came by to enjoy the food, give us their congratulations, and take a peek around the new facility. Gary Ayers from WBHN was there to tape interviews for his morning radio show. Earl Douthit, the hospital administrator, showed his hospital staff around the office. He struck us as a proud papa.

Even Louise came by to see the place. "Just wanted to see where I'd be referrin' folks," she whispered as I walked around with her.

"You know, I wanted you to come over here and interview for a job," I told Louise.

She stopped and turned toward me, cocking her head and asking, "You did? Dr. Larimore, you tellin' the truth?"

"I'm as serious as a heart attack, Louise. You could have a job here anytime you want."

She smiled and then looked away. "I'm not sure I'd know what to do away from *my* emergency room. I ain't ever known nothing but that ole ER. Reckon they'll carry me outta there feet first with my boots on one day."

It was my turn to smile. "Louise, I think the hospital would just close up if you ever left."

She seemed intensely pleased.

During the open house, Katherine and Elizabeth served the finger foods they had prepared at the Fryemont Inn kitchen. Ella Jo Shell brought trays of baked goods from the Hemlock Inn, including my personal favorites—her famous pumpkin chips and apple chips. Not to be outdone, Eloise Newman and her hospital kitchen staff provided goodies. "They must have the best hospital food in the world," one of our visitors commented. I could only nod in agreement—my mouth being full.

The entire rescue squad, including Monty and Diana Clampitt, came by. John and Becky Mattox from Super Swain Drugs stopped in for a visit. During his tour, John kept looking behind every door and in every closet. My curiosity overcame me. "What in the world are you looking for, John?"

He seemed to blush. "Just checkin' to see you don't have a small pharmacy up here. Don't want any young whippersnappers puttin' me outta business!"

I laughed. "Doc John, you know your clients won't go anywhere else. And you know it would take me ten years to learn how to mix all the potions you concoct. Furthermore, I'll never have your gift of gab. So don't worry. There will never be a pharmacy up in this office—at least while I'm here. You can depend on that."

He beamed.

The entire hospital board, the city councilmen, and the county commissioners all attended. The ribbon-cutting ceremony was photographed by Pete Lawson from the *Smoky Mountain Times,* and the Reverend Kenneth Hicks (as he liked to be called during formal occasions) shared a wonderful prayer of blessing for the practice, the facility, and our town.

After the crowd had left, Rick, Katherine, Barb, and I were alone in the lobby of the new building. We were drinking a last cup of coffee and just enjoying the quiet of the moment. Kate and Scott were playing in the new children's area of the waiting room.

"Boys," Katherine began, "you two have a mighty fine building here."

We nodded in silent agreement.

She continued. "I'm serious. There's not a finer office building between here and Asheville. And I'm not sure there's a nicer medical office building even in Asheville."

"Didn't Barb do a great job decorating it?" Rick asked.

Barb quickly added, "With Sally Jenkins's help, I might add!"

"Well," Rick responded, "you did a great job. I think it's going to be a very comfortable place to practice."

Katherine smiled. "Do you mean the building or the town?"

We all smiled, and I chuckled. *Both!* I thought to myself.

But only time would tell.

chapter thirty-one

MOUNTAIN BREAKFAST

It was just past 5:00 a.m. when I completed the forty-five-minute drive from Bryson City to Fontana Village, a large resort by Fontana Dam. I followed the directions from the main highway to the home of John Carswell, who was the head of security at the Village.

We first had met in the emergency room over a year ago when he had brought in a heart attack patient. John invited me at that time to come out and go fishing with him. Today the rain check would be collected.

When I arrived at the Carswells, it was still dark, but the house was brightly illuminated. John Carswell came bounding out of his house and jumped off the front porch as I pulled up in our old Toyota. Now, John was a rather portly person, and for him to bound anywhere, especially off a four-foot porch, was a sight to behold indeed.

Still smiling from the spectacle, I crawled out of the car as John bounced over, smiling from ear to ear and extending his large, calloused hand. "Great to see ya, Doc! Just great to see ya! Can't wait to show you around the place a bit!" He kept pumping my hand like the handle of a pump as he turned toward the house, pulling me in tow. "Come on in and meet the wife and kids. We got some vittles ready for ya."

The fragrance of frying bacon smacked my nose as John released his ironclad grip on my rapidly paling hand and began to beat my back as we walked toward the house.

"Doc, the fish have really been bitin'. Can't wait for you to catch a mess of 'em!"

We entered the house. It was small, and family pictures covered the walls. Family heirlooms crowded tabletops and bookstands. Introductions were made all around. John's kids were school-age, and his son was a physical look-alike of his dad—and his handshake just as vicelike.

"John Carswell!" a shrill voice called from the kitchen. "Y'all best git in here right now if ya wants to eat. Now, I say!"

"Best be movin' in that there direction before Priscilla Carswell gets irritated!" John herded me into the kitchen, where his wife, with her back to us, was fast at work over the stove. The kitchen table was covered with a quaint red-checkered tablecloth on which the family's best china lay.

"Good to meet you, Doc! Welcome to our home. Welcome!" Mrs. Carswell exclaimed without turning around. "Y'all have a seat and help yourself to the juice."

Her hair was tied up in a bun on top of her head. She was dressed in a simple blue-and-white-checkered cotton dress with an apron tied around the back.

We sat at the table, and John poured freshly squeezed orange juice. We began to visit, but as we talked, I couldn't take my eyes off Mrs. Carswell. She was a whirlwind of activity that was a sight to behold. Her hands were flying like hummingbirds over the multiple pots and pans, each containing a different delicacy. Scrambled eggs, link sausage, patty sausage, and thick smoked bacon were sizzling in cast-iron frying pans. Grits and sawmill gravy were each gently bubbling in their own old aluminum pots.

Mrs. Carswell was overseeing the preparation of the feast like a composer—a maestro—over an orchestra of her own creation. Not only was it a visual spectacle; the smells were an olfactory bacchanalia instantly filling the room as she opened the oven and pulled out a pan of fresh, hot, homemade yeast bread.

"Got the starter for this bread from my ma's ma. It's been in the family for at least three generations. We girls just keep it goin' and goin'. It's almost like Ma was here herself."

Mrs. Carswell slowly lifted the bread to her nose and deeply breathed in the precious aroma. Her voice softened. "This is heaven," she said, almost to herself. Then she spun toward the kitchen counter, and platters filled with breakfast foods were transported to the table.

There almost wasn't enough room. Already on the table were jars containing several types of local honey, jam, and jelly. A tub of local butter, which looked as if it would taste delightfully creamy, sat next to a small pitcher of heavy cream and a pot of freshly brewed coffee—with steam slowly rising from it and the heaping platters of food.

As Mrs. Carswell sat down, the family members instinctively bowed their heads and at the same time held their hands to the side. I did the same, and as we held hands in a circle, John said a simple, and thankfully a short, blessing—because bowing your head over that table only brought the splendid aromas into more focus. Had the blessing been too long, I'm sure I would have been tempted to lower my head into the platter of sausage right in front of me.

No sooner had the "Amen" been said than the family began to pass around the food.

"Doc," instructed John, "take all you want. Don't want ya gittin' hungry on me out there on that lake. But be sure to leave me some of that sausage. It's my daddy's recipe. We combine boar and venison and pork and . . ." He leaned over toward me and continued with a whisper, "a bit of bear meat."

He paused for effect. I didn't know if the bear was poached or legal, and I was a bit too intimidated to ask—John being a law enforcement officer and all.

"We have to age the meat and then marinade it with an ole family recipe. Doc, if you and me stay together as fishin' buddies for a few years, I may be able to share it with ya. But not till I know ya better."

In many places, such a statement might not have been taken as a friendly one, but I knew it was actually a compliment—that John was offering me a promise, a token if you would, of a mature friendship, when, in fact, ours was just beginning. It was almost as if he was predicting that our friendship would grow and develop.

It was quite a compliment indeed.

I don't remember much else about that meal. I don't remember much about leaving the home and getting into John's truck to take a tour of the Village. But I do remember the food and the laughter and the family feeling.

To this day, I'm convinced that the family that shares meals like this is just a healthier family—the kind we all long for deep down. By his actions John had inspired me and given me a model to follow, for I wanted my family mealtimes to feel like his.

chapter thirty-two

WALKINGSTICK

After breakfast, John kissed Priscilla good-bye, and we headed for his truck. On the way from his home to the marina, he told me a bit about Fontana Dam.

"Son, it's a monster of a dam. I mean, it's the highest concrete dam east of the Rocky Mountains—nearly 480 feet from its base to the top—the highest dam in the TVA system. It's over 2,300 feet long and over 375 feet thick at its base."

His knowledge impressed me.

He continued. "I've seen a lot of dams in my travels, but in my opinion Fontana ranks among the most beautiful in the world—sittin' right smack-dab in the middle of the extraordinary beauty of the Smoky Mountains and its wilderness forests. Man it's gorgeous."

I felt as if I was with a tour guide. But it was good to hear him talk as we wound down the mountain toward the lake—his headlights piercing the mist that was coming off the lake.

John continued his narration. "The dam was built just as America got into World War II. Construction started on New Year's Day in 1942, and they started to fill the reservoir in November 1944. Since the site was so remote, a railroad had to be built to transport supplies. And an entire community for the workers and their families was erected in the wilderness, almost overnight. The five thousand or so men and women who assembled at Fontana in 1942 worked in three shifts, around the clock, seven days a week. And what was once their construction village is now our resort and homes."

John slowed down the truck to turn toward the marina. "The saddest part of the whole project was the effect on the towns and the folks who lived in what is now the lake basin. There were approximately six hundred mountain families in the area when Fontana was built. Some were relocated; some moved east to Asheville or west to Tennessee."

As we drove I reflected on what I had heard locals say about this relocation. They still feel the government stole their land; in fact, many still feel the land is theirs, so that's why they feel justified in hunting in the park—they're just taking what they feel is rightfully theirs.

We arrived at the Fontana Marina at first light. The tree line was nearly fifty feet above waterline. In years gone by, Fontana Lake had produced electricity for the Tennessee Valley Authority. Folks around here saw that project as just another plot by the federal government to steal what was theirs and sell it to others—in this case, the folks over in another state. It caused a great deal of distress and was the topic of frequent discussions.

When the lake was low, a ribbon of unsightly red clay was usually visible above the waterline. There could be as much as 100 to 150 feet of treeless, red shoreline above the water. In the years we lived in Bryson City, I only saw the lake full to the top once—and even then it was only for a few short weeks.

When the lake was full, it was a spectacular sight—with massive, sometimes virgin forests hugging the waterline. The tree-lined canyons and fjords were mesmerizing. Waterfalls and creeks tumbling into the lake were a never-ending delight to fishermen cruising the shore.

Since the north shore of the lake made up much of the southern border of the Great Smoky Mountains National Park, it was totally undeveloped and wild. When the lake was full, the wildlife would come to the shore for a drink during the day. To see deer, bear, boar, or bobcat then was not rare. However, when the lake was down, as it was today—and as it usually was—the wildlife stayed in the woods and drank from the streams.

Because of the unpredictable lake levels, the marinas were all built on floats and would be raised or lowered by a winch and cable system. Aluminum walkways would protect the shore and the fishermen as they walked from the tree line to the marina.

The small marina store was already a beehive of activity. People were purchasing last-minute supplies, day licenses, and bait. Others were filling gas cans. Boats with motors idling awaited their occupants. Coffee cups held in one hand and cigarettes in the other seemed common. Laughter and fish stories merged into a soft bedlam that reverberated around the small cove.

Nearly everyone knew John and spoke to him. He greeted them all, asking about their spouses and families. He shared gossip and tips freely and joyously. He introduced me to each person, and I enjoyed watching the way he made each person feel significant.

At the end of one of the aluminum piers, a small group of Cherokee men were drinking coffee and laughing. As John and I walked up, they stood and greeted him. One of the men was very large, with a headful of waist-length hair that was as black as midnight. I think it was the most beautiful hair I'd ever seen on a man. As he stood to shake our hands, I noticed that his left arm was missing; the long-sleeve flannel shirt arm was tied in a knot on the left side. He must have noticed my slightly too long stare.

"Lost the arm in 'Nam, Doc. Lost the arm but kept my life. Turned out better than most of the boys I was with."

It was my first meeting with Carl Walkingstick. He was about six foot six and weighed over three hundred pounds. Yet he didn't look obese—rather, he was just a very, very big man. And to the Cherokee, who tended to be a bit smaller than average, he was a Goliath.

"Carl, tell Doc about that pike you caught not too long ago," directed John.

Carl seemed almost embarrassed. "Aw, Officer John. Doc don't wanna hear a bunch of fish stories from me. After all, he's gonna be hearin' 'em all day from you!"

The men howled in laughter.

"Carl, this here's Doc's first trip down here and I been tellin' him about the fishin' down here. And you done caught one of the biggest pike ever. I think he'd like to hear a bit about it, wouldn'tcha, Doc?"

John elbowed me. "That's true, isn't it, Doc?"

"Mr. Walkingstick, I've got to tell you. The boys in Bryson who've been telling me about fly-fishing say that lake fishing isn't really that good. But I'd sure like to hear your views about the matter."

"Well, I do like to fly-fish," began Carl. "But, Doc, there's nothin' quite like trollin' for muskie or pike or walleye or lake trout. Some of 'em in the deeper parts of this lake are as big as torpedoes. The muskie is the biggest. And there are some massive trout and pike here also. I love fishin' in the streams and I love fishin' in the lake. My dad taught me both. He loved both. And so do I. But if I had to choose, I'd choose lake fishin' most any time. The fish are huge—especially that pike I caught."

The conversation paused for a moment. I felt like all eyes were on me. It was almost as though the group was waiting for me to speak next. Unfortunately, I did.

"Well, Carl, just how big was that pike?"

I had no sooner spoken than I knew I shouldn't have. The snickers started almost immediately. The men tried to hide smiles and chortles behind shirtsleeves and nodded heads.

Carl's pearly white teeth gleamed as he rose to attention. His right arm was fully extended, his hand outstretched like he was going to applaud, but there was no left arm to match it. "Doc, he was this big!"

The group could not contain itself. John Carswell and the younger men howled in laughter—belly-shaking, bone-deep laughter. I couldn't help but join in. No doubt, this joke had been told a hundred times before—and would be told again and again in the future.

"You boys have a good day," said John as we turned to head to his boat.

"Doc, good to meet you," chimed the group as it broke into peals of laughter again.

"You all got me on that one." I chuckled to myself.

As we turned to leave, Carl yelled out, "Hey, Doc!"

I turned back toward him. "Yes."

"You know how you can tell Carswell is lyin'—at least when he's talkin' about the fish he done caught?"

I paused—then took the bait. Again. "How?" I asked.

Carl smiled and then exclaimed, "His lips will be movin'!"

The men howled again in laughter—one of them laughing so hard he fell off his bench onto the dock. Again I couldn't help but join in.

If there was some way I could have bottled Carl's humor and prescribed it to every patient I saw who had to live with a physical disability, I know I'd have healthier patients.

Actually, I've come to believe this might be a true principle for us all. And as I would soon learn, it was his and his friends' humor that would help save Carl's life.

⊷

We readied John's bass boat, and as the light began to build, we slowly left the cove.

Steam and mist rose from the water as we headed out toward the lake. The mountains surrounding the lake were clothed, as they usually were on fall mornings, with their petticoats of smoke, drifting slowly, almost daintily, over the trees. With each chug of the motor, we moved away from civilization and toward freedom, and my sense of expectation increased.

Behind us, echoing off the walls of the cove, we heard peals of laughter—almost certainly from Carl and his friends. I smiled. Once outside the cove, John gave the motor its full throttle, and we were off.

As the boat pulled out of the cove, the massive dam came into view. John turned the throttle, and we shot off in the mist, headed for the other side of the lake. I loved the feel of the cool mist and air swirling against my face and hair. I could almost feel my pulse and blood pressure drop. I loved being out on this lake.

We went several miles up the lake and turned into a mountain cove. Some of the coves had gently sloping banks up to the tree line and then rolling hills above. This cove was more like a fjord, steep sides, nearly cliffs, soaring hundreds of feet into the air. It was like cruising up a canyon. John turned the motor off, and we coasted several hundred feet. The silence, other than an occasional birdcall, was deafening. We slowly drifted by a waterfall that tumbled dozens of feet into the lake.

"Tell ya what, Doc. I love fishin'. I do. But sometimes it's so beautiful out here I just come and listen to myself think."

He was quiet for a moment and then continued. "I can get away from about everything out here except the Lord. He's out here. This is where I meet 'im and talk to 'im. This here's my cathedral."

He surprised me with his openness about his faith. Yet the setting and the conversation were so natural—not at all contrived or forced. He was expressing a normally hidden side of himself—and in a very comfortable way. I felt honored he was comfortable enough to share this with me. I made a mental note to consider how I might do the same with my friends and patients. I sighed. "None finer," I commented.

"Amen" was the reply.

"This sure is a big lake, John."

He smiled. "You betcha Bob!" He exclaimed. "It's over 24 miles long and has almost 240 miles of shoreline."

He paused for a moment to take in a deep breath.

"Well, let's see if we can get some smallmouth bass. They say this is the best smallmouth bass lake in the world."

For the next two hours we trolled the shores of various coves, catching scores of nice smallmouth bass. Some we kept, but most we released.

After we had fished one spot, John would rev up the boat and sometimes head miles away to another cove—always working the north shore of the lake.

By late morning, we had several fish in the live well and John was steering the boat back toward the dam and turned up the Hazel Creek cove. John slowed down the boat and then stopped in the middle of the cove—a pristine wilderness as far as the eye could see. John took out the lunch his wife had packed. We drifted down the cove, carried by the slow current from Hazel Creek.

After our lunch, John started up the boat, and we headed back up the large cove leading to Hazel Creek. We pulled all the way to where the creek came tumbling out of the trees, down the clay banks of the lake and into Fontana.

"Let's take us a little hike."

We scurried up the bank, following what looked like an old road. Indeed it was. When we got into the trees, the road became more obvious.

"The Park Service still uses this road. It makes a nice hikin' trail. Some folks ride horses over here, so watch your step." John laughed out loud.

"I'm surprised at just how lush it is."

John nodded in agreement. "Guess so. After all, we get over seventy-five inches of rain down on this end of the lake each year. Sure helps keep the flowers a bloomin'!"

We hiked for a bit in silence and then came across some brick ruins. The ruins reminded me of some of the old Civil War forts along the Gulf Coast I'd explored as a child.

"These are the ruins of the old sugar mill and the dryin' kilns. After they'd cut up the hardwood, they'd bring it in the kiln to dry it out. Then they'd send the wood up the East Coast and to Europe. At one time, the Ritter Lumber Company that clear-cut this valley was one of the largest lumber companies in the world."

As we were walking around the ruins, John pointed out where the various structures stood and described what they were. He suddenly stopped and put his index finger to his mouth. "Shhh."

We were quiet. I couldn't hear a thing.

"You smell that?"

No sooner had he asked than my nostrils picked up a malodorous, pungent smell.

"Pigs," he groaned. "Follow me. Be quiet."

We crept forward among the ruins. The smell became more noticeable. He began to squat, and I followed suit. He peered over a low wall and then quickly ducked down. He turned to me, smiling and pointing across the wall. I came up beside him.

We both slowly peered over the wall and saw just on the other side and down in a small hollow a small herd of the largest, blackest, meanest pigs I'd ever seen.

"Russian boar," he whispered. "The male's the big one with the tusks."

I saw him. He was huge, with long ugly hairs sticking up on the nape of his neck. Just seeing and smelling them, hearing their grunting as they rooted through the brush, made the hairs on *my* neck stand up. I felt my arms chill with gooseflesh.

"Besides the male," John whispered, "there's a bunch of mature females—his harem. There's also a bunch of piglets—I'd guess about six months old."

We watched in amazement. "I'd guess that male is over 250 pounds," John said.

"Are they native?"

"Heavens no! Some wealthy fellow who stocked 'em in his hunting game preserve up by Robbinsville imported them from Russia. Bunch of 'em escaped, and they've been breedin' in the Snowbird Mountains and the Smokies ever since. We see 'em down in this valley all the time. And there's a fair bit of poachin' over here since it's so close to public land."

The boars began to move away into the brush, although their odor hung in the air like a morning fog. We stood. "Don't want to startle those guys. More times than not, when they're startled, they attack. And I wanna tell ya, there's not a nastier gash than a gorin' by a mad boar. No question about it."

chapter thirty-three

ONE BIG FISH

After our hike, we returned to the boat.

"Son!" John exclaimed as he pushed the boat away from the shore, "let's go catch us some big fish."

He started the motor, and we were off—out of the cove and down the lake to the back side of the dam.

After he turned off the motor and set the boat up to troll, he commented, "Son, there's some monster bass along this dam. No one fishes for 'em but me. Catch and release is what I practice up here, so these fish have gotten mighty big. But they're also hard to catch—they've gotten awfully smart."

We changed lures and began trolling the dam. Several hikers waved to us from the dam, heading to and from the national park.

John noted, "The Appalachian Trail crosses right across the dam. But people can access all sorts of trails into the park. But the Appalachian Trail brings the most."

"Just how long is it?"

"Well, the Appalachian Trail starts down in Georgia and extends over two thousand miles—all the way up to Maine."

He pointed to the south end of the dam. "There's a trail shelter just up there. The hikers call it the Fontana Hilton."

"Why's that?"

"Well, I think it's because of the hot showers at the TVA Visitors Center."

Suddenly John dropped his pole and his eyes got as wide as saucers. I looked over to the edge of the dam—perhaps thirty feet away—and saw an amazing sight. It was a hole in the water. The hole was perhaps ten inches in diameter, and in an instant it closed.

"What was that? I've never seen anything like that!" I exclaimed.

John dropped to his seat and was rapidly opening his lure box. "There must be a nest up in the works under the edge of the dam." He was cutting off his lure. "I seen a little baby bird fall out into the water." He found a huge lure that looked like a small mouse. "Was gonna point it out to you—when this huge bass come up and opened her mouth and done sucked in that chick."

"I saw the end of the action but never saw the bird!" I cried.

He had the lure tied on and in seconds was flipping the lure to the exact spot. He played the lure for only a few seconds, when the hole opened again.

John set the lure, and the fight was on. The enormous fish would run fifty to seventy yards of line off John's reel, and then John would begin reeling her in. Then she'd run again. The process was repeated over and over, until he got her close to the boat.

"Oh my goodness! Looky there. Looky there! Grab the net, Doc. She's a monster!"

Then I saw her. She *was* huge!

"Bet she's twenty pounds!" he cried. "Oh my goodness!"

He played her up to the surface—less than four feet from the boat. She looked like a small barracuda—not a largemouth bass.

John was slowly lifting the end of his rod, drawing her closer and closer. "Oh my! Goodness gracious, looky here! Get that net over here and in the water under her! Slow and gentle. Don't scare her!"

I dipped the net in the water and began to work it out toward the fish.

"Oh my ever-loving goodness!" John exclaimed.

Then she turned her head to the side, gave a flick, threw off the lure, slapped her gigantic tail on the surface, and was gone.

"Oh no! No!" John whispered as he slumped into his chair.

He took a deep breath. "I've been tryin' to catch her for years. That's as close as I've ever gotten." He smiled at me. "Least I got to see her eye to eye."

"Man, that was some fish, John."

"Yep. She was a beaut. Well, what say we go home?"

"Sounds good to me."

Back at the dock, we cleaned the fish and wrapped them in freezer paper. John handed me the fish and pulled out a piece of paper from his pocket.

"Take these fish back to Barb. And here's my favorite recipe for grillin' or fryin' or broilin' these fillets. They'll be some good eatin'."

"Thanks, John. I appreciate it."

As we were walking off the floating docks, we heard a voice thunder across the piers. "Doc, Carswell tell ya any fish stories?" We looked across the water to see Carl Walkingstick sitting on a bench.

I cupped my hand to yell back. "No need for him to tell me any stories, Carl. I saw him catch a monster bass."

"How big was she?" he hollered back.

I held up my right arm—my right hand stretched out in the air—while keeping my left hand in my pocket. "This big!" I exclaimed.

Carl's laughter ricocheted off the walls of the cove.

John and I laughed.

He slapped me on the back. "Let's go home."

I felt I was already there.

chapter thirty-four

MEMORIAL DAY

It started out as a very warm day for the end of May. Little did I know when the alarm went off that morning it would be my most unforgettable Memorial Day for decades to come.

The excitement had been building in town for weeks. Not only would today host one of the largest town parades in recent memory—as the Olympic torch would pass through town—but it also would be marked by a full eclipse of the sun!

Some unknown purchaser was rumored to have ordered dozens of flowers from Libby's House of Flowers for his float. They had been delivered to Libby's back parking lot and then clandestinely picked up, after hours, by two shadowy figures driving a rental truck.

The most devilish part of the whole surreptitious operation was that the truck from the wholesale company opened its back door just as the rental truck, with its back door open, backed up to it. The trucks were back-to-back, like two lovebugs, while the contents of one was secretly disgorged into the entrails of the other.

The rescue squad had been secretly planning its float for weeks. The Smoky Mountain mental health office had only recently begun their planning process. But it was rumored that they were planning a "Crazy Float." No one really knew what to expect from them—after all, most of the staff members were out-of-towners!

The rest home, the library, Sneed's Restaurant, and Bennett's Drug Store were all planning minor entries—probably just some folks riding in the back of a decorated pickup truck.

There was a community buzz about John Cope and the folks at Cope Chevrolet. Word was that a bright red Corvette had been delivered to the dealership and was discreetly hidden in a locked shed that had no windows. Super Swain Drugs hadn't announced any plans, but everyone knew Doc John couldn't miss out on the free advertising the "parade of the century" would bring. Several of the women at Willa Jean's Hair Shop were sure Doc John was the one who had ordered all the flowers.

For some reason, the hospital, doctors, and dentists all decided to sit out the parade—at least as far as hosting a float. It was generally conceded that the medical and dental professionals would have an unfair financial advantage. Why this thinking wasn't applied to some of the tourist venues—such as the Fontana Village Resort, the Nantahala Outdoor Center, and the Cherokee Holiday Inn—was a complete mystery to me.

A number of churches had signed up to have floats. Of course, the high school marching bands from Swain County, Robbinsville, and Cherokee were signed up. But everyone knew the Swain County High School marching band would have the premier position at the end of the parade—just before the Olympic torch. No one knew who might be carrying the torch through town—or if it might be several different individuals. And everyone was abuzz about who he or she or they might be. Riders from the Graham County sheriff's cavalry would be there, and there were rumors that the Shriner clowns from Asheville might even be coming.

Why, there were more topics for gossip about this event than any in recent memory. Every hair shop, restaurant, service club, and store in town was buzzing!

Rick was on call for the practice that day, and since there were no patients in the hospital, I didn't have to make morning rounds.

Even though it was a Wednesday, our office, like the others in town, was planning to be closed that day. Everyone would be downtown. There would be food and craft booths. A dunking booth featuring local celebrities would be very busy. We were expecting the town to be packed.

The kids and Barb were asleep, and I got up and made a pot of coffee. The smell of her favorite coffee brewing was enough to awaken her, and pretty soon, in her robe and slippers, she was sniffing her way into the kitchen.

"Happy Memorial Day, honey," she announced, shuffling sleepily into the kitchen.

I turned to give her a big hug and a good-morning kiss.

"Have you made rounds already?"

"Nope. I don't have anyone in the hospital."

"Isn't it funny," she mused, "how the hospitals always seem to empty out at holidays? Your census is down on Christmas, New Year's, Easter, and Thanksgiving."

"That's true. I'm not sure why that is. Certainly folks put off elective surgery and procedures, but even the acute hospitalizations seem to be down on holidays—except for the accidents."

"Well, I hope Rick doesn't have to take care of too many of those. He's coming over to go downtown with us for the parade, and then y'all are grilling dinner for us."

"I am? I didn't know that."

"Yes, you are! Rick and I decided that on his day off."

I smiled as I poured our coffee. Rick and Barb were extremely close, and on his off day, he'd go to our house to have coffee with Barb and chat.

"Come on," I invited, "let's take advantage of the quiet. How 'bout we go sit on our bench?"

"Count me in." Her beautiful smile caught my eye and, as always, relaxed and attracted me. It had since I was five years old.

"Not too long until Independence Day," Barb observed as we walked to the bench outside our house. The morning was still cool, and the scattered clouds and mist—for which the Smoky Mountains are famous—drifted slowly over the peaks bordering Deep Creek.

"Why are you thinking about Independence Day?" I wondered out loud.

Barb was quiet for a moment as we settled on the bench.

"Wow, it's so beautiful here," she softly commented as she took in a slow, deep breath. I smiled to myself. This deep breath was one of the ways Barb told me she was comfortable and felt safe. But I still suspected something was up.

"So what's the deal about July Fourth?" I asked again.

"Oh, nothing," she replied as she stared at Deep Creek Valley.

"Something, I think."

Then she turned to me. "Walt, you know how you docs are not really doing anything for this Memorial Day. And you all usually don't do anything special for the Fourth of July?"

"Well, it's kind of a tradition that we don't. At least that's what Mitch said."

"But don't you think it'd be good for the docs to participate in a community event?"

I was beginning to smell a fish. "Barb, we donate our time to the athletes. We give money to the athletic fund, the community theater, and every kid who comes to the office asking for any sort of charitable donation."

"But you're not really giving yourself."

"What? Of course we are. Either Rick or I are at every football game and most home basketball games."

"I know, but that's in your profession. I think you should do something personally."

"Where are you going with this?" I asked very suspiciously.

"Well, I volunteered you to participate in a community event on the Fourth of July. And it's for a good cause. It's to raise money for the rescue squad and the fire department."

I was quiet for a moment—imagining myself flipping pancakes at a community breakfast, serving a meal at the senior center, or, in the worst case, sitting in a dunking booth at a local carnival. I wasn't even close.

"Walt, I've signed you up to compete in the Miss Flame contest."

I was in shock! Absolute shock!

I began to feel a bit of a chill and got up to walk into the house and pour myself a fresh cup of coffee. Barb came with me.

I had never heard of the Miss Flame contest. I had no idea what it was. But I was certain of two things—one, I didn't want to know more, and two, I didn't want to participate.

"Walt, this is going to be community service at its best. The rescue squad and fire department are having their first annual Fireman's Day on July Fourth. Diana Clampitt and the fire department auxiliary are planning a really big event. And the highlight will be the Miss Flame contest. Best of all, we can do this together."

"Do what together?"

"Everyone is volunteering. The president of the bank, the mayor, several of the doctors and football coaches, the athletic director, and the director of the health department will all be participating. And it's all to raise money for the fire department and the rescue squad."

I was speechless as I poured us both a second cup of coffee.

"And as a member of the rescue squad, you really *do* have to participate."

"Whose idea was this?"

"Well, I think Diana Clampitt heard about it somewhere. All the wives have talked about it, and we think it's a great idea. Will you do it? Please? Pretty please?"

"Barb, I don't even know what *it* is."

"Oh, *it* is no big deal."

"So what is *it*?"

"Well, *it* is a beauty contest."

"A beauty contest! What does *that* mean? We're a bunch of men!"

"Not that afternoon."

"What do you mean 'not that afternoon'?"

"Well, that afternoon you gentlemen are going to be ladies. We'll dress you all up like you are beautiful young women. The winner will be declared Miss Flame."

Now I was in shock *and* speechless. I almost dropped my coffee cup. I'm sure my jaw had dropped open. "Dress up like ladies!" I could barely squeak out the words.

"Yes," Barb matter-of-factly explained. "You are each going to dress up as ladies. There will be an evening gown competition, a bathing suit competition, and a brief onstage interview."

"Ladies!" I groaned.

"Oh, don't worry. I'm going to be there to take care of you. I'll show you how to do everything."

I was nauseous and walked into the dining room to sit down. "There's no way. Not me! Not in *this* lifetime!"

"Oh, just think about it a bit. It's going to be fun," Barb cried from the kitchen.

As I was continuing to whine, Rick knocked on the kitchen screen door. "Uncle Rick!" yelped Kate, who ran as fast as she could to the door to greet him.

"Hey, Rick," called Barb. "Come on in."

Rick came in and picked up Kate. "How you doing, Kate?" Kate gave him a big hug, and he walked through the kitchen into the dining room. "Where's Walt?" he asked Barb.

"He's either sitting or lying down in the dining room. I think he's still in shock."

"So you must have told him about Miss Flame?"

"This is *not* funny!" I called out from the dining room.

"Yes. And obviously he didn't take it very well," Barb commented.

"Is he going to do it?" Rick asked.

"It isn't looking very positive right now."

"We'll just give him time. He'll come around."

They both laughed. I pretended not to hear them. For now I knew for sure that Rick had been in on this all along. He still wasn't even a member of the rescue squad—well, at least he hadn't gone through the initiation like I had the previous year. Now I even more wanted to be there when he went through it.

"Hey, Barb. Did you hear about who they've chosen to carry the Olympic torch in the parade?" asked Rick.

"No. Who is it?"

"Steve Streeter."

"Who's that?"

"He's a kid from Sylva who played defensive back for Sylva. Then he went to play football at the University of North Carolina. He broke his neck playing there and is now a quadriplegic. So Swain County is honoring him today. I think the county is trying to make peace with the folks over in Jackson County—where he's from."

"Rick, you're just too cynical." Barb commented. "I think it's a nice gesture."

I was still lying on the floor, feeling very nauseated. *Miss Flame!* I thought. *That's not a nice gesture!*

chapter thirty-five

THE PARADE OF THE CENTURY

I was feeling better by the time we needed to leave. We all loaded into our little yellow Toyota and drove down Hospital Hill to Mitch and Ray's office and parked there. I carried Kate on my shoulders and Rick had Scott on his. Barb walked between us. The streets were packed with people waiting for the parade, and we worked our way up Everett Street, past Cope Chevrolet and Super Swain Drugs, then crossed the Tuckaseigee River bridge and walked past Fred Moody's office and Bennett's Drug Store.

It was 11:30, and the parade was about to start. The sun was scorching, so we crossed the street to stand under the awning in front of Charlie Robertson's CPA office. We could hear the first band coming down Main Street. The music got louder and louder and the children got more and more excited as the Cherokee High School Band turned the corner. The crowd was six to eight people thick.

"I had no idea there were so many people who lived here," Barb shouted to me.

"Me either."

Once the parade started, we began our critique. The rescue squad float was wholly unimpressive—just the new inflatable rescue raft with several of the guys dressed up in wet suits and pretending to paddle the raft down Everett Street. The Smoky Mountain mental health office's "Crazy Float" was really just staff dressed up as crazy doctors and nurses riding in the back of a pickup truck. Doc John and Becky were, of course, riding on the Super Swain Drugs float. It was a rendition of the old-timey soda fountain, with high school girls dressed up in 1950s-style white shirts, poodle skirts, and bobby socks tossing candy to the kids. It was totally covered with carnations and other flowers.

"Maybe they're the ones who purchased the flowers!" Rick yelled to me over the noise of the crowd.

The Shriner clowns on their miniature motorcycles followed them. The kids squealed in delight—both at the clowns and at the sheriff's cavalry that followed. The horses were magnificent. We could hear the crowd murmuring even before the bright red Corvette convertible turned the corner by the courthouse. It was an impressive car, made more impressive by the roaring of the engine. However, the sight of John Cope sitting on the back waving to the crowd was not as impressive as John Mattox's soda fountain girls!

Following the Robbinsville High School band came the church floats, all on the back of pickup trucks. The most impressive of the three church floats was the float from one of the Baptist churches, featuring a mock-up of the pearly gate and the pastor dressed up as Saint Peter himself. He was a very large man, and Barb shouted out, "That's one impressive Saint Peter, don't you think?"

I nodded my assent.

But by far the most impressive float was Clampitt Hardware's flower-covered pickup truck. Rick leaned over to shout above the cheering of the crowds. "This must be the closest Bryson City is going to get to the Rose Parade."

I smiled and nodded my head in agreement once again.

Barb leaned toward me and exclaimed, "Maybe that's where the flowers from Libby's went." She was probably right.

Just before the final float appeared, the Swain County High School marching band—the pride of Swain County—paraded down the street. As good as the football team was year after year, the band was as good or better, and their halftime shows were always superb.

Following the band, there was a gap and a pause. Then came the last "float" around the corner. It was strikingly simple—just a motorized wheelchair decorated with red and blue streamers and balloons.

The young black man riding in the motorized wheelchair was strikingly handsome, and his smile was beaming as his eyes swept from one side of the road to the other. Behind the wheelchair walked an older African-American man and woman dressed in red, white, and blue, each waving to his or her side of the crowd.

"I bet they're his parents!" Barb shouted.

I thought she was probably correct.

The young man was dressed in white shoes with a white shirt and pants. The blackness of his skin was a stark contrast to both the whiteness of his clothes and—as I looked around at the cheering crowd giving the Streeters a standing ovation—the whiteness of the crowd. It suddenly struck me how lily-white the town was—racially speaking. Other than Louise and her husband, Dr. Pat, and a couple of high school football players, I didn't know any non-Caucasians in the town—or even in the county.

As the Streeters passed, the large crowd of locals continued to give this young man a standing ovation.

"They say he'll never walk again," Rick shouted near my ear.

They said that about Kate! I thought to myself as I smiled.

Then the crowd grew strangely silent. No one moved. For a moment, I was confused. *What is happening?* I thought.

Then I heard a whispered gasp spread through the crowd. We were standing under an awning and didn't realize as quickly as others that the eclipse had started.

It began to get dimmer and dimmer. People were in the streets, looking up at the sun with specially designed glasses. As it grew dimmer, the air grew palpably cooler—almost like a spring evening. Suddenly a cool breeze blew across the street and rustled the edge of the awning. I felt chill bumps growing quickly on both arms.

Then Rick exclaimed, "Look!"

I had been looking at the crowd and missed what was right at our feet. Rick was pointing down at the sidewalk. There at our feet were hundreds of small suns, each beaming its way through the pinholes in the awning.

The cool breeze, the approaching dusk, and the chill in the air combined with the scene at our feet to create a surreal, almost haunting setting. We watched the pavement in amazement. As dozens and dozens of moons slowly moved in front of an equal number of miniature suns, we saw the suns slowly begin to disappear.

When the full eclipse reached its peak, the entire town was suddenly dark—not completely dark, but twilight dark. As I looked around, it appeared that the entire town was frozen. And the town was completely silent. Hundreds of people were standing in the streets—and not a single person was making a sound.

Under the awning of Charlie Robertson's office, we saw not one full eclipse of the sun but hundreds.

Then slowly the street became brighter, and the crowd began to come alive.

We stayed under the awning, watching a hundred suns come back to light.

"What an eclipse! Wow, I've never seen one!" cried Barb as little Scott snoozed in his carrier.

"Wow, what a parade!" Kate chimed in.

"What a day!" exclaimed Rick.

If we had only known what lay ahead.

chapter thirty-six

LOST BOY

*L*ater that afternoon, we were back at our little green house on Hospital Hill. Rick and I were outside firing up the grill. Barb was inside preparing the rest of the meal. Kate was taking a nap, and Scott was making a nuisance of himself in the kitchen under Barb's feet.

We heard the screen door creak open as Barb came out carrying Scott.

"Hey guys," she shouted, "can I leave Scoot with you?"

"You bet, Barb!" replied Rick.

"Don't take your eyes off him, okay?"

I assured her, "Ten-four, honey!"

Rick walked over to help Scott down the stairs and then held his hand as they walked over to the grill. I smiled to myself. I was so delighted to have an eighteen-month-old son. And he was such a cute kid—a towhead with Paul Newman–blue eyes. Rick sat in a lawn chair and pulled Scott onto his lap as I put the hamburgers on the grill. As we talked and laughed, Scott got down to play in the grass.

Rick and I kept talking, and I kept flipping the burgers.

Barb interrupted our conversation as she called out the kitchen window. "Hey guys, where's Scott?"

"Oh, he's right here," said Rick—suddenly looking around for Scott.

We both quickly looked around and couldn't see him in the small yard between our home and Dr. Bacon's home.

"Where is he?" asked Barb, more alarmed, as she sped down the stairs.

"Honey, he was just right here!" I assured her.

"Not to worry, Barb. We'll find him," Rick exclaimed as he quickly stood.

I turned off the grill. "Rick, you take the driveway, and I'll look behind the garage."

Barb stripped off her apron and threw it on the steps. "I'll take the apple orchard."

I went out back and frantically looked behind the house. There was no Scott. I began to get distressed. I turned and searched behind the garage and looked down the back side of Hospital Hill—down to the recreation park. No Scott.

I could hear Rick and Barb calling for Scott. Their calls, like mine, were sounding more frantic by the moment.

I met Barb behind the garage. Her eyes reflected a storm of raw emotion—fear, anger, despair—as they filled with tears. I gave her a quick hug. "We'll find him."

Barb pulled away from me—looking at me in disbelief. I felt awful.

"Honey," I told her, "you go search around Dr. Bacon's house and I'll go search around Dr. Bacon's office."

I quickly walked around our house and Dr. Bacon's office. No Scott! Then I began to walk more quickly—out toward the street, where I ran into Rick.

"No luck!"

"Me either."

"Rick, you take behind the hospital, and I'll look behind Dr. Sale's and Dr. Mathieson's offices. We'll meet at your house."

"Sounds good, Walt."

As we separated, a Swain County sheriff's car drove slowly between us toward the hospital. There was a man in the back-seat—probably a prisoner headed to ER. We waved to the patrol-man. He waved back. I was scared to death we'd have to call the sheriff or police at any moment. I berated myself for not watching Scott more closely.

I could again hear both Barb and Rick calling for Scott as we all frantically continued our search.

As I called for Scott, my pace quickened and my forehead began to break out in a cold sweat. I felt dreadful—awful—com-pletely unqualified to be a father, unless you counted me as the worst father on earth. Why couldn't I have kept a closer eye on him? Did someone take him? Would they hurt him? Was he hurt or crying out for his mom or me? How could I ever face Barb again? I was beginning to feel nauseated.

When I got to Rick's house, Rick was coming up from behind the hospital. I could see the alarm on his face and the sweat on his brow. Our eyes met, and no words needed to be spoken.

Together we jogged back to the house. As we came up the driveway, Barb was sitting on the stairs panting.

There was no Scott on her lap.

When she saw us jogging empty-handed, she put her head between her knees and began to sob as Rick and I jogged up to her.

Rick spoke first. "Barb and Walt, I think we should call the police."

I nodded.

⎯⎯⬝⎯⎯

As Rick went inside to call the police, I felt like crying or throwing up—or both. I sat down on the stoop next to Barb and tried to put my arm around her shoulder. She pulled away from me, her head in her hands—continuing to sob.

As I turned my head away from Barb and toward the hospi-tal, I saw either a mirage or a miracle. I couldn't believe my eyes!

I actually rubbed them and looked again. There at the end of our driveway and walking toward us was Louise in her crisp, white nurse's uniform. No, she wasn't walking. She was marching! And smiling—a brilliant, white "I know something you don't know" smile. And in her arms was Scott!

I slowly stood—in disbelief—as my jaw fell open for the second time that day. "Barb, look! Rick, come here!" I heard Barb gasp and then felt her brush by me as she began to run down the driveway toward Louise, with Rick and I hot on her tail.

"Barb, is this your son?" cried Louise before Barb reached her.

"Scoot. Oh my goodness. Oh yes!" exclaimed Barb between sobs.

Louise held Scott out, and Barb grabbed him into her arms, holding him tight and continuing to sob—but this time tears of relief and joy.

"Where'd you find him?" asked Rick as he ran up beside us.

"I didn't find him, Dr. Pyeritz."

"Then who did?"

"Well, the sheriff was drivin' up Hospital Hill bringin' a prisoner up here for you to see. Halfway up the hill, about two hundred feet from your house, he saw this little blond-headed boy walkin' right smack down the middle of the road. So he stopped to pick him up, put him in the backseat for the prisoner to hold, and brung him up to my emergency room."

"And you knew it was Scott!" Barb cried.

"Well, not really, Barb. I just knew he was a little boy. I began to think to myself, 'Louise, who do I know what has a little boy?' I gotta confess, I didn't think of you and Dr. Larimore. I knew you took better care of your kids than that."

That stung. But Louise picked up the pain in my expression. "No offense meant."

"None taken, Louise."

Louise continued. "Well, Maxine came down and saw him and said, 'That there is Dr. Larimore's little boy. Shore 'nuff is.' I was confounded for sure. 'Cause I'll tell you the honest truth—I can't tell the difference between white kids. They all look the same to me."

Rick and I smiled at each other.

"Thanks, Louise. You're a lifesaver!" exclaimed Barb. "Thanks for bringing my baby home!"

Barb turned to go inside with Scott in her arms. Rick and I were left with Louise.

"Were one of you supposed to be watching that young'un?" asked Louise in her most condescending voice.

We both nodded our heads like schoolboys caught red-handed in a prank.

"I wouldn't want to be in your shoes." She turned and left.

"I don't want to be in my shoes either," I said.

"Well," Rick said, "let's go in and face the music."

chapter thirty-seven

FACING THE MUSIC

At the next Swain County General Hospital medical staff meeting, all doctors were present and accounted for. There were no items listed on the agenda under new business. However, when the chief of staff, Ray Cunningham, called for new business, Ken Mathieson slowly stood up.

"Dr. Cunningham, I'm sorry to have to do this again. But I must."

"What's on your mind, Ken?" asked Ray.

"It's come to my attention that there has been a serious breach of medical ethics in our hospital, and I would like to bring a formal complaint to the medical staff."

I began to feel sick. Only last year Dr. Mathieson had asked for Rick and me to be expelled from the medical staff. I had a sneaking suspicion he was behind the allegations about the nursery. And now here he was up to his old tricks. It didn't take long for my suspicion to be confirmed.

"I'd like to charge Dr. Larimore and Dr. Pyeritz with a breach of ethics."

"I second that charge," blurted out Dr. Bacon.

"I call the question," exclaimed Dr. Mitchell.

"What's the charge?" cried Rick, standing to his feet. "You can't do this again!"

I'm sure I was red-faced and caught totally off-balance. This was wholly and absolutely unexpected. Why hadn't Ray or Mitch let us know this was coming?

Then I realized all the men were smiling. Ray was snickering.

Dr. Mathieson answered, "The charge is failure to properly babysit. I move that these men lose their privilege to babysit. I further move that if they should babysit, they do it under the preceptorship of Mrs. Larimore or one of the other competent spouses of an active member of this medical staff."

Dr. Bacon seconded the motion while laughing hysterically.

Ray called out, "All in favor say 'aye'."

There were "ayes" all around, while the other doctors were laughing hysterically, and as a result there were only four dry eyes in the house.

"We've been had, partner," whispered Rick.

I smiled and nodded my head in agreement.

The other doctors, still laughing and snickering, slapped us on the back as they left.

"Those scoundrels planned and rehearsed the entire ambush," I muttered to Rick.

After the other doctors left the conference room, we were left alone with Mr. Douthit, who was still wiping his eyes and trying to smother his laughter.

"Hope you boys didn't mind that bit of humor on your account."

Rick commented, "I guess it was pretty funny."

"Indeed it was," Earl commented. Then he became serious. "But I'll tell you this. That couldn't have happened just a year ago. I think they like you boys. I think they consider you part of the team. I think your honeymoon is over, and I think this marriage is going to last. Congratulations!" He stood and left.

Rick chuckled. "Guess we had it coming, didn't we, Walt?"

I smiled. My thoughts returned to the evening Louise brought Scott home to us. Compared to the horrible round of possibilities, this embarrassment was a small price to pay.

—

$\mathcal{A}$fter the lights were out that night, I turned to hug Barb. Instead of turning toward me, as she usually did, she turned away—as she did only when she was frustrated or angry.

"Honey, we've already talked this through. I've told you how sorry I am. This was all my fault. I was a terrible babysitter. I know that. And I promise it will never happen again."

Barb was quiet. She didn't say a word or move a muscle.

"Honey, is there anything I can do to make this up to you?"

Barb instantly turned over to me. "Yes, there is!"

"Name it, honey. Just name it."

"Will you be in the Miss Flame contest?"

There was a long, long silence as Barb waited. I had been had—big-time. I had been had, and I had no one to blame but myself. I nodded my head in silent assent.

She laughed in delight as she hugged me and said, "And to all a good night!"

part five

ANOTHER SUMMER

chapter thirty-eight

FLESH-EATING
BACTERIA

$\mathcal{U}$nlike most of my older colleagues, I couldn't remember a time in my training or practice when we hadn't had the blessing of antibiotics for severe bacterial infections.

However, after decades of a steadily declining morbidity and mortality due to bacterial infection, the early 1980s saw a resurgence of severe, invasive bacterial disease. And in those days, none was worse than a bacterium called group A streptococcus.

The first case I saw was in a young woman named Georgia. About a week after a normal menstrual period, she came to the office with vaginal pain and a purulent vaginal discharge. At first I thought it was a severe form of vaginitis, but her fever, pain upon examination, and low blood pressure worried me enough to admit her to the hospital. Fortunately, intravenous antibiotics stopped the potential killer in its tracks. Only the next year would this type of infection be officially named—then labeled streptococcal shock syndrome or toxic shock syndrome.

But toxic shock syndrome was a mere lamb compared to its nasty cousin necrotizing fasciitis, which was reputedly one of the most severe and potentially fatal forms of invasive streptococcal disease around. With this illness, patients would suffer from rapid, local, deep soft-tissue destruction, severe septic shock, and multi-organ failure. It would often kill its victims quickly and very painfully. My first victim survived—albeit barely.

I didn't learn about his admission until I entered the nursing station to make Monday-morning rounds. Vernel met me as I entered the station. "Dr. Larimore, Dr. Sale admitted Carl Walkingstick to you last night. He's a diabetic patient of yours who has some cellulitis on his back. He was fishing down on Fontana and hooked himself in the back. Apparently that led to the infection. He's in the isolation room. I'd suggest you see him first. He's not really doing very well."

I quickly looked over his chart and became alarmed. His initial labs from the previous evening showed an extremely high white blood cell count—indicating a severe infection. However, even more ominous was an elevated creatine phosphokinase (or CPK) level. This enzyme is found in the blood only when muscle or brain tissue is dying. I quickly walked to Carl's room.

When I entered, he was alone and appeared to be sleeping. When I tried to awaken him, he only moaned—and that only came with a deep pain stimulus. Carl was unconscious, and his respirations were dangerously slow and his pulse perilously high. I punched the nurse call button. "Vernel, get down here right away!"

I quickly examined him. His heart and lungs sounded fine. His abdomen was soft and had normal bowel sounds.

Vernel appeared behind me. "Help me roll him over!"

We worked together to slowly roll the enormous man on his side. I lifted up his gown and gasped. Carl's back looked dreadful. Instead of being indurated and red or pink, as I would expect in a case of mild cellulitis, Carl's skin was thickened and swollen, with an ominous bluish or purplish coloration. However, the violet blisters covering the surface of his back were the most dooming.

"Dr. Larimore, his back didn't look like this when I came on my shift this morning—I promise!" Vernel exclaimed.

I nodded. "I believe you, Vernel." The skin was thick and tense. As my fingers probed, Carl moaned in pain.

"Vernel, get me the biggest syringe with the largest bore needle we have—and I'll need some culture tubes. I need to culture the leading edge of this infection. Let's switch him to stronger antibiotics, start oxygen immediately, and let's get him to ICU! Stat!"

"Yes sir!" Vernel exclaimed as she turned to leave the room.

"Oh!" I added, as Vernel turned toward me. "Call Ray or Mitch to come down here stat."

"Yes sir!" she responded as she exited.

I knew as soon as I saw his back that Carl had necrotizing fasciitis, which had been called streptococcal gangrene when I was in my training. It would be many years before it would be named flesh-eating bacteria by the lay media. It's a deep-seated infection of the subcutaneous tissue that results in progressive destruction of the fascial tissue and fat below the skin, but it may actually spare the skin itself. It is an infection that advances with striking rapidity and can eat away an entire limb or denude the tissue of the torso or the abdominal flesh in hours.

I knew that if we didn't get at least three powerful antibiotics into his system *and* get him to the operating room to clean out the deep infection, within a very short period of time the purple areas would become gangrenous. Then the dead skin would begin to slough off, revealing extensive necrosis of the subcutaneous tissue. Without emergency surgery and intensive care, Carl would likely die very soon.

Vernel returned with Betty and the equipment. "Ray will be here in a few minutes." A respiratory therapist ran into the room and set up the oxygen mask.

I quickly put on sterile gloves and took a sterile syringe and aspirated fluid from several of the blisters. I handed the syringe to Betty, who squirted the ominous dark fluid into a culture container.

Then Vernel handed me another syringe, and I plunged it into the skin on Carl's back, near the edge of the advancing infection.

Carl only moaned. I knew he didn't feel much of the pain. When the needle reached just below the skin, I pulled back on the plunger and thick, yellowish-green pus oozed through the large-bore needle into the syringe.

Just that moment, Ray entered the room.

"Look at this, Ray."

"Oh no!" he replied.

I gave him a quick history as he gloved and then examined Carl's back.

"Walt, I agree with you. We've gotta get 'im to OR. *Now!* I need to do an aggressive fasciotomy and debridement. It won't be pretty, but if we're lucky, we'll save his life. If we don't, this infection will spread over most of his body."

"Yep," I replied, trying to sound calmer than I was feeling inside.

"Are you changing his antibiotics?"

"I've already ordered high doses of triple antibiotics to be given stat. I'll get the pre-op labs, EKG, and chest X-ray if you can get OR ready."

"I'll do it!"

Ray turned to leave, and then he turned back to me. "Walt, I hope we're not too late."

Me too! I thought.

Early recognition is the key. Ray and I both knew that successful management of necrotizing fasciitis was dependent first and foremost on early detection.

In Carl's case, the appearance of the infection on his back actually helped me. In the 50 percent or so of the patients who develop necrotizing fasciitis without a defined portal of entry, the infection begins deep below the skin, frequently at the site of a muscle strain or traumatic joint injury. In these folks, the disease can mimic deep vein thrombophlebitis or a mild cellulitis. However, the presence of fever, increasingly severe pain, an unexplained fast heartbeat, a marked elevation of the white blood cell count, and an elevated creatine phosphokinase level all suggest necrotizing fasciitis and should prompt surgical cleansing of the deep tissues.

In the OR, Kim had no problem getting Carl under anesthesia. However, before we could start surgery, his blood pressure began to drop quickly.

Kim yelled out to Ray and me, who were scrubbing in the hall, "Dopamine okay?" Dopamine was a medication that would increase his blood pressure.

"You bet!" cried Ray, who shouted out the dose he wanted Kim to start. He then turned to Louise. "Louise, let Betty know I'll need some albumin and intravenous gamma globulin from the lab ASAP."

"Yes sir!" Louise responded as she quickly left the surgical suite to go to the lab.

"Albumin and gamma globulin okay with you, Walt?" Ray asked.

I was a bit embarrassed because I hadn't thought of these two medications—which were standard interventions for systemic infections that resulted in low blood pressure or shock. "Sounds good, Ray," I mumbled.

After finishing our scrub, we entered the operating room and quickly gowned and gloved, while Kim and the OR staff placed Carl on his side and scrubbed his back with Betadine. We placed the sterile surgical drapes in place, then Ray made an initial large incision across Carl's back. The skin was thickened from the infection, and it took a moment or two for us to slowly deepen the incision and control skin bleeders until we were finally able to enter the fat-filled space between the underside of the skin and the fascia, the thick leatherlike tissue overlying the back muscles.

What we found was astounding. Upon entering the space, the putrid smell nearly knocked us off our feet.

"Nice aroma, eh?" Ray kidded.

My surprise must have shown in my eyes.

"First case of necrotizing fasciitis?" he asked.

"Well, the first case I've accompanied to OR."

"It's not pretty. We've got lots of tissue to remove. Let's go to work!"

As we extended the incision, pus poured from the wound. We'd first irrigate out the pus and then break apart and remove any necrotic tissue and irrigate again and again.

"The solution to pollution is dilution with solution," Ray would mutter to no one in particular as he continued to cut out more and more gangrenous necrotic tissue. "Once we get all the necrotic tissue out, we'll have to leave the wound open to drain. It won't be pretty, and it's going to take weeks to heal—if he even survives. But we'll sure give it every shot we can."

chapter thirty-nine

THE BEST MEDICINE

Carl's recovery was long, slow, and painful. During the first week in ICU, he suffered from shock and multi-organ failure. For a short time he was on a ventilator and a dialysis machine. Because of intractable hypotension and diffuse leakage of fluid from his back, I had to give him massive amounts of intravenous fluids (up to 10 liters per day at one point). He also required lots of albumin replacement IV.

By the second post-op week, Carl was out of ICU. He suffered a lot of pain, but when his sense of humor returned, I knew he was out of the woods.

Fortunately, Carl had a good bit of help exercising his notorious sense of humor. One or more of his fishing buddies sat by his bedside for most of his hospitalization. When he felt discouraged, they were there with their terribly sophomoric jokes, and they'd incessantly kid him about his hospital gown. When he felt like giving up, they encouraged him and cheered him up.

One Saturday I was rounding with Kate at my side. I'd often take the children on rounds with me. The patients enjoyed getting to know them, and the kids seemed to enjoy entering their dad's world. On this day, Kate and I went to see Carl. They seemed to have an instant bond, and from that day until his death they were close.

Carl's pals were in the room that day. One of them looked across the bed at Kate and commented, "Katie, you are really walking well!"

Kate scowled at him. "My name's Kate!" she corrected.

He laughed and set her on his lap. "Well then, Kate. You are walking very, very well."

"My surgery was a success," she bragged. "Dr. Fitch says I am one of *his* best patients ever!"

"You're not fibbing to me, are you, Kate?"

"No sir. I don't tell stories. Mama says that's bad."

"Honey, do you want to know how you can tell when big Carl is lying?"

"How?" she asked.

"His lips are moving!"

The entire group melted into shrieks of laughter.

Another day, one of them told me, "Doc, Carl says you used a monster needle on his back. Carl, show Doc how big that ole needle was!"

Carl's effervescent smile filled the room as he held up his one arm. Where a man with two arms might have held out his hands to show how long the needle had been, Carl had only one. Holding out his hand and pretending to eyeball the length of the needle, he exclaimed, "It was this big!" And just as it had brought laughter on the docks of the Fontana marina, the effect was even greater in the hospital.

I smiled, but Carl's friends shook in laughter—causing Maxine to enter the room. "You all better shush up!" she scolded. "Don't make me come back in here and throw you out of the hospital like I had to last night!" They thought she was angry, but I could see the twinkle in her eye.

On another day, I walked into the laughter emanating from Carl's hospital room. One of Carl's friends was able to stop laughing long enough to look at me and remark, "Morning, Doc. We was just talkin' about Carl's funeral. I was asking Carl what he wanted me to say when I saw him in his big ole coffin." The man began to snicker. "Tell Doc, Carl. Tell him what you told me you want me to say!"

The men were all laughing so hard that tears were running down their cheeks. Carl wiped his tears and between guffaws looked at me and said, "Doc, when I'm in my coffin, I want Jimmy here to say, 'Looky there, he's breathin'!'" The room erupted in laughter—including mine.

Carl's pals provided for me a powerful lesson on the incredible healing influence of friends and community. It was true Ray and I had played a crucial role in recognizing Carl's pathologic process and then initiating a treatment plan that made his healing possible. But it's equally true that his friends were critical to his healing and even truer that they were responsible for his recovery.

As I left Carl's room that day, I thought back to Sam Cunningham, who believed that no one really cared for him. I reflected on Anne Smith and the other patients of mine who didn't feel close to anyone, who felt they had no one in whom to confide or to help them out of a bind. I considered my patients, such as Tim Johnson, who seethed in anger or harbored bitterness and grudges—those who simply could not practice forgiveness. It was my impression that these types of people had far more difficulty recovering from disarray, disease, or disaster—and premature death was much more likely to visit them. Thankfully, Tim had overcome his disability. Even more thankfully, Carl never suffered from it.

I learned in Bryson City in those early days of my practice that the impact our relationships and our attitudes have on our becoming or staying healthy cannot be overstated. My patient's friends taught me that, apart from our immediate family relationships, friends who love and care for us, who assure us that their unconditional support or help is available, provide a powerfully positive health benefit.

In fact, Solomon, considered one of the wisest teachers of all time, wrote, "As iron sharpens iron, so one man sharpens another."

He also wisely pointed out that "a cheerful heart is good medicine, but a crushed spirit dries up the bones." (See Proverbs 27:17 and 17:22.)

Finally, four weeks after admission, Carl was ready for discharge. It would be another six weeks before the large wounds on his back would be completely healed, and then six months of rehabilitation before he'd be back down to the dock at Lake Fontana, laughing and clowning around with his fishing buddies.

But if it weren't for them, I'm not sure he would have made it in the first place.

Carl was blessed to have friends who were happy and who laughed easily—and they were good medicine for his heart, his spirit, his soul, and his body.

chapter forty

THE BLESSING

$\mathcal{B}$y June, Kate's therapy had progressed far more quickly than expected—and her walking, although not normal, was far superior to any other form of mobility she had used in the past. When she tried, she could even run a few steps! With this increased ambulation came increasing independence—and when combined with the strong-willed nature of her brother, life became even more interesting for the Larimore household.

As was typical at that time of year in the Smokies, the days were becoming considerably warmer. The pool at the recreational park was open, and even though it was just down the hill from our house, we never chose to become members. Rather, we'd take the kids on hikes along Deep Creek and find a quiet, still pool where we could sit and read and the children could frolic and play.

As much as we enjoyed our time at Deep Creek, we had never tried the most popular tourist event at Deep Creek—tubing. So on this particularly delightful Saturday morning, we took advantage of the free passes that had been hanging on our refrigerator since Mrs. Nichols had given them to me the previous year.

"I hope they'll still honor these passes!" Barb exclaimed as we closed the door to the house behind us. We—and most of our neighbors—never locked our homes. There was just no need to do so back then.

The short drive up the Deep Creek road brought us to the Deep Creek Tubing Center, which was located at the entrance to the Great Smoky Mountains National Park. Peter Nichols welcomed us as we entered the store. He helped us pick out two appropriately sized tubes and then helped me load them in our trunk. He then gave me advice on how to "tube the creek."

We drove away from his store and headed up the creek. We parked at the end of the road. I carried the tubes as Barb held Kate's hand. Her walking was *so* much better. Scott toddled alongside us, exploring every large rock, summer wildflower, and small waterfall along the road. Any significant finding would elicit cries of "Dad, Mom, Kate! Come look!" We'd all stop to admire his discovery.

The creek echoed with the laughter and shrieks of others who were already tubing down the creek. I smiled as I heard the laughter.

After passing a waterfall that tumbled a hundred feet down from a small stream high up the side of the valley and then crossing an old bridge, we finally arrived at the tube "put in" spot. As we stepped into the tumbling creek, we all sucked in deep breaths. "This is ice-cold!" Barb shouted.

With Scott in Barb's lap and Kate in mine, we launched and were off! Years and years of previous tubers had moved rocks and small boulders so that the "tubing channel" was obvious. As the tubes bounced off rocks and over small waterfalls, the children shrieked and laughed with delight.

Before we knew it, we had arrived back at the parking lot.

"Let's go again, Dad!" Kate and Scott cried in unison.

Barb smiled, and I laughed.

We hiked up and rode down again and again. *We* hiked. I felt the tears welling up in my eyes. I could still hear the pediatric neurologist's prognosis: "She'll likely never walk or talk. She'll grow bigger, but she'll never get better."

Ah, I thought, *if only he could see her now!*

$\mathcal{I}$ had just finished seeing Mr. Walkingstick at the office one afternoon. The horrible wounds on his back were nearly healed. I expected the resulting scars to be lifelong, but I fully expected them to finally heal. As we were walking out of the exam room, he looked down and said, "Doc, I know you saved my life."

"Carl, I admit I did a lot of work. But as I often say, the healing comes from God—not me. And the will to live comes from you—not from me. And, last but not least, those scoundrels you call friends added enough laughter to drive away *any* unhealthy morale. So let me give you, your friends, and the Lord the credit. How's that sound?"

"Well, Doc, I'm gonna give some to you and Dr. Cunningham. And I've got somethin' for you."

He reached into his pocket and pulled out a small necklace. "I had this necklace made for your little girl. The woman who made it told me to tell you it's a gift from her also. Her name is Mrs. Black Fox." He handed it to me. The intricate beadwork was beautiful, and in the middle was a small piece of stone carved into the shape of a bear.

"Doc, in my tribe we believe the Great Spirit looks at a man and a woman before he gives 'em their first child. If the man and woman are strong and brave and spiritual, then the Great Spirit will give them one of what we call his special children."

I must have looked puzzled. He smiled and placed his hand on my shoulder. "Doctor, we believe these are the children many white people call handicapped or defective. We believe they are wrong. We believe these special children are specially gifted—that they'll have the ability to accomplish much for the Great Spirit, that they have a special call from him and a most special heart and spirit."

I continued to listen.

"This necklace was made in love. It is given in love and admiration of a powerful healer. It is for your special girl and the gifts you'll come to see in her. It is from me, the son of a chief, *da-na-wa-ga-we-u-we-e u-we-tsi*, to your daughter, who I call *u-tse-li-dv u-we-tsi ga-na-ga-ti a-le tsi-sa*."

"What does that mean, Carl?"

He smiled. "The precious daughter of a doctor and Jesus."

I felt tears welling up in my eyes as I looked into his kind, dark eyes. I knew this was a very special moment—and I vowed to remember and cherish it.

"Would you like to give it to her?" I asked him.

He smiled and shook his head. "It is best to come from her father—her *a-gi-do-da*. Dr. Larimore, there is great power in the father. No person can bless a child like a father. Do not forget that."

"I won't, Carl. Thank you."

And I never have forgotten the lesson.

Or the blessing given to me and my daughter by this gentle giant.

chapter forty-one

THE RUNAWAYS

*L*ater that afternoon, as I was standing and writing in a chart, I felt a small hand pulling on my pant leg, and looking down, I saw Kate and Scott, holding hands and looking up at me. I bent down to eye level.

"Hey guys!" I exclaimed as I gave them each a hug. I always wanted my children to know they could interrupt me at any time—and I made sure my staff knew it too. My children were one of my most wonderful responsibilities and priorities. I loved it when Barb walked them over to the office, which she did at least once a day since we had opened the new office. Having the office so close to our home offered many advantages.

"Where's your mom? In the front office with Dean?"

The kids looked at each other, and then Scott spoke up. "She's at the house."

"What house, Scoot?"

Scott smiled that "it's amazing how much you don't know" smile and said, "*Our* house."

Kate added, "We had a problem."

Now I was concerned. "What is it?"

They looked at each other—trying to decide who would spill the beans. Kate took a deep breath and then looked back at me. "Daddy, we *had* to run away from home."

"You did? Why?"

"Well, it was not very nice."

"What? The heat?" I asked, thinking of the fact that we still didn't have air-conditioning in the house.

"No. Mommy." Tears formed in her eyes.

"Here, let's walk into my office and chat." I looked up to see Beth standing in the hall just outside an exam room, tapping her watch.

"Five minutes. Okay?"

She smiled, and I turned to go into my office. Kate and Scott were hopping up onto the sofa. I sat in my desk chair and pulled it up in front of them.

"Tell me more."

Kate began. "This morning after breakfast Mommy told us she would take us to Deep Creek to go swimming. Then after our nap she broke her promise and said we couldn't go swimming."

"Why not?" I asked. Both kids shrugged their shoulders.

"We don't know," Kate replied. "But we knew we couldn't stay there anymore. We decided to run away. And this was the best place we could think of."

"Does your mom know you're here?"

Both kids shook their heads. "She was taking a nap on the couch in the living room. She said we had tired her out and she'd had enough," Kate explained.

I nodded and thought for a moment. "Well, a couple of things. First of all, I'm delighted you came over here. If you had run away to Asheville or Sylva, you probably wouldn't have had enough money to live very long. That would have meant getting a job. Work can be very hard, eh?" They both nodded.

"We don't have any money," Kate confided—almost in a whisper.

"Second of all, maybe we should let your mom know where you are. If she wakes up and you're not there, don't you think she'll be worried?"

They both looked at each other, and then Kate nodded.

I rolled the chair over to the desk and punched in our home phone number. "Hi, honey. Did I wake you up?"

"Yes!" I heard Barb yawn. "I was taking a little nap."

"Well, I'm sorry to bother you. I just wanted to let you know that your children ran away from our home."

"What!" she exclaimed. I could tell she was fully awake now.

"It's true. They're here in my office. Something about their mother breaking a promise to take them to Deep Creek. Know anything about this very serious allegation?"

I could hear her chuckle. "Who appointed you judge, Dr. Larimore?"

"I'm just trying to be a good family physician here."

"Hmm. Well, perhaps the little delinquents didn't tell you that the promise to go to Deep Creek was contingent on their cleaning up their rooms. When it didn't get done, I told them I was taking a nap. I told them if their room was clean when I woke up, we'd go. If not, I'd just start supper."

I smiled. "Well, Mrs. Larimore, I must confess I wasn't made aware of these additional facts by the defendants. Perhaps I can talk to your children and see if they'd be willing to return home and clean their rooms for you."

Suddenly both Kate and Scott looked very guilty.

Barb laughed. "Well, while you're doing that, I'll just take a little walk over there. Maybe you'd have time to give us a little family therapy."

"I'll have to check with my nurse, Mrs. Larimore. But I think we'll be able to squeeze you in."

I hung up and turned back to the kids. "I just talked to your mom."

They both nodded—having heard the entire conversation.

"Your mother says you didn't clean up your rooms."

"It's just not reasonable!" Kate exclaimed, with her brother nodding in concurrence.

"Why not?"

"Because it's our room. We know where all our toys are. And besides, isn't *your* room messy sometimes?"

I looked at the magazines and charts strewn all over my desk.

"Good point," I admitted. I thought quickly and only for a second, which is a critical skill for a parent—quick thinking, that is. "How 'bout this? If I clean my desk and Mom cleans our room and you all clean your rooms, then we'll go to the swimming hole together. How's that sound?"

"Yippee!" was the unanimous agreement.

"Okay, you stay in here—or let Miss Beth know if you go to the kitchen or waiting room. Your mom will be here in a few minutes. Let me finish seeing my patients, okay?"

Both nodded.

"Well then, let's shake."

We all shook hands.

I knew that later that evening I'd have to confront the issue of their running away. But for now I was in awe. The miracle was that Kate could walk at all. The marvel was that she could talk and make decisions. It was a wonder that she was beginning, for the first time, to show independence. And she and her brother were bonding in a very special way. When Barb and I were long gone, they'd still have each other. And what others saw as a disability in Kate, I could clearly see as a blessing.

That day I fell in love with my kids as never before.

chapter forty-two

GREAT SCOTT

The next day, I saw patients by myself at the office. Rick had the day off. He and Katherine planned a day hike with George and Elizabeth Ellison.

While I was standing in the hall writing on a chart, the back door flew open. I looked up to see Barb, obviously distressed, carrying Scott. She was holding a bloody washcloth on his head, and he was crying.

I quickly put the patient's chart in the rack. "Beth!" I called out to my nurse as I ran toward Barb. "What happened?"

I could tell Barb was upset, although she bravely tried to remain calm. "Scott was over at Georgianna's house playing with little Mitch. They were eating chocolate chip cookies. When there was only one left, Mitch wanted it. Scott didn't give it to him, so Mitch picked up a hammer and hit him over the head with the claw end. I was just walking up to their front door to pick him up when it happened. Georgianna gave me a washcloth, I applied pressure, and we walked right over."

As she talked, I reached out and took Scott from her and gave my sobbing son a hug. "It's going to be okay, Scoot." His sobs lessened to cries. I slowly removed the bloody cloth, and when I saw the bright red blood gush into the large scalp wound, I quickly reapplied pressure and lifted Scott and carried him down the hall toward our surgical room as Beth came running up. I was trying to remain calm. "Beth, Scott has a little cut on his head. Let's set up to fix it."

I carried him into the surgery room. "Scoot, I'm going to lay you down on the table here, partner."

I slowly laid him down as Patty quickly entered the room. "Patty, Scott's got a little cut on his head. Can you glove up and hold pressure for me?" After Patty's hand replaced mine, I performed a quick neurological exam on Scott. Other than his whimpering and deflated pride, his mental status and neuro exams were normal. Good news! There was no sign of a concussion. While I examined Scott, Beth unpacked a suture tray.

"Two percent lido with epi?" she asked. She was double-checking the type of local anesthetic I would want to use. For scalp wounds we'd usually use an anesthetic like lidocaine with epinephrine added—the lidocaine would numb the wound and the epinephrine would constrict the arteries, thus slowing down or even stopping the bleeding.

I nodded.

Beth asked, "Do you want 4-0 or 5-0 suture?"

With the question, Scott's eyes almost bulged out. "Sutures?" he asked, and his crying restarted with a vengeance. Suddenly I wished I didn't need to be both his dad and his doctor.

"Beth, let me take a look first." She could tell she had made an error. Later I would talk to her about not using the word *suture* when asking this question in front of kids. Knowledgeable nurses knew this—but every one of them had learned from experience.

"Scoot, I don't know if you'll need sutures or not. I just want to take a look and put some numbing medicine on your boo-boo to make the pain go away."

He was still crying. "Are you going to give me a shot?" he asked between sobs.

I didn't want to lie, as that was exactly what I was going to do. "Son, first I just want to take a look and take the pain away. Is that okay?"

He nodded his head, and the crying muffled to soft sobs. He sniffled, and I helped him sit up. I pulled out my handkerchief and had him blow his nose. Suddenly a thought came to me.

"Scoot, do you remember the bedtime story your mom read last night?"

He thought for a moment and then smiled. "Yes sir!"

"What was it about?"

"A little boy who had bad things happen."

"That's right. The little boy's father taught him that when you're sad or when bad things happen, you need to remember that God loves you and that he'll walk with you through the tears. You just gotta trust him."

Scott's smile spread across his face. "Sounds like you were listening."

It was my turn to smile. "Yep. And it's true for you right now. You've got a boo-boo, but God loves you, and he'll be here with you and me while I fix things up. Okay?"

Scott reached out, and we hugged each other.

Closing the wound was not traumatic—yet I purposefully avoided being my family's doctor whenever possible. I wanted to be family and not physician for my relatives—especially Barb, Kate, and Scott. One of my professors had said, "The physician who doctors his or her family has fools for patients." Although that sounded a bit harsh to me, I understood his intent.

⟞⟝

That evening, after saying our bedtime prayers with Kate and Scott, Barb and I walked out to the bench to share a few quiet moments. We both gazed out over Deep Creek Valley—deep in our own thoughts.

"Walt, you did a good job with Scott."

I put my arm around her and pulled her close. "Thanks. I'm just glad little Mitch didn't crack Scott's skull or give him a concussion."

"Me too!" Barb paused for a moment and then continued. "You were sweet with him."

We locked eyes and then just spent some time in silence. Barb broke the silence. "When we first found out about Kate's cerebral palsy, do you remember how it shook us to the core?"

I felt a sudden shudder in my heart. Had it not been for Barb's faith in God and her prayers, I wonder if our marriage would have survived. I felt my eyes filling with tears. I had not been a good husband during that time. I had turned from my family, and Barb had to carry too much of the load.

"Barb, I remember getting so angry at God when that happened. I remember shaking my fist at him and asking, 'God, why did you do this to me?' I now know those 'why' questions usually have no answer—at least on this side of eternity. I think I've learned over time that the proper approach is to realize that God is in control, and the appropriate question is 'God, what is it you're doing here—what do you want to teach me?'"

Barb sighed. "I think you're right on target, honey."

I pulled her close, and we hugged for a few minutes. When I let go, she looked up into my eyes and smiled.

"What are you thinking?" I asked.

"So, Dr. Larimore, I guess the moral of the story is that when you're sad or mad or when you have a problem, don't blame it all on God, because he loves you. And he'll walk with you through the tears. You just gotta trust him. Okay?"

I smiled, realizing that what Barb and I were trying to teach our children mirrored what our Father in heaven was trying to teach us.

chapter forty-three

MISS FLAME

The dreaded day finally arrived.

July 4 dawned clear and bright—unfortunately—with not a cloud in the sky. But even if it *had* rained, I still would have been up a creek without a paddle. They would have just moved the dreaded competition to an indoor location. The contest was to include an evening gown competition, a swimming suit competition, and a live interview. Barb had been working with Michelle Robertson to gather my wardrobe. I had no desire to model for them or to try on my feminine attire any sooner than absolutely necessary. If there was any consolation, it was that the group of contestants would include other prominent members of the community—including two of the assistant football coaches, a dentist, a banker, an attorney, and other such notables.

The Fireman's Day fund-raiser included a road race, lots of food booths along Main Street, games for the children, a dunking booth, and rides for the kids on the fire engine. While the town folks were enjoying their day, the other contestants and I were holed up in the old courthouse, getting readied by our all-too-eager wives and friends.

Michelle and Barb continuously giggled as they placed me in an overstuffed bra and then squeezed me into what would become an overstuffed midnight-blue sequined evening gown. Then came a long blond wig donated by some cruel person, plenty of face and lip makeup, gaudy earrings, a pearl necklace, and then—to end it all—stiletto high-heeled shoes. I determined that whoever invented high-heeled shoes had a warped sense of humor. I also determined, after only a few practice steps, that my ankles and knees were in grave and imminent danger.

"Did we tell you your name?" Michelle asked.

"My what?" I replied.

"Oh, Walt, I forgot to tell you," said Barb. "Monty wanted each of you to have a name. So Michelle and I named you Waltina Larina Bustmoore."

I was now in official—perhaps even irreversible—shock. I just moaned and tried to hide my face in my hands, but I was jerked back to a sitting position by Michelle. "No!" she exclaimed. "You can't ruin your makeup!" Nevertheless, I'm sure there was no makeup that could hide the dismay and apprehension on my face!

When the time for the contest began, each of the unhappy contestants was paraded before what appeared to be the entire town—all gathered on the lawn of the old courthouse. The cat-calls and whistles were drowned out by the laughter as each contestant was recognized and then verbally harangued and berated.

My walk down and back the contestants' ramp seemed to take an eternity. And when each contestant stumbled in his high heels or over a long skirt, the crowd's howls only grew in intensity.

After my walk on the stage, I was whisked back into the court-house by Barb and Michelle. They tried to encourage me as they changed me from an evening gown into a one-piece swimsuit. It was bright red and very shiny.

"Where'd you get this?" I asked incredulously.

Barb and Michelle giggled. "Believe it or not," Barb replied while stuffing an amazing amount of padding into the soon-to-be overstuffed cups of the swimsuit, "this came from Eloise Newman's closet."

I was stunned. "You mean Pastor Newman's wife?"

"Yep," replied Barb.

"The registered dietician at the hospital?"

"One and the same," Michelle confirmed.

"Stand still, Walt!" commanded Barb. "I need to tie this over-sized scarf around your waist."

"Why?" I asked.

Barb looked at Michelle, and they both laughed.

"What's up?" I inquired.

"Just hiding the family jewels!" Barb explained between giggles.

"Next we're going to give you the tanned look," Michelle stated.

They turned me around, applying what they called a bronzing makeup. Then they turned me like a top, inspecting their work. Barb gave me a kiss on the cheek. "Break a leg, honey!"

"Where are you going?" I pleaded.

"The kids and I will be out there watching the contest and rooting for you."

Before I could protest, she was gone. As I looked around the room, the sight of a group of very uncomfortable men disguised as women made me laugh. *Some of these guys,* I thought, *are incredibly ugly women.* I took a mental picture I've never forgotten. The hairy legs and chests were a sight to behold. Seeing the beer bellies stuffed into bikini bathing suits was even more hilarious!

As the Miss Flame contestants were paraded out together on the stage, the town must have agreed. The laughter and applause were deafening.

One by one, like sheep to the slaughter, we were escorted down the aisle between the crowds by fire chief Monty Clampitt. Monty was laughing as hard as anyone else. When I walked down the aisle, the crowd erupted in catcalls, whistles, and laughter. I tried to keep my chin up and flash a smile—but it was pretty difficult. Not as difficult as walking in stiletto heels, mind you, but difficult nevertheless.

After we all had been paraded before the crowd, Monty asked each of us a question. Most of the questions were humorous, and the answers only added to the laughter—especially since the voices of the Miss Flame contestants were so very testosterone deepened.

As Monty approached me, I began to feel a bit nervous.

"Miss Waltina," he began, gawking at the size of my upper torso to the chuckles of the crowd, "just what size cup do you have there, ma'am?"

The crowd howled, which gave me time to think.

"I don't use a cup for my coffee, Monty," I responded. "I use a mug."

Monty smiled, again gazing at my padded anatomy. "Indeed, Miss Waltina, you have very admirable mugs."

The crowd roared its approval.

"One more question, Miss Waltina."

I nodded my approval—as if I had any choice at all.

"What would be the best and the worst thing about becoming Bryson City's first-ever Miss Flame?"

I tried to smile, but it felt so forced. "Well, Monty, the best thing would be for the rest of the contestants—who wouldn't have to bear this, uh, incredible responsibility for the next year."

The femininely dressed men standing next to me applauded their approval.

"And the worst thing?" Monty asked.

"Having to dress up like this next year to crown next year's Miss Flame."

The crowd both laughed and applauded. Now the pressure was off, and we had to stand and await the decision of the judges.

It had finally come time to name Bryson City's inaugural Miss Flame. The only reward I would obtain by participating was that I'd *never* have to compete again—that was the one guarantee we contestants had in writing from the fire department.

Thus, when the announcement was finally made that one Waltina Larina Bustmoore was the city's first Miss Flame, I nearly cried—and if I had, they would *not* have been tears of happiness, I'll tell you that!

That evening, after putting the children to sleep, Barb and I slipped out back to sit on our bench and look across the mountains.

"I'm proud of you," Barb whispered as she nuzzled under my arm.

"Barb, today was so embarrassing."

"I know, honey. But it was for a good cause. It really was."

"I guess so. At least I have the solace of knowing that Rick's going to have to enter next year."

Barb laughed. "Yes indeed. In fact, Katherine and I are already talking about how we're going to dress him up. The only problem is going to be his beard. We'll have to figure out something to do about that."

"Well, I'll tell you this, Barb. I have a lot more respect for women—what with the wig and makeup and bra and high heels. It's just *too* much."

Barb chuckled.

"Honest, Barb," I said. "If I had to dress up and get made up like that every day, I think I'd want to cry."

Barb laughed softly. Then she pushed away from me and turned to face me. "Oh, I forgot to tell you."

"Tell me what?"

"Do you remember walking down the aisle after being named Miss Flame?"

"Unfortunately."

"And do you remember wearing your tiara and carrying the bouquet of kudzu vines and waving to the crowd?"

"Regrettably I do. Why?"

"Well, your son was sitting on my lap, and he turned and asked me, 'Mom, who is that lady?'"

"I said, 'Son, that's *your* dad.'"

"And?" I asked, sure that *my* son would have been so proud of my sacrifice—of my donating my body and my reputation to such a worthy community event.

Barb paused and then sighed. "Well, Walt, he began to cry."

"Are you serious?"

Barb nodded.

We sat in silence for a few moments.

Slowly Barb began to chuckle. Then I followed.

Before we knew it, we were both laughing and hugging—Mrs. Larimore and the new Miss Flame, embracing on a bench overlooking one of the most special of towns in one of the most special of places, a place we now called home.

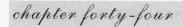

chapter forty-four

THE SUMMONS

$\mathcal{B}$eth walked quickly into my office. "Dr. Larimore, I need you in the treatment room. Now!"

I threw down the chart I was reading and quickly followed her down the hall and into our procedure room. Inside the room, Patty was placing a blood pressure cuff on a distinguished-looking gentleman with beautiful gray hair and a tanned face—but he was ashen. I instinctively felt his forehead, which was cold and clammy. His lungs were clear, and his heart and abdomen sounded normal to a quick check with the stethoscope.

As I examined him, Beth gave me some history. "His name is Dan Autrey. He lives in a development above the Nantahala Outdoor Center. He was working in his yard, clearing some brush, when he was stung on the head and neck by several yellow jackets. His wife said he began to get welts and then began itching all over. She drove him down here to the office after giving him a 50-milligram Benadryl capsule."

Patty finished taking his blood pressure. "His BP is only 60 systolic!" she exclaimed, indicating an abnormally low blood pressure. "Pulse is 100 and thready. Respirations 32."

"Patty," I barked, "let's get an IV started. Lactated ringers wide open."

"Yes sir!" Patty responded as she turned to the supply cabinet.

"Beth, get an EpiPen and give one dose sub-q, stat."

I turned my attention to the patient. "Mr. Autrey, can you hear me?" He nodded. "Can you say anything?"

He appeared to try, but he could only whisper. I could not understand his words.

"Beth's going to give you a shot in a second. It should help."

He nodded again.

Although reactions to insect stings were not uncommon in the mountains, the more severe variety, such as this one, were, fortunately, less common. I knew that with the treatment, he'd likely be better in just a few moments.

Patty had the IV started quickly. I always admired how well and how quickly she and Beth worked under pressure. It was probably their experience in the hospital that had helped the most.

Beth took the cover off the epinephrine syringe, wiped the patient's skin with an alcohol swab, and then plunged the short needle through the skin and into the subcutaneous tissue.

I stood back, waiting for the inevitable response, which happened within just a few seconds. Dan's color improved and his breathing slowed down. He blinked his eyes a few times, and I nodded to Patty to take his vital signs again.

"Blood pressure's up to 90 over 60, pulse 90, respirations 22."

I felt Dan's forehead. It was warmer.

"Feeling better?" I asked.

He smiled. "I am."

It was my turn to smile. "Mind if your wife comes back to sit with you?"

"That would be fine," he said.

I turned to Beth. "Let's give him another 50 milligrams of oral Benadryl. Okay?"

She nodded, and I left to go see another patient.

*W*hen I returned to the treatment room, Dan was sitting up on the procedure table. He looked much better. At his side, holding his hand, was a beautiful woman who appeared to be somewhat younger than Dan.

As she stood, I introduced myself.

"And," she replied, "I'm Boots Autrey."

"Where are you from?" I inquired. I was fairly certain they weren't from Swain County, and the development in which they lived was reportedly inhabited—some locals said *infested*—with Floridians.

"We're from a small town in central Florida called Kissimmee. It's near Disney World."

I smiled. "My wife and I honeymooned at Disney World, and we celebrated our tenth anniversary there last fall."

This comment seemed to spark Boots's interest. "Did you like it?"

I nodded. "We did—both times!"

She looked at me. "Then why don't you come practice in our little town? We need some new doctors down there. And I can tell you, you'd have *no* problem building a practice down there."

I chuckled to myself. *Floridians!* I thought. *They come up here in the good weather, buy up our land, and run up our prices. Then they leave in winter. And what's more,* I thought, *they don't know how to drive on mountain roads. Nothing worse than needing to get somewhere and getting stuck behind a Floridian!*

"Mrs. Autrey," I responded, "I think central Florida would be the *last* place in the United States I'd want to set up a practice!"

She smiled at me. "Could those be what are called 'famous last words'? It's awfully beautiful country down in Osceola County. Big lakes with big ole bass and great fishing. Oak trees and Spanish moss. Wonderful people. No snow or ice. Good schools and churches. Great place to raise a family and build a practice. You'd love it!"

I cocked my head at her. "Do you work for the Chamber of Commerce down there?"

It was Dan's turn to laugh. "She should, Dr. Larimore. She should!"

I smiled. "Tell you what. If the Lord ever leads us away from here, I'll give you all a call. Sound okay?"

"It's a deal!" Boots responded.

I finished my visit with them and gave Boots instructions on how to care for Dan and the bites. I handed her a prescription of an antihistamine for him to take over the next three days, and I also gave her a prescription for an Epinephrine Pen to keep at the house.

I had Beth explain to them how to use the EpiPen in the event of future bites that resulted in a severe reaction, and I had her suggest they take the prescriptions down to Doc John to get them filled. I knew he'd give them other potions for the bites, instructions on avoiding future bites, and an abundance of other advice they probably neither wanted nor needed but would certainly be entertained by!

I felt fairly certain they couldn't get his type of service in Kissimmee, Florida.

⌐

Just three days later, Barb and the children left Bryson City to visit Barb's parents at their summer home on a beach near Pensacola, Florida. Unfortunately, we started planning the trip a bit too late, so it coincided with a long-scheduled vacation that Rick had planned to the Outer Banks with George Ellison—with whom Rick was developing a fast friendship.

Also, I'm delighted to say, Barb left town before Pete Lawson's coverage of the Fireman's Day in the weekly *Smoky Mountain Times,* which came out on Thursdays. His coverage of the day was excellent, with one glaring and conspicuous flaw—his poor choice to place a picture of one Miss Waltina Larina Bustmoore in the paper!

I knew I could not put this awful "triumph" into my past—at least not yet. But I did have the consolation of knowing that Barb wasn't there to collect copies of the article and its pictures to mail to family across the nation. *Maybe,* I mistakenly thought, *we can keep the news of this so-called marvelous event confined to the general vicinity of the southern Smoky Mountains!*

So I found myself deserted by my family and my partner to endure the seemingly endless ridicule of physicians, hospital staff, our office staff, and my patients. The most insufferable comments flowed from Louise and Vernel, who'd incessantly ask for my makeup and hair-styling suggestions—and then laugh hysterically as I muttered and mumbled in consternation. I wondered if my life would *ever* return to normal!

The only good news I received that week was that my good friend and mentor during my internship, Dr. John Hartman, and his wife, Cleta, would be coming through the area that weekend and had called to express their interest in visiting Bryson City for a night. My hope was that they'd at least be able to come and go without being exposed to the local gossip tabloid—as I now called the *Smoky Mountain Times.*

The Hartmans arrived in town late Friday afternoon while I was seeing patients. Dean took them over to the house and showed them the guest room. After they had gotten settled, they came over to the office to take a look around. Although there were only two of us practicing in the office, it was designed to easily expand to hold additional staff and physicians—although we weren't sure if that might ever happen.

After they toured the office, I took them on a very brief tour of the hospital. Fortunately, Louise was off that night, and equally fortunately, the hospital was busy enough that none of the staff had any time to mention the events of the week. The Hartmans seemed impressed by the scope of staff and services available at our small, forty-bed hospital. I realized how proud I was of our small facility.

When it came time for supper, I knew that a visit to the Hemlock Inn or the Fryemont Inn would invariably produce comments about the Fireman's Day activities. I thought about escaping to the Jarrett House in a neighboring community or to Mabel's Table at the Holiday Inn in nearby Cherokee, but it seemed too much trouble, especially given the fact that the somewhat more decorous and much smaller Frye-Randolph House was available.

Since the Frye-Randolph House was normally fully occupied by tourists, the chance of a "safe" visit and private conversation were vastly increased. I called Bill Adams, the proprietor, and he indicated he would gladly provide a private table for me and my guests.

The house was located just below the Fryemont Inn and could easily be accessed without being seen at the inn.

I parked the car at the house, and we walked up to the gracious manor where we were to dine. What was then known as the Frye-Randolph House was initially a small Victorian lodge built in 1895 by Captain Amos Frye. The captain later expanded it to an L-shaped plan, complete with lovely gables and a stone-pillared porch.

Captain Frye and his wife, Lillian, lived in the house while the captain's palatial Fryemont Inn was being constructed just up the hill. After the captain's death, Lillian, by then the first practicing female attorney in western North Carolina, continued to practice law and run the inn until her death in 1957.

We sat outside in the courtyard until the dinner bell was rung and then were escorted into the beautifully kept home. Only the tourist brochures on one wall distracted from what appeared to be a very comfortable and luxurious private home.

We were shown into a private dining room where linens covered the table and candles glowed warmly. Our five-course meal was highlighted by light, friendly conversation. Bill and Ruth, the proprietors, were in and out of the room and were, as was their habit, always present when needed and absent when not.

After dinner, Ruth escorted us to the sitting room. A small fire was burning in the fireplace, which, given the coolness of the evening, was warming and comfortable. Our conversation turned to the future.

"Walt," John began, "I'm finishing my commitment in the Navy next year. Cleta and I are beginning to consider practice options."

I nodded and took a sip of my after-dinner coffee.

John continued. "This seems like such a lovely little town. Any chance we might be able to settle here?"

I thought for a moment before replying. John was a wonderful friend. We had become very close during my internship year at Duke University Medical Center when he was a senior resident.

"John," I responded, "practicing medicine with you would be a dream come true—especially since you, Rick, and I were such good friends at Duke." I paused, as there was a check in my spirit, and then continued. "But I'm not sure there's room for another physician here. This town has about a thousand residents, and our referral area has about 25,000 folks. But there are two surgeons here who both practice general medicine and another five GPs if you include Rick and me. I'd absolutely love for you to come here, but I'd be somewhat concerned about whether our practice would be busy enough for all of us."

"When you came here, weren't you told that some of the older physicians were planning to retire? Any retirements in the future here?"

I smiled. "You're right about our being told there were physicians who wanted to retire. But it doesn't appear to be true. And to tell you the truth, I don't see any in the foreseeable future."

John nodded. "Any chance you'd ever leave here?"

I smiled. "I haven't given it a thought. Why?"

"Another option we're considering is joining a couple of my Navy colleagues. They're FPs who are finishing their commitment about the same time I am. We all work together in the Family Medicine residency program at the Pensacola Navy Station. They are really good doctors, and we're looking at working together in a small town in central Florida."

"Where?" I asked, suddenly curious.

"Oh, it's just a small town. I doubt you've ever heard of it."

"Try me."

"It's a small town near Disney World called Kissimmee."

I laughed out loud.

"What's so funny?" Cleta asked.

"You won't believe this, but a couple from Kissimmee came into my office just this week. And they tried to encourage me to move my practice to Florida."

"Would you?" she asked.

"Cleta," I responded, "I think Barb and I would be so happy to practice with you guys. But central Florida would be the *last* place in the world we'd want to set up a practice!"

She smiled at me. "Walt, you should *never* say never. The area is gorgeous and has big lakes surrounded by majestic oak trees covered with Spanish moss. The people are wonderful, and the pace is slow. They also have good schools and churches."

Cleta sounded just like Boots Autrey. And I did not consider it a mere coincidence that two people had mentioned the same town in the same week. Was I being summoned to another path—another place?

chapter forty-five

DISTANT THUNDER

That night, after the Hartmans had turned in for the evening, I walked out back to sit on the bench behind our home.

A full moon lit up Deep Creek Valley all the way to the distant ridge lines, over fifteen miles away, which separated North Carolina and Tennessee.

As I sat there, just reflecting and contemplating, my mind thought back over my time in Bryson City. Barb and I had arrived as strangers—more unwelcome and unwanted by many than we ever could have imagined. Yet this small town served as the formative setting for my first medical practice experiences.

My marriage was maturing here. I was deeply in love with the wonderful woman God had given to be my wife-for-life. Kate was growing and doing so much better with her cerebral palsy. For a child who had been predicted never to walk or talk, she was doing just fine with *both,* thank you. Her surgery had permanently changed her physically and me professionally. Scott, despite his strong-willed and independent nature, was developing into a fine young boy—one who was molding his environment and his parents by his energy, enthusiasm, and exuberance. Although the day I "lost" him was still an embarrassment, it sure did remind me of how incredibly important he was to me and his mom.

I had a wonderful family, and my memories of spending time with them along Deep Creek and during our mountain drives and hikes were especially vivid.

I had grown so very much, not only as a person, a husband, and a father but also as a physician. I had learned how bitterness, anger, and loneliness could kill—and had seen firsthand the healing salve of friendship and laughter. I smiled as I remembered Carl and his friends.

Katherine had gone out of her way to help us feel welcome—as had the rescue squad, the Park Service rangers, Pastor Hicks, and, especially, Doc John and Becky. John and Ella Jo Shell at the Hemlock Inn had become special friends, as had the Douthits and the Jenkinses.

I practiced medicine with my best friend—an incredibly skilled physician with our patients and my family. Thankfully, Mitch and Ray had given us a practice home in which to start—and then allowed our staff to train under the experienced eyes of their staff. Dr. Bacon's vote had helped us survive an attempted coup, and my relationship with him was both warming and maturing. Mitch and Ray had become both professors and friends.

Peggy taught me about the importance of women attending women in labor and delivery—women who would two decades later be called "doulas." I had also been taught much by the granny midwives, the Cherokee people, and my patients.

Most of the nurses at the hospital seemed to be comfortable with Rick and me—despite our many ways that were new to them—and Louise in particular had made me feel welcome. In fact, I had developed a fond affection for her.

I had seen my first patients with HIV/AIDS, toxic shock syndrome, and flesh-eating bacteria before those diseases were even described in the medical literature. I also had experienced the dramatic impact of sensitively, and with permission, integrating spirituality into my medical practice. It was exhilarating and inspiring to see some of my patients' medical problems become the foundation and initiation of their own spiritual growth. And to be at the bedside of a patient who began a new life spiritually on the day he died physically had been a profound experience.

I sighed and then bowed my head to thank the Lord for my many blessings.

Most of all, I was thankful for a God who would call me into a personal relationship with himself—a Creator who desired to know me, One who deeply and unconditionally loved me. I simply could not imagine my life without his presence and peace. I was immeasurably thankful for his blessing, for my practice, and for my family.

As I looked up and across the silvery mountains, I felt the cool summer breeze blowing across my face. I knew I could be satisfied here in Bryson City—for many years to come. Barb and I desired a large family, and I knew this would be a great place to grow a practice and raise a family.

After what seemed to be an eternity of education—college, medical school, fellowship, and residency—not to mention the not-so-easy initiation into the private practice of medicine in a small, somewhat closed mountain town, it finally seemed to me that life had a rhythm and a meaning, a deeply satisfying and rewarding cadence.

Yet I sensed a deep, nagging disquiet. To have two couples suggest a move to Kissimmee in the same week seemed to me more than a coincidence. I had come to believe that apparent coincidences were only God's way of staying anonymous. I wondered if a change in my plans for myself and my family's life wasn't looming.

As I looked across Deep Creek Valley, I could see dark clouds and lightning on the horizon. Then the distant sound of thunder echoed across the valley. I didn't realize that the storm gathering on the horizon was symbolic of one on the horizon of the Larimores' life. I had no idea that within a month I would receive some terrible news—news that would shatter me, my family, and my future.

But for the moment, I decided I was finally at home—at least as at home as I could be on this planet. By the end of my quiet time, I had pushed Kissimmee out of my mind and was sensing a deep tranquility and harmony—despite the unforeseen storms that were coming.

I was convinced that although I did not and could not know what the future was to hold, I could be and was utterly certain of the One who did hold it—and me—in his hands. For now, that was all I needed to know. It was enough.

As I stood to go inside, a loud clap of thunder boomed across Bryson City. I looked over my shoulder. A storm was moving toward me faster than I could have imagined.

$\mathcal{S}$ome of the characters revealed herein are real and some still reside in Bryson City, while others have moved away. Some still keep in touch with me, for which I am appreciative. Many are still friends—even after having their stories divulged in both this book and its prequel, *Bryson City Tales*—for which I am even more thankful.

However, virtually all of the characters described in this work are only composites of one or more real people, and most bear names that are purely fictional—primarily to protect the identity of those on whom the story was based and secondarily to protect those who are either blameless or grumpy or both. Many times I've changed the name, gender, and age of people (and especially patients) to protect their confidentiality and privacy—as they never planned to have their stories divulged in the public square. Therefore, those readers who think they recognize a friend or acquaintance in these pages should consider it a most unlikely happenstance.

Some of the influential characters mentioned in this book have passed on and will have no opportunity to tell their side of the same story. Some, I suspect, would be pleased with what I have recorded about their impact on my life; others, I'm sure, would protest—perhaps vociferously.

Some of the stories in this book are recorded as they actually happened, or at least how I remember them happening; however, most of the stories did not occur exactly how or when they are written. Artistic license was employed frequently and unapologetically. You see, I'm hoping one day to be a "certified storyteller."

Working to obtain such a license, I've been led to believe, allows a writer to use his or her imagination to rearrange history to improve a story—as long as the chronicle is still true in its essence. I attempted to write this book in such a way that I might not be disqualified from eventual certification.

Thanks to Donna Lewis for reviewing the rough draft of this book. Thanks to Traci Mullins for expertly and professionally tearing apart the original submission and helping me put it back together again into a much more coherent and pleasant read. The best book editor I've ever worked with, Cindy Hays Lambert, depleted a case of red ink pens and several months of incredibly valuable time while making the innumerable and incredible suggestions that have improved this book dramatically. Then, when I had rewritten the book for the fifth time and everything was correct and in order, Dirk Buursma read it and corrected at least a thousand additional errors. Thanks, Dirk! Nevertheless, for any remaining mistakes, I take full credit.

Thanks to Barb, my wife-for-life, for not only reviewing the manuscript for accuracy but allowing me, along with Kate and Scott, to share their stories with you. I owe a debt of gratitude to my elder board at the Little Log Church in Palmer Lake, Colorado. My books are reviewed and approved by my elders. Thanks to Pastor Chris Taylor, Jeff Ball, Rick Fisher, Tom Nicholls, and Ron Rathburn for their review and insightful comments.

Thanks to the team at Zondervan (Bruce, Scott, Lyn, Cindy, Sue, Cris, Sherry, Greg, and Verne), who upon hearing some of these stories believed in this book before it was ever written and in me before I was ever published. Thanks to Rick and Deb Christian and Lee Hough at Alive Communications, who not only represent me but have become special friends. Thanks also to my longtime legal counselor, Ned McLeod.

I owe a debt to Ben Skillman, who allowed me to invade his Pontalba apartment on Jackson Square in the French Quarter of New Orleans to write a great deal of this book. The baroness

Micaela Almonester de Pontalba built the apartments over 150 years ago. She designed the brick building in grand European style, with shops on the street level and apartments above. She is said to have personally ordered the decorative cast iron of each apartment's balcony from a firm in New York and had it shipped down the Mississippi River. The initials of her maiden and married names (an "A" and a "P" intertwined) can still be seen in the iron railings of the balcony behind which I wrote—overlooking the eighteenth-century slate-covered streets, the statue of General Andrew Jackson in the middle of the park bearing his name (with my view being the west end of his east-facing horse), and the steeple of the St. Louis Cathedral, the country's oldest cathedral. Each morning I wrote to the nostalgic music of the steam calliope playing from a paddle-wheel steamer—the *Natchez*—and listened to the quarter-hour chimes of the cathedral bells.

Thanks also to Norm and Carolyn Boeve and Stan and Inez Shaw for allowing me to use their vacation homes (the former in the Rocky Mountains and the latter on a quiet Florida beach) for writing. Without these quiet, inspirational places to retreat, meditate, think, pray, and then write while avoiding the office, TV, email, phone, and so many other instruments that promote the urgent over the important, this book simply would not have happened. I also appreciate Mort and Lainey White, the current proprietors of the Hemlock Inn (Lainey is John and Ella Jo Shell's daughter) for allowing me to call them and to check innumerable facts. They also provided resources used to create the Bryson City map in this book. I'm thankful for Tammi Burns, who provided Swain County High School yearbooks for me to use in the checking of facts.

I also owe a debt to Bryson City and its people. These selected stories represent only a small portion of all that could be told about these special people—our "southern highlanders"—who represent, at least once you come to know them, a warm and gentle people. They slowly took me in and welcomed me into their community. This book represents a special thank-you from me to them—for who they are to me, what they mean to me, and what they've taught me.

As you read about the events that occurred at the dawn of my medical career, I want you to know that similar books could have been recorded by countless other family physicians across rural America—with, of course, some personal and geographic variations. This particular composition is intended to be more a record of this type of practice (vanishing as it is)—and the personal and professional growth it produced in almost any young physician of that era—than the partial autobiography of any single one.

Walt Larimore, M.D.
Colorado Springs, April 2004

chapter one

BLOODY MESS

*H*ey, Walt."

I recognized Rick's voice on the other end of the line. Rick Pyeritz and I were both family physicians and had practiced together for four years. Before moving to Bryson City in 1981, we had been family medicine residents together at Duke University Medical Center.

"What's up?" I asked him.

"I need some help, partner. I'm over in the ER sewing up a woman who stabbed herself several times. When the EMTs brought her in, she was hysterical, so I had to sedate her pretty heavily. Anyway, Don and Billy said she apparently murdered her husband in their home and then tried to do herself in. Since I'm going to be here awhile, would you be willing to go to the crime scene and do the medical examiner's report?"

My heart began to beat a bit more quickly, as it always did when I received a call from the emergency room or a summons to the scene of a crime, and I suspected that the suspense of the unknown—of the surprises one might find waiting—would keep on giving me a sense of nervousness and trepidation every time a call came. Nevertheless, I tried to sound cool, calm, and collected. It's a skill doctors are taught early in their training. "Be glad to help, Rick. Where's the house?"

"It's up a hollow just off Deep Creek. Don and Billy are taking the ambulance back over there. They say you can follow them."

"Let me throw on some scrubs. Five minutes?"

"I'll have them wait in their unit at the end of your driveway."

"Sounds good, Rick."

I hung up the phone and walked to our bedroom to put on my scrubs. I smiled as I looked at the bedroom furniture I had given to Barb, my wife, for our tenth wedding anniversary over a year earlier. Right out of medical school in Durham, North Carolina, we had moved to this quaint little house in this charming village with our then nearly three-year-old daughter, Kate. Bryson City is the county seat of Swain County, in the heart of the Great Smoky Mountains. The county is spread over 550 square miles, yet in 1985 it only had about 8,000 residents. Less than a thousand people lived in the town. The population was small because the federal government owned 86 percent of the land—and much of it was wilderness.

Since pathology-trained coroners lived only in the larger towns, the non-pathologist physicians in the rural areas often became certified as coroners. We were not expected to do autopsies—only pathologists were trained to perform these—but we were expected to perform all of the non-autopsy responsibilities required of a medical examiner.

Having obtained my training as a coroner while still in training at Duke, I knew the basics of determining the time and suspected cause of death, gathering medical evidence, and filling out the copious triplicate forms required by the state authorities. Not long after receiving the fancy certificate of competence from the state of North Carolina, I was required to put my new forensic skills to work. Through the subsequent years as a medical examiner, the work had become more routine, but never boring.

After putting on my scrubs, I left our house, which was located across the street from the Swain County General Hospital, and jumped into our aging Toyota Corolla. Billy was in the driver's seat of the ambulance as I pulled up to the end of the driveway. He smiled and waved as he gunned the accelerator and disappeared behind the hospital and down the backside of Hospital Hill.

I had no idea what awaited me at the murder scene, and I tried not to think about it as I followed the Swain County ambulance.

———

 *B*ecause medical examiners were required to gather medical evidence for all deaths that occurred outside the hospital, during my first four years in practice I was called on as a coroner in dozens of cases. Nevertheless, I still found my stomach in knots whenever I approached the scene of a crime or unexpected death.

After observing the scene, determining the cause of death was usually straightforward, at least from a medical perspective. But every instance continued to remind me of the finality of death, helping me realize again that death almost always comes unexpectedly, without warning or opportunity for preparation. An even more troublesome aspect of my work as an ME, at least when exploring a murder scene, is that it was an unnerving reminder of people's inhumanity to people—of the intrinsic evil that can potentially bubble out of any person's heart, even in an idyllic town I had come to love and call home.

I followed the ambulance up the narrow dirt road into a small mountain hollow. It was a typical winter day in the Smokies—gray, overcast, damp, dreary, and cold. Most who visit the Smokies in the spring and fall revel in its temperate and lush glory. But most aren't aware of how stiflingly hot and steamy the summers can be—and virtually none know how dismal a Smoky Mountain winter can be. This day would prove to be far more dismal than most.

As we reached the end of the road, I saw several sheriff vehicles in a small field in front of a diminutive white farmhouse surrounded with bright yellow crime scene tape. After parking and hopping out of the cab, Billy walked over and extended his hand. "Howdy, Doc."

"Greetings, Billy."

As Don walked up from behind the ambulance I nodded at him. "It's a mess in thar, Doc," Don explained.

"What happened?"

"On first look, it seems the woman stabbed her husband. She used a big ole butcher knife. Pretty much got him straight in the heart, at least judgin' from all the blood on his chest and the floor. Then she turned the knife on herself."

"Cut her wrists?" I asked, assuming a common method of suicide.

"Nope," Billy responded. "First she cut her arm a couple of times, and then she tried to stab herself in the chest a couple a times. When we got here, she was out like a light. Don't know if she fainted or was in shock. But her vitals were good. We got her stabilized and then transferred her up to the hospital."

We began to walk to the house. "Were you able to talk to her at all?"

"Not at first," Don explained. "I got the bleeding stopped with compression dressings. Her heart and lungs seemed fine, so I think her chest wounds are superficial. I got an IV started, and then we put her in the unit, and Billy aimed our nose toward the hospital. Once we were underway, I used some smelling salts on her, and she woke up real quick like."

"What'd she say?"

"She was hysterical—absolutely hysterical. Seemed real scared and tried to fight me. I had to restrain her for the entire trip to the hospital. Then when we got there, Dr. Pyeritz had to give her a real strong IV sedative to calm her down. When we left the ER, she was deep asleep, and he was sewin' her up."

"Just doesn't make sense to me," I commented.

"What doesn't?" asked Billy, as we ducked under the crime scene tape.

"Folks usually don't stab their chest to commit suicide. Did she leave a note?"

"Don't know, Doc. We just stabilized her and transported her as soon as we could."

We walked up the steps to the porch as the sheriff walked out the front door to greet me. "It's a strange one, Doc," he said as we shook hands. "The neighbor man told one of our deputies that this here family had the ideal marriage. Good churchgoin' folks. Never a cross word, at least publicly. But you never know what goes on behind closed doors, do you?"

"What've you put together so far, Sheriff?"

"Apparently the woman was gettin' dinner ready. He came in the back door, and they musta' had a bit of a scuffle. There's some broke plates on the floor, and the kitchen table was pushed over a bit. Anyway, she got him in the chest with a big knife she was usin' to cut vegetables. Looks like he died on the spot. Then she tried to stab herself. Had cuts on her forearm and her chest. Her left hand was all bloody. The butcher knife was by her side, even though she was fainted out on the floor. That's where we found her—still out cold."

"How'd you all get notified?"

"We think she musta' called 911 before she fainted."

"What makes you say that?"

"Millie down at dispatch said a call came in, but there was no voice on the other end of the line. Then she heard a muffled sound, and the phone went dead. There's some bloody finger marks on the phone. The phone was hangin' off the counter right beside her."

"This does sound like a strange one!" I remarked to no one in particular.

"Yep, it shore 'nuff is," the sheriff answered. "We've got the state crime scene van on the way from Asheville."

"Sounds good. Let's go take a look."

As I walked through the small dining room, I could see the kitchen table. It looked like it had been set for dinner, except that the glasses and silverware were haphazardly strewn across its surface.

I entered the kitchen, and I could see a middle-aged man sitting in a slumped position against the cabinet below and to the right of the sink. Two deputies walked in from the back porch as I set down my crime scene bag and pulled out a pair of disposable latex gloves. My eyes slowly swept across the scene, gathering whatever facts the site was willing to tell me.

The man had a huge bloodstain on the center of his muscle shirt, and a pool of coagulated blood was on the floor beside him. The blood loss explained why his face was pale and not the cyanotic blue usually seen in a fresh corpse. There was a cut in the shirt that was two or three inches long—oriented diagonally from his left shoulder toward the lower part of the chest bone. A large amount of blood had flowed down his shirt and soaked the left side of his denim jeans before pooling on the floor at his left side. I suspected the pathologist would find a punctured lung and heart—as well as a chest cavity full of blood.

I walked over to the body and squatted down. I felt along his right wrist. The radial artery had, as I expected, no pulse. I noticed several lacerations on the top of his left forearm. "Looks like he tried to defend himself. See the cuts here on his arm?"

The sheriff and deputies nodded.

I raised the left arm and found it to be fairly supple. "No rigor mortis yet."

My eyes were then drawn to the man's left shoulder, where I saw what appeared to be two cuts or puncture wounds—filled with coagulated blood. I looked behind the shoulder and saw that the wounds had bled down the back of his shirt, which explained the streaked bloodstain on the cabinet just above him. "He'd been stabbed up here before he collapsed," I commented, mostly to myself.

I looked to my left and saw more bloodstains and streaks on the floor by the sink. "That where you found her?" I asked.

"Yep," Billy answered. "We figure she intended to cut her wrists and then panicked and stabbed herself in the heart. When that didn't work, she called 911, got Millie, and then fainted. We found her right there—just below the phone."

I could see the phone receiver hanging from its cord, dangling about halfway down the cabinet. The phone base was on the kitchen cabinet.

"We unplugged the phone from the wall, Doc," Deputy Rogers explained. "It was making an awful racket."

I nodded and looked carefully at the receiver. I could see a faint bloody thumbprint on the inside. I peered around the other side to see three faint and slightly smeared fingerprints on the top.

"Look here, Sheriff."

"Whatcha see, Doc?"

"It looks like someone tried to wipe the blood off this phone, doesn't it?"

The sheriff walked over and stooped down to look at the receiver. "You know, Doc, I think you're right."

I was getting more confused by the minute. I stood and backed up just to observe the entire scene at once. My intuition was telling me things were not exactly as they appeared. I had learned that crime scenes could speak to you—but you had to learn to look very carefully, and listen even more carefully to the soft whispers of the scene itself. My instincts were telling me that this crime scene was trying to scream a message to me. But what? What was it?